Fun

with
Grammar

**Communicative
Activities
for the
Azar Grammar
Series**

Suzanne W. Woodward

Contributing Editor
Betty Schrampfer Azar

PRENTICE HALL REGENTS

DEDICATED TO

Kyle, Scott, and Sarah

Publisher: Mary Jane Peluso
Editor: Stella Reilly
Development Editor: Janet Johnston
Production Editor/Electronic Page Composition: Nicole Cypher
Interior Design: Wanda España, Merle Krumper
Manufacturing Manager: Ray Keating
Art Director: Merle Krumper
Art Production: Marita Froimson

PRENTICE HALL REGENTS

Printed in the United States of America

10   9   8   7   6

ISBN 0-13-567926-5

Contents

Chapter 5   QUESTIONS

Chapter 6   NOUNS

Chapter 7   PRONOUNS

Chapter 8   PREPOSITIONS

Chapter 9   ADJECTIVES

Chapter 10   MODALS

Chapter 11   PASSIVE VOICE

 # Foreword

Fun with Grammar describes exactly what teachers and students should do with grammar: they should have fun with it. For me as a teacher, grammar class is always an opportunity for fun. I cannot imagine dry and dull ESL/EFL grammar classes. During classtime there are, of course, periods of focused concentration, especially during the first phases of a new unit when the students are trying to grasp an initial understanding of the form and meaning of a structure. We, as teachers, should know that even during those phases, explanations and examples can be enlivened by funny sentences using the students' names or by fun demonstrations or pantomimes.

Fun and humor are essential in ESL/EFL classrooms. Interaction and group participation engage students and make information more memorable and relevant. In my experience, many people approach grammar far too seriously, with long, unsmiling faces, in plodding academic style. That is not how I approach grammar nor how I intend teachers to approach my textbooks. Perhaps it should go without saying, but I am going to say it anyway: I heartily endorse having **Fun with Grammar**!

This resource book by Suzanne Woodward is exciting because it collects, categorizes, and details fun communicative activities to use in the classroom. Many teachers make up games as they go along and create interactive activities out of grammar exercises. With this book, teachers have an excellent resource for ideas and materials to support and expand upon the activities that make grammar fun.

The text is subtitled "Communicative Activities for the Azar Grammar Series" because the author's activities grew out of actual teaching experience using the Azar series. The exercises and activities in **Fun with Grammar** fit beautifully with the approaches and material in the Azar grammar textbooks, but are independent enough to be suitable for use with any grammar textbook. The activities in **Fun with Grammar** can also be used in other kinds of classes such as writing classes or speaking/listening classes quite independent of any grammar text or grammar focus to the class. For grammar (whether presented and practiced deliberately or not) underlies all skills.

This resource book is a practical and welcome tool for busy teachers. It provides all the resources needed, and they are right at your fingertips! The games and worksheets reflect and give structure to what actually goes on in effective ESL/EFL classrooms. In addition, teachers have a wealth of material for fun, interesting classroom activities. This book presents clever, innovative ways of creating authentic communication in a cooperative learning environment. Enjoy!

Betty Schrampfer Azar

To the Teacher

INTENDED USE

Fun with Grammar is a collection of communicative activities and games designed to supplement grammar lessons and "jazz up" ESL/EFL classes. Expanding upon text exercises and presentations, these games reinforce the grammar the students already know by providing realistic settings in which they may practice their knowledge. Included are types of activities and games to satisfy all teaching styles. Some games are competitive; some, such as activities that involve problem-solving and a sharing of information, are noncompetitive. All activities are interactive, designed to be done in class with other students. Some of the activities can be assigned as homework, but that is not the main intention of this book.

Fun with Grammar has been designed to assist you in several ways:
- to reinforce points that have been covered in a grammar text
- to provide oral or written practice with grammar forms and rules the students have already learned
- to provide practice in communication skills
- to liven up a grammar class (or any class).

Because **Fun with Grammar** contains activities for all levels and grammar points, it can be used as a source of activities for any grammar class or, indeed, for any other ESL/EFL class. Many writing classes focus on editing skills. This text provides activities (on articles, agreement, subordination, etc.) that a writing teacher can use to highlight those skills. The book can also be used in a conversation or listening/speaking class because all the activities and games are communicative and require spoken interaction with classmates. (For this reason, do not give out worksheets and let the students work individually.) In some cases the goal of the activity is to create sentences or paragraphs, but the students must work together to discuss what they will produce. The games, especially the competitive ones, work extremely well in a conversation class. They are fun, active, and allow the students to react spontaneously. Cooperation and conversation are keys to the activities.

Finally, a number of the activities are very short (5 to 10 minutes). They can be used as a warm-up activity or in the few minutes remaining at the end of a class.

ADAPTING LEVELS

One useful aspect of this book is that the activities are keyed to the Azar books: *Basic English Grammar* (the red series, low level), *Fundamentals of English Grammar* (the black series, intermediate level), and *Understanding and Using English Grammar* (the blue series, high-intermediate). The activities or games that are appropriate for two or three levels have more than one color designation. The color designations help you to find an activity quickly when you have only a few minutes before class. When you do have more time, you will want to look at some of the activities and games that are coded higher or lower than your level. Often they can be adapted to your level easily by using a more (or less) advanced form or more (or less) advanced vocabulary. You know your class best; use the color-coding as a guide, but do not let it limit your use of the activities.

If you are not using the Azar series, the games and activities in **Fun with Grammar** are still easy to use. If you are teaching a low-level class, choose activities designated "red." If you are teaching a higher-level class, remember that "black" designates intermediate and that "blue" designates high-intermediate. The games and activities are organized in this book by grammar point, so whichever grammar book you use, you will be able to locate the grammar point you need in the table of contents or index.

It is important to be open to adapting the games or activities from one grammar point to another. Again, notes or suggestions for variations are often contained within the description of the activity. As you will note, several varieties of activity types (**Line-ups**, **Concentration**, and so on) are repeated in different chapters. You may find a type of activity you like and devise your own unique way of using it with a grammar point.

MATERIALS

Each game or activity lists the materials needed to implement it. If no materials are needed, that fact is stated. The worksheets are located at the ends of the chapters. When a worksheet is required, its number is given. Sometimes several worksheets are provided, either for different class levels or to include variations. Any other materials needed are easy to obtain. For example, if the directions call for 3" x 5" index cards, you may cut up the worksheet and use the slips of paper as cards, or paste the papers onto index cards for repeated use. (Index cards are also easier for students to handle than small pieces of paper.) If an activity uses an optional tape recorder, of course any other type of play-back instrument (CD player, LP player) may be used instead.

SUGGESTED TIME

The time suggested for each activity is the minimum amount of time needed to play a reasonable version of the activity. Many factors must be taken into consideration here. Some activities, such as **Line-ups**, are not affected by class size, but many, such as **Role Plays** and **Pantomimes**, are. You will need to adjust the playing time according to the number of participants. Because many "types" of activities are repeated, if you use them more than once (with a different grammar point), the explanation time will be greatly reduced or even eliminated. Also, many games can be played in several rounds. If the students are enjoying the activity, you may want to play several rounds; if not, cut it short. In addition, many of the activities list variations. The time required depends on whether the variation is used instead of the main activity. In one case, an activity is done entirely outside of class. In a few other cases, the activity is started in class and then continues as homework or outside of class. In these cases, it is not possible to give a definite time for the completion of the activity. Whether you want to conduct the activity entirely in class (more teacher-controlled) or send students out on their own will also affect the time needed for completion.

WORKSHEETS

The worksheets are located at the end of each chapter and are numbered consecutively throughout the book. They may be photocopied for class use. Also, do not feel you must use them as is. Instead, use them as models for your own worksheets. For example, if you have covered only the first half of the irregular verb list, you will not want to use a worksheet for **Concentration** that includes words from the entire verb list. Make your own worksheet that is appropriate to your class. Some of the activities are more fun and effective if you use the names of students in your class. To play **Human Bingo** and **Are You the One?**, among others, use information related to your students. If, for example, no one in your class is married, it makes no sense to use a worksheet that requires the students to find someone who is married.

On the other hand, many of the worksheets are generic and can be used in any class. You can use the printed worksheet the first time you do the activity and then, if you are reviewing at the end of the quarter or semester, make your own based on the model. Do not hesitate to adapt.

GROUPING

All of the games and activities in this manual involve student interaction in groups of two on up to the entire class, although most involve pair or small-group interaction. There are many ways to divide your class into groups. The simplest and quickest is to group them where they sit, which you will do occasionally, especially if pressed for time. But because students tend to sit next to the same students, it is beneficial to have them work with other classmates during these activities. When the students work on the exercises in their textbook, they probably work with those sitting next to them. Doing any of the activities in this book, then, provides a good excuse for mixing up the class. Here are a few suggestions for ways to divide the class into pairs or groups.

1. ***Count off.*** Decide how many groups you will need (usually determined by the size of the class) and have the students count off up to that number, then repeat. Group all the 1s together, all the 2s together, and so on.

2. ***Cut-up cards.*** Postcards work well for this activity, or you can use magazine covers. Cut each picture into the number of pieces according to the size of the groups you want (a minimum of three in each group). Hand out one piece to each student. The students circulate, trying to put the pictures back together. The students holding the pieces of each picture are the members of that group. The first time you do this activity, the students usually think that once they have put the picture together, the activity is over and they can return to their original seats. (They may or may not wonder what this has to do with grammar.) Therefore, you may need to call them back to get into the groups formed by their pictures. After the first time, they'll know what to expect. Hint: Try to use similar cards so that the students have to fit the pieces together, not just look for someone with a piece of the same color. If you pick up multiples of the same postcard while on your vacation, you may want to try using all the same card, but be sure to cut them differently. This method works well if you have an odd number of students. Cut some cards into four and others into three, and use the ones you need on any given day. Having sets of cards cut into different amounts will also help you group quickly when one or more students are absent.

3. ***Deck of cards.*** There are three ways you can use a deck of cards to group students. First, have students get into groups by the number of the cards they are holding (all 2s in one group, all 3s in another, etc.). If, for example, you have seventeen students, you would separate out four 2s, four 3s, three 4s, three 5s, and three 6s.

   Another way to use a deck of cards is to group students by suit (all hearts in one group, all clubs in another). This limits you to having four groups at most.

   You can also group students by card color. Obviously, this limits you to two groups, but the method works well for pairs or teams. For team division, half the class would receive red cards, the other half, black. For pair division, use a combination of color and number: the two red 2s are one pair, the two black 2s are another, the two red 3s are another, and so on.

   Cards work well in dividing students for jigsaw activities by combining two of these methods. Imagine that you want to divide students into small groups and then, after a certain activity, divide the original groups and have one member of each group form a new group. This can be accomplished by having students get into groups by number. When you are ready to split them up again, have them reform by suit.

4. ***Paper draw.*** This is a quick way to group, especially if you forget to bring your cards. There are two ways to do it simply. The easiest is to cut or tear up pieces of colored paper (such as five pieces of red, five pieces of blue, four pieces of green). Put the papers in a

hat and have students pick one out without looking, then form groups by color. If you do not have colored paper, simply cut up enough pieces of paper for your class and number them (or if you want to be creative, use nouns—dogs, cats, and so on). All students with the same number (or noun category) form a group.

5. **Class list.** Group the class by reading off names from the class list. After the first time, it's better to skip around rather than to read alphabetically. For example, skip every other name. The first three names you call form one group. Then continue with the next three names. You can start from the top, the bottom, or somewhere in between. You may need to mark off names as you call them to avoid getting confused.

6. **Student choice.** To form pairs, you can put the names of half of the class on papers in a bag, then have the other half pick out a name to be a partner. You can put the name of every other student in the bag, or the names of the first half of the class list. This can be a somewhat controlled pairing, so if you have some strong and some weak students, put the names of the strong students in the bag and have the weaker ones pull the names out. This avoids having two very strong or two very weak students pairing up. Keep track of whose name is in the bag so you know who should be picking out a name. You can also do this by nationality. If your class is fairly well divided between two nationalities, put the names of all one nationality in the bag and have the others draw names. Even if your class is not divided neatly in half, this can be useful. If you have a large group of the same nationality who hesitate to mix, put all their names in the bag (or have them all draw names) so they cannot possibly end up with one another.

7. **Match.** This division is also for pairs. Prepare some quick matching activity related to the grammar point (or to review one). For example, you might prepare cards, half of which are questions and the other half, answers. Distribute them and have the students find their match. Once they have found the partner whose card matches theirs, you're ready for the "real" activity.

8. **Miscellaneous.** There are other ways to divide into groups that work well in a conversation class. In a grammar class the time is usually limited and it is not possible to spend much time on activities not directly related to grammar. If you have more time or teach an integrated-skills class, you may find some other method useful occasionally. For example:

   a. **Line-ups.** Have students line up according to some criterion such as hair color or birth month. Once they have formed the line, divide them into groups (the first four, the next four, and so on).

   b. **Interests.** Have all students whose favorite season is spring go to one corner, summer to another, and so on. This method has a few disadvantages: you can have only four groups, and the groups may end up being very uneven (five summers, six springs, one winter, three falls). Any interest can work: favorite ice cream, type of movie, color. If it works, this is a fun way to divide, but it is not as predictable as some of the other methods described above.

NUMBER OF STUDENTS PER GROUP

Most of the games and activities specify the number of group members. Although a certain number is sometimes necessary (**Tic Tac Toe** with handout, for example), this is just a guide for the instructor. How many students you put into each group will depend mainly on how many students are in your class.

If the instructions specify pairs and you are left with one extra student, you can solve this in a couple of ways. (a) Make one group of three, either randomly (the last three students) or intentionally (two stronger students with one weaker, or three quiet students who will not be overpowered by more outspoken classmates). (b) Work with the last student yourself, a useful stratagem, especially if one of your students is not quite up to the ability of the others. Be aware of the student's feelings. It may be better to form a group of three so one student does not feel singled out.

Do not let one student work alone. Sometimes a student says he/she is willing to do the activity alone (or even prefers to), but these activities and games are interactive and often cannot or should not be done alone.

When dividing into small groups, use your judgment. Again, the division will be a direct result of the number of students in your class. While it is nice to have even groups, it is not always possible. Keep the numbers as close as possible. If you are doing groups of five and then are left with two students, do not let them work as a pair. Either have two groups of six or create a new group by borrowing students from some of the other groups.

What happens when your groups are all set up and working and a student walks in late? If you have some smaller groups, add the late student to one of them. If all groups are equal, randomly assign him/her to a group, or put him/her in a weaker group (so that there are more students to generate ideas) or in a group that needs someone of a different nationality.

Just remember to be flexible. It won't matter if you have one more or one less than the suggested number. Even when an activity calls for a specific number because of assigned roles, a different-sized group can be accommodated. Simply assign two members of the group to the same role and have them split the role.

Acknowledgments

Many of the ideas for games and activities in this book have grown out of conversations and interaction with my colleagues and fellow ESL professionals. In particular, my colleagues at UC Irvine–Extension have encouraged me and helped me to clarify these activities by offering feedback and requesting activities for specific grammar points. Some of these games and activities, which were developed and refined in my classes over the years, were created with instructors who are no longer at UCI–Extension, but I would like to acknowledge their valuable input.

In addition, I would like to acknowledge the invaluable help of several individuals. Eric Bredenberg, always an enthusiastic supporter, was instrumental in helping me get started on this project and has been a dynamic presenter of my ideas in workshops and at CATESOL and TESOL conferences.

Betty Azar has been indispensable in helping me find my way through the publishing world. She has encouraged me and was always available to talk ideas through. I greatly appreciate her insights into the games and activities and would like to thank her for all her helpful comments during the book's editing phase.

I greatly value the opinions and help of Ellen Bartlett. In addition to submitting several activities to this book, she gave me feedback on many of the activities, reminded me of others we had done at different times in our careers, and reviewed the entire manuscript. Most important, perhaps, was her enthusiasm for the project and her overall support.

Mary Woodward, who unofficially contributed ideas to the book, also supported this project from its beginning. Her assistance with day-to-day activities freed me to concentrate on writing.

I also want to thank Kyle Woodward for his support and encouragement, for his help with computer problems, and for the time he spent at the computer, helping to put the manuscript into its final form.

Finally, I would like to thank all the instructors who contributed activities to this book. Acknowledgments for specific games and activities are due to the following individuals:

Wendy Baldwin, English Language Institute, SUNY at Buffalo, New York: 15.2.1, 15.3.10, 16.5.2

Ellen Bartlett, Oceanside Unified Schools, California: 2.3.3, 5.1.12, 13.3.4

Kathy Bates, Fullerton, California: 13.2.1, 13.2.4

Elizabeth Cadwalader, Baltimore, Maryland: 15.3.6

Jeanne Clayton, Intensive English Language Center, St. Petersburg, Florida: 10.2.1, 12.5.3

Bonnie L. Dahnke, International Language Institute, Washington, D.C.: 8.2.5

Eileen F. Kelley and **Diane Sweet**, Holyoke Community College, Holyoke, Massachusetts: 5.1.11, 5.1.15, 14.2.1

Linda B. Leary, Intensive English Language Program, SUNY at Albany, New York: 3.3.1

Thomas G. Long, Educational Unlimited International (EUI), Cambridge, Massachusetts: 6.4.5, 8.1.3, 8.2.6

Patricia Ann Previdi, Catonsville Community College, Catonsville, Maryland: 4.2.7, 6.4.4

Michael Prili, Intensive English Language Center, St. Petersburg, Florida: 8.2.7, 12.5.2

Alice Savage, Houston Community College, Houston, Texas: 2.4.4, 5.1.13, 8.2.8, 10.3.2, 13.1.5, 15.2.3

Jane Shore, Lado International College, Arlington, Virginia: 5.1.14, 9.2.4, 14.2.5

Marlene Sprigle, UCSD Extension, San Diego, California: 10.3.3

Rose To, Rancho Santiago College, Santa Ana, California: 12.5.1

James Toepper, Northern Virginia Community College, Alexandria, Virginia: 3.3.2

Toni Zona, Intensive English Language Center, St. Petersburg, Florida: 8.2.4

CHAPTER 1

Verbs: Present

SIMPLE PRESENT

1. IN COMMON

RED BLACK BLUE

Materials: Worksheet 1

Dynamic: Whole class

Time: 20 minutes

Procedure:

1. Create a worksheet, perhaps by using the blank Worksheet 1, by listing your students' names in the left column. Another way to do this is to use the attendance list, block out everything but the name column, then draw lines across.

2. Give each student a copy of the handout. Instruct students to cross out their name and the names of any absent students.

3. Instruct students to circulate and find one thing they have in common with each other student on the list. They must find a different thing for each student. For example, Soheyla might write:

   Juan: We both like sports.
   Maria: We both have dark hair.
   Akiko: We both have two older brothers.
   Kimtien: We both drive a car.

4. When two students have discovered something in common, each writes it down on the line next to the name of the student he/she is talking to. In the above example, Soheyla writes *We both like sports* next to Juan's name, and Juan writes it next to Soheyla's name.

5. When they have finished, the students sit down. Ask which verb tense they used most often (simple present) and why (facts). If the students cannot provide these answers, give them clues by soliciting some of the sentences they wrote down. Ask if these are true statements, etc.

6. For fun and to learn more about the students, ask individual students at random what they have in common with someone on their list. (It would take too long to go over all the answers.) You may want to collect the papers to use as a source of information for preparing other activities or exercises.

   NOTE: *This is a good culmination game at a lower level, after completing the present tense chapter. It also works well as a review for higher students to see if they remember why they use the present tense.*

2. ARE YOU THE ONE?

RED BLACK BLUE

Materials: Worksheet 2

Dynamic: Whole class

Time: 20 minutes

Procedure:

1. Distribute one copy of the worksheet to each student. Tell students to circulate, asking the questions on the worksheet.

   Example: **On the worksheet:** is afraid of spider
   Student A: Are you afraid of spiders?
   Student B: Yes, I am.

2. When the questioning student gets a *yes* answer, he/she fills in the answerer's name. If the answerer answers *no*, the questioning student continues until he/she finds someone who answers *yes*.

3. When a student completes the worksheet, he/she sits down, but still answers other students' questions. Not all students may be able to complete every entry. If they have asked all their classmates a question and no one has said *yes*, they can also sit down.

4. Go over as many of the questions/answers as time allows.

   NOTE: *You can limit answers to only one* yes *answer per student. This avoids students pairing up and talking to only one or two other students. Or you may allow students to write a classmate's name as many times as that student answers* yes.

3. SHORT ANSWERS 1

RED

Materials: Strips with answers (Worksheet 3)

Dynamic: Pairs/Small groups

Time: 20 minutes

Procedure:

1. Divide the class into pairs or groups of three or four.

2. Give each group several strips with short answers on them. Have the students work together to write questions for the answers.

3. The members of each group can take turns reading their questions and answers aloud, or one student can read for the group. The rest of the class judges whether the questions are appropriate for their answers.

4. SHORT ANSWERS 2

Materials: None

Dynamic: Pairs/Small groups

Time: 30 minutes

RED   BLACK

Procedure:

1. Divide the class into pairs or groups of three or four. There should be an even number of groups if possible.

2. Each group writes five short answers on a piece of paper, exchanges answer papers with another group, and writes appropriate questions for the other group's answers.

   Examples:

Group 1:	**Group 2:**
Yes, I do.	Do you walk to school?
No, he wasn't.	Was John late for class?
No, you aren't.	Am I from Korea?
Yes, they did.	Did they leave at 12:00?
No, she didn't.	Did Keiko lend you her car?

3. Put the two groups together and have them return the answer papers. The group who wrote the answers checks that the questions are appropriate.

   NOTE: *This activity can be adapted to a higher level by using different tenses, such as a mixture of perfect tenses.*

   SUGGESTION: *Before dividing your class into pairs, tell them what tense to use or, for the higher-level class, if the activity is intended to be a verb review.*

5. INFORMATION, PLEASE

Materials: Worksheet 4 (optional)

Dynamic: Pairs

Time: 30–45 minutes

RED   BLACK   BLUE

Procedure:

1. Divide the class into pairs. Assign each pair a different topic to discuss. Partner A asks the questions; partner B provides his/her own answers. Partner A can use the worksheet questions as a guideline, but encourage students to think of other, more specific questions. For low-level students, you may want to provide answers for partner B or have the partners work together to create answers. Higher-level students can use the worksheet as a guide and then develop their own questions based on the situation.

SUGGESTED TOPICS: mall information desk
airline information
ticket booth
county fair information office
bus information
college information line
library
hospital information desk
local tourist attraction

2. Have the students practice their questions and answers several times. They will do a telephone role play for the class, so they should be familiar with the questions and answers. Circulate, helping the pairs with their grammar and checking their answers.

3. The partners take turns presenting their role plays to the rest of the class.

6. HUMAN BINGO

Materials: Worksheet 5

Dynamic: Whole class

Time: 15 minutes

RED   BLACK   BLUE

Procedure:

1. Go over question formation if necessary. If this is used as a review, the students should be able to form questions from the prompts. Give a copy of the handout to each student.

2. Tell them to circulate, asking their classmates questions as indicated by the prompts on the bingo card. If a student answers *yes*, they write that student's name after the prompt. If the student answers *no*, they continue asking until they find someone who answers *yes*.

3. As in Bingo, there are several ways to win.

   a. The first student who gets five names in a row wins.

   b. The first student who fills in the four corners wins.

   c. The first student who completes the board wins.

   d. The first student who makes a cross wins (third row down and third row across).

   e. Use any other variation you choose.

4. After you have a winner, go over the tense used and why (fact or habit?) and some of the answers ("Whose favorite color is green?" "Who gets up at 7:00?").

Variations: a. Make your own grid from information you know about your students. They will be more likely to be able to complete the game.

b. Use at holiday times with prompts geared to the holiday.

   Examples: Has seen a ghost, Will go to the costume party tonight, Has eaten candy corn, Knows what a ghoul is.

7. TWENTY QUESTIONS 1

RED   BLACK   BLUE

Materials: None

Dynamic: Whole class

Time: 10 minutes

Procedure: 1. Choose a category, such as famous people, occupations, food, or animals. Choose one student to answer questions from the rest of the class. Show the student a piece of paper with a word telling what he or she is (an object or person in the category). This student sits in front of the class and may answer only *yes* or *no* to any question.

2. The class may ask a total of 20 *yes/no* questions to discover the "identity" of the student in front of the class (the word on the paper the student was shown). If they guess the student's identity before or by the 20th question, the class wins. If the class does not guess correctly, the student wins. (Although this is based on the popular Twenty Questions game, you may want to vary the number of questions the class can ask. Be sure to make the number clear before the game begins.)

Variation: To make the game more challenging, especially at the higher levels, omit step 1 so that the students use up some of their questions determining the category.

8. TWENTY QUESTIONS 2

RED   BLACK   BLUE

Materials: Small pictures

Dynamic: Whole class

Time: 10 minutes

Procedure: 1. Tape a small picture on the back of each student, staying within the same category, such as famous people or occupations.

2. The students circulate and ask each other *yes/no* questions to discover "who" or "what" they are. The responding students look at the picture on the back of the questioner before answering. Circulate around the class to help out if the students are not sure of an answer. Instruct the students that they can answer *I don't know* if they are unsure and you are not available to ask. In the example below, the first two questions can be answered with *yes* or *no* just by looking at the picture. The third question requires that the student know the identity of the person in the picture.

   Examples: Am I a woman?
   Do I have blond hair?
   Am I a singer?

3. For a competition, the first student to discover his/her identity wins. If it is not a competition, set a time limit and try to have as many students discover their identities as possible. When students discover their identity, have them continue to participate by answering questions from those students who are still trying to guess their identity.

9. CLUE

Materials: None

Dynamic: Whole class

Time: 20 minutes

RED BLACK BLUE

Procedure:

1. This is another variation of Twenty Questions. Choose one student to come to the front of the class. This student will be given an identity and will give clues to the class. The class tries to guess the identity from the clues and can ask only *yes/no* questions.

2. Before starting the game, discuss strategy with the class. Tell them that the student who is giving clues will give the most difficult clues first and the easiest last.

   Example: Identity: baseball

   SAMPLE CLUES: Many people like me.
   You can watch me.
   It is (or I am) done outdoors.
   I am a game/sport.
   You need a mitt to play.

3. If the class guesses the identity, it wins. If the class cannot guess the identity after a preannounced number of clues (between 5 and 10), the student wins.

Variation: Send one student out of the room. Give the class an identity for that student, discuss clue strategy, and go over possible clues. When the student returns, the class members begin giving clues. The student may ask only *yes/no* questions, or you may limit his/her questions to identity questions ("Am I a teacher?"). If the student guesses his/her identity, he/she wins. Otherwise, the class wins.

10. MEMORY ROUND (Frequency adverbs)

RED   BLACK   BLUE

Materials: 3″ x 5″ cards with a frequency adverb written on each

Dynamic: Whole class

Time: 20 minutes

Procedure:

1. Prepare one card for each student. The words should be large and in dark ink so that all the students will be able read them. Depending on the size of the class, you may have to duplicate cards or play in two rounds. (For example, divide the class in half and have the first group come to the front of the class. When they are finished, have the second group come up.)

   FREQUENCY ADVERBS: *always, almost always, usually, often, sometimes, frequently, generally, occasionally, seldom, rarely, never, almost never, hardly ever*

2. The students form a circle, either sitting or standing. Ask who has the best memory. Start with the person next to the volunteer so that the person who said he/she has the best memory will be last. (If you know who your weaker/quieter student is, start with him/her.)

3. Each student makes a sentence using his/her frequency adverb, but no writing is allowed at any time.

   Examples: *Never:*   I never eat fast food.
   Always: I always brush my teeth.
   Seldom: I seldom study for tests.

4. Holding the card with the frequency adverb toward the circle, the first student says his/her sentence. The second student says his/her sentence and repeats the first student's sentence. The third student says his/her sentence and repeats the first two sentences, and so on around the circle until the last student, who says his/her sentence and repeats the sentences from everyone in the group. Don't allow any writing, but do allow gestures and even one or two helpful words from the other students.

Example:

Student 1:	I never eat fast food.
Student 2:	I always brush my teeth, and Jae never eats fast food.
Student 3:	I seldom study for tests, Akiko always brushes her teeth, and Jae never eats fast food.
Student 4:	I usually go to bed at 11, Maria seldom studies for tests, Akiko always brushes her teeth, and Jae never eats fast food.

SUGGESTION: *You may want to choose a topic before playing so everyone's sentences will relate to that topic.*

11. BALL TOSS (Frequency adverbs)

RED   BLACK

Materials: Any soft ball or beanbag

Dynamic: Whole class

Time: 10 minutes

Procedure:

1. Arrange students in a circle, either standing or at their desks.

2. Ask a question using a frequency adverb, and toss the ball to a student.

   Examples: Do you always eat breakfast before coming to class?
   How often do you wear jeans to class?

3. The student who catches the ball must answer, using a frequency adverb in a complete sentence. The same student then asks a question with a frequency adverb and tosses the ball to a classmate.

12. HOW OFTEN? (Frequency adverbs)

RED

Materials: Worksheet 6

Dynamic: Pairs

Time: 20 minutes

Procedure:

1. Divide the class into pairs. Give each student a copy of the worksheet, and have students interview each other, writing the answers on their worksheet. Have the pairs work together to do Part 2.

2. Share answers from Part 1 with the entire class. Check the answers for Part 2 and discuss any incorrect ones with the group.

13. PICTURE SEARCH (Be / Have)

Materials: Magazines or catalogs

Dynamic: Small groups

Time: 15 minutes

RED

Procedure:

1. Divide the class into groups of three or four. Give each group several catalogs or magazines. (You may want to ask each student the previous day to bring in a magazine or catalog.)

2. Have each group make ten sentences, using a form of *to be* or *to have*.

    Examples: The man has a hat.
    The man is tall.

3. Have the groups read their sentences aloud while showing the class the pictures the sentences describe.

Variation: To make it a competition, the first group that shows you 20 correct sentences wins. For a higher group, you may want to assign more sentences.

14. WANT / NEED

Materials: Worksheet 7

Dynamic: Groups

Time: 20 minutes

RED

Procedure:

1. Cut up Worksheet 7 into separate situations. Divide the class into groups of approximately four, and give each group a different situation card.

2. Instruct the groups to make a list of things they need and want for the situation on their card. You may want to limit them to five items each.

3. Each group reads its situation and tells what it needs and wants, and why.

    NOTE: *You may fill in the blanks on the worksheet before distributing to the class, or the class can name a popular singer and actor.*

1.2 NONPROGRESSIVES

1. RELAY

RED BLACK BLUE

Materials: Board and markers/chalk

Dynamic: Teams

Time: 10 minutes

Procedure:
1. Divide the board in half. On each side, write the words *progressive* and *nonprogressive*.

2. Divide the class into two teams. Have each team form a line. The first person from each team comes to the board.

3. Call out a verb. The students check either *progressive* or *nonprogressive*. The first one to choose the correct answer gets a point for his/her team.

   NOTE: *Have students check in front of the words on the board. You will have to erase the checks between rounds.*

4. After each verb, the students at the board are replaced by two more students for the next verb. The team with the most points at the end of the game wins. Both speed and accuracy are important.

2. BALL TOSS

RED BLACK BLUE

Materials: Any soft ball or beanbag

Dynamic: Whole class

Time: 10 minutes

Procedure:
1. Arrange students in a circle, either standing or at their desks.

2. Call out a verb, and toss the ball to a student. The student who catches the ball answers *progressive* or *nonprogressive*, then tosses the ball to another classmate while calling out another verb.

PRESENT PROGRESSIVE

1. ACT IT OUT

Materials: Worksheet 8, or small pieces of paper similar to Worksheet 8

Dynamic: Whole class/Teams

Time: 20 minutes

Procedure:
1. Cut up Worksheet 8 into activities, or make your own. One student comes to the front of the class, draws a piece of paper with an activity on it, and acts out the activity silently. The class tries to guess what he/she is doing.

2. The students can take turns acting out the activities, or you can divide the class into teams. A student from each team presents the activity to his/her team. If the team guesses correctly in the allotted time (30 seconds?), the team scores a point. You may also allow the other team to "steal" after the time limit is up. This keeps all students involved.

   NOTE: *If you make up your own activities rather than using the worksheet, make the activities involved. "Jumping" is too easy even for low levels. "Jumping on your left foot" is better.*

2. PICTURE SENTENCES

Materials: Worksheet 9 or pictures with a lot of activity going on

Dynamic: Small group

Time: 25 minutes

Procedure:
1. Divide the class into groups of three or four. Give each group the same picture, or put it on an overhead.

2. Instruct the groups to describe the picture in as many sentences as possible in the time allowed, using the present progressive. The sentences must be grammatically correct and accurately depict what is happening in the picture.

3. Each group reads its sentences or writes them on the board. The group with the most correct sentences wins.

12

Variation 1: Give each group a different picture.

Variation 2: Give each group a different picture. Follow step 2. After 15 seconds, say "Pass" and have the groups pass their picture to the next group. Continue until all groups have written sentences for all pictures. Score the correct answers as in step 3.

> **NOTE:** *Good sources for pictures are a picture dictionary (especially if the students have the same one), lower-level student ESL books containing drawings for students to discuss or write about, and magazine advertisements.*

3. WHAT'S HAPPENING IN YOUR COUNTRY?

RED   BLACK   BLUE

Materials: None

Dynamic: Whole class

Time: 15 minutes

Procedure:

1. Ask any student in the class what time it is in his/her country at that moment.

2. Then ask the student who he/she lives with when in his/her country. (Sample answers: "In Japan, I live with my mother, father, two brothers and a sister." "In Brazil, I live with my wife and two children." "In Taiwan, I live with my mother, father and grandmother.")

3. Have the class speculate on what their family members are doing at that time. Ask questions of students at random.

   Example: Is your mother making breakfast?
   Is your mother working?
   Is your brother watching TV?
   Is your brother attending classes at the university?

4. The student who has provided time and family information should try to answer as best he/she can. For example, "I think so" or "Probably" are acceptable answers.

> **NOTE:** *Be sure the student provides only the names of family members in step 2 and does not give any additional information. He/she should not say* I have a ten-year-old brother, and my mother is a nurse. *Just have each student give the relationships:* I have a brother and a mother.

4. DESCRIPTION (Simple present and Present progressive)

Materials: None

Dynamic: Whole class

Time: 25 minutes

RED

Procedure:

1. Each student writes a one-sentence description of a classmate on a piece of paper, without giving the name of the person being described.

   Example: She is wearing sandals.
   He has a mustache.
   She is wearing a dress and has short hair.

2. Take turns reading the descriptions aloud. The other students try to guess who is being described.

   NOTE: *Caution students not to be too general if the description applies to most of the class ("She is wearing jeans").*

5. IMAGINATION

Materials: None

Dynamic: Whole class

Time: 30 minutes

RED   BLACK   BLUE

Procedure:

1. Ask students to imagine a place where they would like to be. (Sometimes it helps to play music, but this may influence them.) Have them close their eyes and imagine this place in great detail: What are they doing? How is the weather? What do they see? Where are they sitting or standing? Who is with them? Give them several minutes to think about this place.

2. Have them take a piece of paper and write a description of what they just imagined, beginning with the place they imagined. They can write as informally as they want. You might suggest they write this as a letter to a friend ("I am sitting on a quiet beach") or in their journal or diary.

3. Ask for volunteers to read or tell about the place they would most like to be.

   NOTE: *You may want to demonstrate by telling them where you would most like to be and what you see yourself doing there.*

6. COMPLAINTS (*Always*)

Materials: None

Dynamic: Small groups

Time: 15 minutes

BLUE

Procedure:

1. Divide the class into groups of three or four. Give each group the same (or a different) topic to complain about. They must use *always* in their complaints. The groups make as many complaints as possible before you tell them to stop.

   SUGGESTED TOPICS: school
   family member (choose one)
   transportation system
   city they are in
   roommate
   classmates
   friend

   POSSIBLE COMPLAINTS:

   Topic a: The teachers are always assigning too much homework.
   The teachers are always giving too many tests.

   Topic b: My brother is always leaving his dirty clothes on my bed.
   My brother is always telling me what to do.

2. Have each group read its list of complaints aloud.

NAME	IN COMMON

Worksheet 2: ARE YOU THE ONE? (PRESENT)

FIND A CLASSMATE WHO ...	
Has more brothers than sisters.	
Speaks more than two languages.	
Has a pet.	
Is not from a large city.	
Is older than you.	
Is wearing socks.	
Walks to school.	
Has a car.	
Likes to dance.	
Likes fast food.	
Has a name that begins with the same letter as yours.	
Drinks coffee.	
Is married.	
Has a birthday in April.	
Is afraid of spiders.	

Yes, I do.	No, he doesn't.
Yes, they do.	No, they don't.
Yes, I am.	No, I am not.
Yes, he is.	No, he isn't.
Yes, she does.	No, she doesn't.
Yes, she is.	No, she isn't.
Yes, it is.	No, it isn't.
Yes, it does.	No, it doesn't.

1. <u>Mall information desk:</u>

   a. What are your hours?
   b. How do I get there?
   c. Is there a bus stop nearby?
   d. Is there a _____ (store name) in the mall?
   e. Are there any restaurants in the mall?

2. <u>Airline information:</u>

   a. Is flight 62 on time?
   b. At what gate does it arrive?
   c. Which terminal is it in?
   d. How do I get to the airport?
   e. Is there short-term parking?

3. <u>Ticket booth:</u>

   a. Do you have tickets for _____ (group/event name)?
   b. How much are they?
   c. Can you send them to me?
   d. Can I buy tickets at the door?
   e. Do you have student rates?

4. <u>County fair information office:</u>

   a. What dates are you open?
   b. What are your hours?
   c. Is there a bus stop nearby?
   d. How can I get there by car?
   e. Is there parking nearby?

5. <u>Bus information:</u>

   a. Which bus goes to _____ (city name)?
   b. How much does it cost?
   c. Which bus goes to the university?
   d. Are there special buses for disabled people?
   e. Is there a child's fare?

6. <u>College information line:</u>

   a. When does the semester begin?
   b. Is it too late to register?
   c. Do I have to register in person?
   d. How do I get there?
   e. Is there a bus stop nearby?

7. <u>Library:</u>

   a. Are you open on Sundays?
   b. What are your hours?
   c. How do I get a library card?
   d. How do I get there?
   e. Is there parking nearby?

8. <u>Hospital information desk:</u>

   a. What are visiting hours?
   b. Are children allowed?
   c. How many people can visit at once?
   d. How do I get there?
   e. What room is _____ (patient's name) in?

Gets up at 7:00	Likes chocolate	Is from a small town	Is married	Has a dog
Lives in an apartment	Likes to go bowling	Favorite color is green	Favorite class is grammar	Has more brothers than sisters
Drinks coffee	Eats health food	**FREE**	Likes to swim	Is studying a subject besides English
Sometimes forgets to brush teeth	Takes a shower in the morning	Is wearing black shoes	Wears contact lenses	Is dating someone from another country
Eats lunch at 12 noon	Takes the bus to school	Is taking more than two classes	Has a pet	Drinks milk at breakfast

Blank grid for making your own

		FREE		

PART 1: *Answer with a frequency adverb whenever possible.*

1. How often do you go to the movies?

2. How often do you play soccer?

3. How often do you eat Mexican food?

4. How often do you brush your teeth?

5. How often do you eat breakfast?

6. How often do you visit your mother?

7. How often do you go to the library?

8. How often do you go to the bank?

PART 2: *Read the story together and circle the correct answer.*

John lives in San Marcos. He works in a restaurant. He works six days a week. After work he plays soccer or baseball with his sons. He tries to play every day, but sometimes he can't. John's wife works too. She goes to school three nights a week. Sometimes she can go only one night a week because her children are sick or she has to work late. She works late only one or two nights a month.

1. John seldom works.	**True**	**False**
2. John usually plays with his sons.	**True**	**False**
3. John's wife never works.	**True**	**False**
4. She rarely studies.	**True**	**False**
5. She almost never works late.	**True**	**False**

Worksheet 7: WANT/NEED

✂ --

You are going to change your image.

1. What do you need?

2. What do you want?

You are going to make lunch for the mayor of your city.

1. What do you need?

2. What do you want?

You are getting married.

1. What do you need?

2. What do you want?

You are stranded on a desert island.

1. What do you need?

2. What do you want?

You are going to make a music video with _____.

1. What do you need?

2. What do you want?

You lost all your books and assignments.

1. What do you need?

2. What do you want?

You are going to be in a movie with _____.

1. What do you need?

2. What do you want?

You are taking a trip around the world by boat.

1. What do you need?

2. What do you want?

Hop on one foot while holding your other foot.	Change a baby's diaper.
Drink a cup of coffee or tea.	Drive a car in rush-hour traffic.
Pick up trash alongside a busy highway.	Put on make-up.
Do sit-ups.	Lock a door.
Eat spaghetti.	Wash a car's windshield.
Meet a friend unexpectedly.	Play with a kitten.
Take your dog for a walk.	Use a computer.

You and your partners will write sentences to describe this picture, using the present progressive. Write as many as you can in ____ minutes.

CHAPTER

2

Verbs: Past

SIMPLE PAST

1. DETECTIVE 1

RED

Materials:	Worksheet 10
Dynamic:	Pairs
Time:	30 minutes
Procedure:	1. Divide students into pairs. Have them read the situation together and fill in the blanks with a past form of *to be*.

2. Assign the roles of police officer and witness (or have the students choose). As a class, brainstorm some questions using a past form of *to be* that the police officer might ask the witness.

   Examples: Was the thief tall?
   Were you across the street from the office?
   Where did the thief go when he left the office?

3. Have the two students practice asking and answering questions. (For a low class, you may want to copy the list of questions in the worksheet.)

4. Encourage the "police officer" to ask both *yes/no* and *wh-* questions.

2. DETECTIVE 2

BLACK   BLUE

Materials:	Worksheet 10 (optional)
Dynamic:	Whole class
Time:	30 minutes
Procedure:	1. Choose five students to be "suspects." The five draw slips of paper from a bag. Four are blank. The student who chooses the one with an X is the "thief." The five do not tell the rest of the class who the "thief" is.

2. Divide the rest of the class into groups of four or five. Using the situation in Worksheet 10 (or your own), have the class brainstorm or adapt the questions in Worksheet 10 to ask the "suspects."

3. While the rest of the class is brainstorming, take the five "suspects" outside. The four without the X should think of answers or an alibi for the questions they will be asked. Work with the "thief" to help him/her to look or sound evasive and give contradictory answers. This student should not make it obvious that he/she is the guilty one, but will have to give some clues to the class.

4. Reassemble the class with the five "suspects" sitting in front of the room. The groups take turns questioning the "suspects." After a time limit or when they have run out of questions, the groups decide who the "thief" is.

NOTE: *This can be used as a follow-up to **Detective 1** in a high-beginning class, or it can be used as an independent activity.*

3. DETECTIVE 3

Materials:	Worksheet 11	

BLACK BLUE

Dynamic: Groups

Time: 25 minutes

Procedure:

1. Divide the class into groups of four. Each group will contain a "detective" and three "witnesses."

2. Give each "witness" a section of Worksheet 11 that contains the situation and a witness statement, all three of which are different. Give the "detective" the situation and the list of suspects.

3. The detective questions the witnesses (using the past tense) to determine who is the "thief." In order to choose from the suspect list, the detective will have to decide who is the best (most believable or accurate) witness and rely most heavily on that witness' information.

NOTE: *There is no right answer. The most logical suspect based on the given information is John Peters, but if the students can come up with good reasons for another suspect, their answer should be accepted. This activity is meant to be open-ended. The students decide which testimony has the most validity.*

4. MEMORY ROUND

Materials: A 3″ x 5″ card per student, with a verb in past tense written on each

Dynamic: Whole class

Time: 20 minutes

RED

Procedure:

1. Give each student a card with the simple form of a different verb, written large. (You may mix irregular and regular pasts, or just focus on irregular past forms.) Let each student decide what the correct past form of his/her verb is.

2. Have students sit or stand in a circle. Instruct them to think of a sentence that uses the verb on their card. They will have to remember the sentences, so they should not be overly long.

3. Students hold their cards facing the circle at all times. The first student says his/her sentence. The next student in the circle says his/her sentence and repeats student one's sentence. Continue around the circle. The last student repeats all the previous sentences.

Example:

Student 1:	I needed to buy groceries yesterday.
Student 2:	I ate breakfast at 7:00, and he needed to buy groceries yesterday.
Student 3:	I drove to the mountains last weekend, she ate breakfast at 7:00, and he needed to buy groceries yesterday.

NOTE: *You can begin with a student who seems weak (he/she will not have to remember so many sentences) or with the person next to the person who has the best memory. No writing is allowed; students must focus on what their classmates are <u>saying</u>.*

5. CHAIN STORIES

Materials: A 3″ x 5″ card per student, with a verb written on each

Dynamic: Large groups

Time: 20 minutes

RED   BLACK

Procedure:

1. Give each student a card with the simple form of a verb written large. The verbs may have regular or irregular past forms, or you may use a mixture. The students supply the past form.

2. Put students into groups of five or six. Give each group a sentence to begin their story. Going around in their circle, the students each add a sentence to their story, using their verb. The stories may be serious or funny, but they should make some sort of sense.

Example:

Starting sentence:	Yesterday, I decided to go to the park.
Student 1:	I saw an old man sitting on a bench.
Student 2:	The old man was reading a newspaper.
Student 3:	The newspaper fell off the bench when the old man got up.

3. After the groups have finished, they may repeat their stories for the class, write their stories, or just end the activity in the groups.

6. SHORT ANSWERS

BLACK BLUE

Materials:	None
Dynamic:	Pairs/Small groups
Time:	20 minutes
Procedure:	

1. Divide the class into pairs or groups of three or four. Have each group write five short answers on a piece of paper.

2. The groups exchange papers with another pair or group and then create questions for their answers.

3. Return the papers to their originators and have the group or pair that created the answers now check that the questions written by the other group or pair are good matches for their answers.

7. LET ME TELL YOU ABOUT THE TIME . . .

RED BLACK BLUE

Materials:	Board
Dynamic:	Whole class
Time:	30 minutes
Procedure:	

1. Write a list of descriptive adjectives on the board.

   Examples: *shocking, embarrassing, funny, crazy, wonderful, ridiculous, terrible*

2. Each student chooses an adjective and writes two to four brief sentences to describe an experience he/she had that illustrates the adjectives chosen. (You might give a real or fictitious example of your own.) Tell the class that you will read their stories aloud, so they should not get too personal unless they are prepared for everyone to know. Students should not sign their papers.

   Examples:

   I had a terrible evening. I ran out of gas and walked in the dark to a gas station, but it was closed. I had to wait for someone to pass by and help me.

   The most embarrassing thing I did was to talk about the teacher when she was standing behind me!

   A crazy thing I did was to go swimming, naked, in my neighbor's pool.

3. Collect the papers and read them aloud. The students (other than the author) should guess who wrote which experiences.

8. TELL THE STORY

Materials: Short video

Dynamic: Small groups

Time: 45 minutes

RED   BLACK

Procedure:

1. Choose a video of no more than 30 minutes. You might use a children's story (such as *Where the Wild Things Are*), a short video (such as *The Red Balloon*), or an excerpt from a longer video as long as the scene is self-contained, that is, tells a story itself. Tell the class to pay close attention to the story.

2. After the class watches the video, put them into small groups of no more than four. You can list difficult vocabulary on the board or give them a handout. Or you may want to circulate and answer questions about vocabulary as they arise.

3. The students discuss the video they watched and retell the story in writing. Each group chooses one recorder, but all group members check over their finished draft.

Variation: Copy a child's picture book. Delete any words on the pages. Put the students into small groups and give one copy of the pictures to each group. Have them write the "text" to correspond to the pictures.

2.2 IRREGULAR PAST FORMS

1. BALL TOSS

Materials: Any soft ball or beanbag

Dynamic: Whole class

Time: 5 minutes

RED   BLACK   BLUE

Procedure:

1. This is a review game for irregular past forms. The game can be played to review all irregular verbs, or you can limit students to the one or two sections they have just memorized.

2. Arrange students in a circle, either standing or at their desks. Call out the simple form of an irregular verb and toss the ball to a student. That student says the simple past form. Then he or she tosses the ball to another student, who provides the past participle. This second student then calls out a new verb and tosses the ball to a classmate.

Example:

Instructor:	swim
Student 1:	swam
Student 2:	swum, eat
Student 3:	ate
Student 4:	eaten, feel

Think of this game as chains of three. The third person must both finish the chain and start a new one.

NOTE: *Encourage students to toss the ball easily. Even though it is soft, you don't want it hurting anyone. Also, if the ball comes close to a student, he or she must attempt to catch it, not avoid it.*

For lower levels:

Instructor:	swim
Student 1:	swam
Instructor:	eat
Student 1:	(throws ball)
Student 2:	ate
Instructor:	drive
Student 2:	(throws ball)
Student 3:	drove

2. RELAY

Materials: Board, 2 markers or pieces of chalk

Dynamic: Teams

Time: 10 minutes

RED BLACK BLUE

Procedure:

1. Divide the class into two teams and have them line up on either side of the classroom. Write the same list of irregular verbs (simple form) on each side of the board, but list them in different order.

2. The first student from each line goes to the board and chooses any verb to write in the past form. (Limit this to either the simple past or past participle.) As soon as he/she is done, he/she gives the marker to the next student in line. Each student can do only one new past form, but may correct any of the answers previously written. Spelling counts.

3. The object is for the team to write the irregular past forms for all the simple forms. The first team to finish correctly wins.

Suggestion: *If you have limited board space or are using a stand-up board that might not work well for this activity, an alternative is to use tag board strips. Write one word on each strip and attach them*

to the board with stick tack or putty. The students write the irregular past form next to the word strip. This way, if a student wants to correct a previous answer, he/she will not accidently erase the words you listed on the board.

Using tag board strips also makes it easy to arrange the words in different order on the two sides of the board. You can have them prearranged in two piles and then just stick them in that order on the board. And you can save the word strips to use again.

3. CONCENTRATION

Materials: Board, Worksheet 12 (optional)

Dynamic: Groups

Time: 20 minutes

RED BLACK BLUE

Procedure: 1. On the board draw a grid with just the numbers. On a paper, you will have the answers written in (see below). Tell students whether they will be matching simple and simple past forms or simple and past participle forms.

On the board:

1	2	3	4	5
6	7	8	9	10
11	12	13	14	15
16	17	18	19	20

On your paper:

1 bought	2 bring	3 found	4 did	5 came
6 brought	7 drink	8 bit	9 drank	10 bite
11 blew	12 buy	13 find	14 do	15 got
16 eat	17 come	18 ate	19 blow	20 get

2. Divide the class into groups of about five. Because this is a memory game, no writing is allowed. Explain that the students are looking for matches and will get a point for each match. They can confer as a team, but you will accept an answer only from the student whose turn it is. Each time the team has its turn, a different member of the team calls out the numbers for that round.

They call out two numbers together the first time (because no one knows where any of the words are), but in subsequent turns, they should wait for you to write the first answer before they call out their second number.

3. As the first student calls out numbers, write the words that correspond to those numbers in the blanks. Ask the class if it is a match. If not, erase the words. If so, leave them there, but cross them out (see below). Whenever a team makes a match, it gets another turn.

On the board:

1	2	3	4 ~~did~~	5
6	7	8	9	10
11	12	13	14 ~~do~~	15
16 ~~eat~~	17	18 ~~ate~~	19	20

4. As a follow-up, students could work in small groups. Divide the class into even-numbered groups and within the groups, divide the students into two teams. Give each group a copy of the worksheet. Have them fold it in half so they cannot see game 2 while playing game 1. Provide small pieces of cardboard or beans to cover the words. Each group will play its own game independent of the other groups.

NOTE: *You may use Worksheets 12A and 12B after you review all the verbs. You can also use the blank form (Worksheet 12C) and fill in your own verbs. This way, you can check the students on the verbs you have just covered in class, especially when assigning certain sections.*

4. TIC TAC TOE

Materials: Board, Worksheet 13 (optional)

Dynamic: Teams

Time: 10 minutes

RED   BLACK   BLUE

Procedure: 1. Draw a tic tac toe grid on the board with the simple form of irregular verbs written in. Decide if you want the students to supply the past tense or the past participle. (You can also draw the grid with the past tense forms and ask for past participles.)

2. Divide the class into two groups. A student from team X comes to the board and writes in the past form for any verb on the grid. If correct, he/she draws an X in the square. If the form is incorrect (spelling counts), he/she cannot draw his/her team mark. Erase the answer.

3. A student from team O comes to the board. That student may choose to correct a square that was done incorrectly earlier, or choose another verb. The teams alternate turns. The first team with three marks in a row wins.

   NOTE: *You will probably want to explain game strategy such as blocking, but often the student's choice is based on which verb he/she knows.*

4. As a follow-up, divide the class into groups of three and use the worksheet. One student is X, one is O, and the third is in charge and can have his/her book open to the verb page to judge whether an answer is correct. After the first game, the students should rotate roles so that the judge is now one of the players. Continue until all students have had a chance to be the judge.

5. LINE-UPS

RED BLACK BLUE

Materials: 3″ x 5″ cards or use Worksheet 14

Dynamic: Whole class

Time: 20 minutes

Procedure:

1. Give each student a question card. If making your own, use two different colors of 3″ x 5″ cards. If copying worksheet 14, use two different colors of paper. Call all students (half the class) with a yellow card (for example) to the front and have them stand in a line facing the class.

2. The other half of the class stands in front of the first line. If there are an odd number of students, either one waits for someone to question, or the extra person in the answer line waits until the line moves.

3. Each person with a yellow question card questions the student standing in front of him/her. When everyone has answered one question, the students in the answer line move down one and are asked a new question. Continue until all the students in the answer line have talked to every student in the question line. (The students in the question line do not move.)

4. The students in the lines now switch positions, and the former answerers are now the questioners. Continue as in #3 above.

6. SPELLING BEE

Materials: None

Dynamic: Teams

Time: 10 minutes

RED   BLACK   BLUE

Procedure:

1. Divide students into two teams and have them line up along the sides of the classroom. Give the first student from line A the simple form of one of the irregular verbs. The student must provide the correct past form and spell it correctly. For lower-level students, this form should be the simple past form. For higher-level students, decide beforehand if you want them to provide the simple past or the past participle.

2. If the student gives the wrong form or spells it incorrectly, the other team gets a chance to answer.

3. After answering, whether right or wrong, the student goes to the end of his/her line. The team earns a point for all correct answers.

4. Alternate until you have gone through your list of verbs or until a certain time limit has been reached. The team with the most points wins.

7. IRREGULAR BINGO

Materials: Worksheet 15 and markers

Dynamic: Whole class

Time: 20 minutes

RED   BLACK   BLUE

Procedure:

1. Give every student a copy of one of the bingo cards and a handful of markers (papers, cardboard disks, beans, etc.).

2. Call out the simple form of an irregular verb. The students cover the past (or past participle, depending on the card).

   NOTE: *You could also make game cards with either the past or past participle and require students to find the other form (in this case the basic form is not used).*

3. The first student to cover five words in a row shouts "Bingo!" Walk over and check for accuracy, or ask the student to call out his/her covered words to see if they are in fact correct.

4. For variety, ask for different completions, as in regular bingo: five up or down, diagonals, across, or four corners. Or use copies of the same card so that all students shout "Bingo!" at the same time.

35

PAST PROGRESSIVE

1. PICTURE SENTENCES

Materials:	Worksheet 16 or pictures with a lot of activity going on
Dynamic:	Small groups
Time:	25 minutes

Procedure:

1. Divide the class into groups of three or four. Give each group the same picture, or put it on an overhead.

2. Instruct the groups to use the past progressive to make as many sentences as possible in the time allowed. The sentences must be grammatically correct and accurately depict what is happening in the pictures.

3. The team with the most correct answers at the end of the time limit wins. To determine accuracy, have each group read their sentences or write them on the board.

   NOTE: *Good sources for pictures are a picture dictionary (especially if the students have the same one), lower-level student ESL books containing drawings for students to discuss or write about, and magazine advertisements.*

Variation 1: Give each group a different picture.

Variation 2: Give each group a different picture. Follow step 2. After 15 seconds, say "Pass" and have the groups pass their pictures to the next group. Continue until all groups have written sentences for all pictures. Score the correct answers as in step 3.

2. PEOPLE WATCHING

Materials:	None
Dynamic:	Pairs
Time:	10 minutes

Procedure:

1. Send students alone or in pairs to different places on campus where there are apt to be a lot of people.

   Suggestions: library, cafeteria, student union, admissions office, outdoor eating areas, bookstore, health center, park area, etc.

2. Tell them to stay there for 10 to 15 minutes and observe what everyone is doing. They will probably want to take notes.

3. Their homework assignment is to write a paragraph about what they observed. They may want to start out with the sentence "Today I went to the _____." They should then describe what the people they observed were doing.

3. VIDEO RECALL

Materials: Short video segment or commercial

Dynamic: Groups

Time: 15 minutes

BLACK BLUE

Procedure:
1. Show the class a short video (2–3 minutes). This could be a short segment from a TV show or video, or a commercial.

2. Tell students to watch carefully and to concentrate on the activity, not on what is being said. They should not take notes.

3. Put students in groups and have them write as many sentences as they can to describe what they just saw. You can set a time limit. The group that has the most correct sentences wins.

4. SONG

Materials: Song lyrics as cloze activity (for models, see Chapter 3 or Chapter 7)
Tape player and tape of song (optional)

Dynamic: Pairs

Time: 15 minutes

BLACK BLUE

Procedure:
1. Find song lyrics containing verbs in the past and past progressive. Try to choose a song that shows a clear contrast, such as "Tennessee Waltz."

2. Divide the class into pairs and give each pair a copy of the lyrics with the past and past progressive verbs deleted. The students work together to decide which tense is more appropriate.

3. Play the song so the students can check their answers or, if you do not have the music, go over the lyrics together. Elicit from the students why they chose one tense over another. ("Are there any signal words in the sentence?" "Is the action described clearly a continuous one?" etc.)

2.4 PRESENT PERFECT

1. ARE YOU THE ONE?

Materials: Worksheet 17

Dynamic: Whole class

Time: 20 minutes

BLACK BLUE

Procedure:

1. Give each student a copy of the worksheet, or make your own with items that are more relevant to your students.

2. The students circulate around the room and ask each other questions in the present perfect, as in the model.

3. Whenever a student gets a *yes* answer, he/she writes down the name of the student who said *yes*. The students need to find only one student who answers *yes*. If a student receives a *no* answer, the student must continue to question others until he/she receives a *yes* answer to that question. Each student continues until he/she fills in all his/her blanks.

2. LINE-UPS

Materials: 3″ x 5″ cards or Worksheet 18

Dynamic: Whole class

Time: 20 minutes

BLACK BLUE

Procedure:

1. Give each student a question card. If making your own, use two different colors of 3″ x 5″ card. If copying Worksheet 18, use two different colors of paper. Call all students (half the class) with a yellow card (for example) to the front and have them stand in a line facing the class.

2. The other half of the class stands in front of the first line. If there are an odd number of students, either one questioner waits for someone to question, or the extra person in the answer line waits until the line moves.

3. Each person with a yellow question card (for example) questions the student standing in front of him/her. The student asking the question fills in the blank with the correct form of the verb given on the card. When everyone has answered the question, the students in the answer line move down one and are asked a new question. Continue until all the students in the answer line have

talked to every student in the question line. (The students in the question line do not move.)

4. The students in the lines now switch positions, and the former answerers are now the questioners. Continue as in #3 above.

Explanation: Using two different colors of cards or papers makes it easy to divide the students into questioners and answerers. When all of the students with yellow cards have questioned all the students with pink cards, switch lines so that the students asking questions now have pink cards.

NOTE: *Before doing the line-ups, you may want to do a sample card on the board so that the students know what is expected of them. Ask them how to fill in the blanks.*

3. USING SIGNALS

BLACK   BLUE

Materials:	Board
Dynamic:	Small groups
Time:	10 minutes
Procedure:	1. Divide the class into groups of three or four. Write a list of signal words on the board.

        Example: *already, ever, for, just, many times, never, since, yet*

2. Set a time limit (2 minutes, for example) and tell the groups they must write a grammatical sentence for each signal word (one per sentence). The students should write sentences using different vocabulary words so you will <u>not</u> get

> I have already eaten dinner.
> I have just eaten dinner.
> I have eaten dinner many times.

3. Have one student from each group read the group's answers. Assign one point for each grammatically correct and logical sentence.

4. FBI FILES

BLACK   BLUE

Materials:	None
Dynamic:	Small groups
Time:	40 minutes
Procedure:	1. Divide the class into groups of three or four. Have each group write an FBI file on a wanted criminal.

Examples:

They have robbed 15 banks so far.
They have been seen in Chicago, New York, and Atlanta.
They have escaped from prison three times.

To liven things up, they might use the name of someone in their group or use the whole group as a gang.

2. Let them work for about 20–25 minutes as you circulate and help them make distinctions between simple past and the perfect tense.

3. Post the reports and let students circulate, look at them, and make comments.

4. To continue the fun, when the students are seated again, ask them to tell you anything suspicious that they have seen. Work with them to make additional perfect tense sentences.

NOTE: *A follow-up detective game is fun (see* **Detective Games 1, 2***, and* **3** *on pages 26 and 27).*

2.5 PAST PERFECT

1. LINE-UPS

— diff. colors

Materials:	3″ x 5″ cards or Worksheet 19
Dynamic:	Whole class
Time:	20 minutes

BLUE

Procedure:

1. Give each student a question card. If making your own, use two different colors of 3″ x 5″ card. If copying the worksheet, use two different colors of paper. Call all students (half the class) with a yellow card (for example) to the front and have them stand in a line facing the class.

2. The other half of the class stands in front of the first line. If there is an odd number of students, either one questioner waits for someone to question, or the extra person in the answer line waits until the line moves.

3. Each person with a question card (in the first row) asks the questions of the student standing in front of him/her. The student asking the question fills in the blanks with the correct form of the verb given on the card. When everyone has answered the question, the students in the answer line move down one and are asked a new question. Continue until all the students in the answer line

have talked to every student in the question line. (The students in the question line do not move.)

4. The students in the lines now switch positions, and the former answerers are now the questioners. Continue as in #3 above.

Explanation: Using two different colors of cards or papers makes it easier to divide the class into questioners and answerers. When all the students with yellow cards have questioned all the students with pink cards, switch lines so that the students asking questions have pink cards.

NOTE: *Before doing the line-ups, you may want to do a sample card on the board so that the students know what is expected of them. Ask them how to fill in the blanks.*

PAST REVIEW

1. QUESTIONNAIRE (Present/Past perfect)

Materials: Worksheet 20

Dynamic: Pairs

Time: 25 minutes

BLACK   BLUE

Procedure:

1. Divide the class into pairs, and give each student a copy of the worksheet.

2. Have them ask each other the questions on the paper, then write their partner's answers.

    Example:

    Anton: What have you done more than three times today?
    Maria: I have drunk water.
    Anton writes: Maria has drunk water more than three times today.

3. After students have completed the questionnaire, go around and randomly ask for answers from the students, or you may collect the questionnaires and correct them.

2. ACT IT OUT (Simple past/Past perfect)

BLACK   BLUE

Materials: Worksheet 21

Dynamic: Pairs

Time: 30 minutes

Procedure:

1. Cut up the cards in the worksheet or make your own.

2. Divide the class into pairs. Have each pair come to the front of the room and draw a card. As in charades, the students will act out the activity depicted without speaking. The students must work together to depict the activity.

3. The class tries to guess what is going on, then states it in a complete sentence.

Fill in the blanks with a past form of to be *(was, were, wasn't or weren't).*

A thief stole a computer and printer from an office on campus Saturday at 10:00. Sandy _____ in the parking lot across from the office, standing next to her car. She saw him for only a few minutes, but she _____ sure she could identify him. The police officers _____ happy to have a witness, but they _____ sure how much Sandy saw from the parking lot. Sandy _____ positive she could answer the detectives' questions.

QUESTIONS:

1. _____ you near the ESL office at 10:00 on Saturday?

2. Why _____ you on campus on a Saturday?

3. _____ the office open when you arrived?

4. _____ you able to see anyone run out of the office?

5. What _____ in his hands?

6. How tall _____ he?

7. What color _____ his hair?

8. _____ his clothes old or new?

9. _____ his clothes expensive?

10. How old _____ he?

11. _____ he someone you knew?

SITUATION:

A computer and printer were stolen from the ESL office on Sunday at 10:00. The police found several witnesses who saw something suspicious on Sunday and have compiled a list of four suspects. The detective is now questioning the witnesses again and then will decide who the probable thief was.

WITNESS 1:

I had just parked my car in the parking lot across from the ESL office. I was planning to go to the library to study. I was taking my books out of the car when a man came out of the office, carrying a computer and printer. He looked familiar. In fact, I'm sure I've seen him at the ESL department several times. I'm not sure if he was a student or if he worked there. He was tall and had light brown hair, I think.

SITUATION:

A computer and printer were stolen from the ESL office on Sunday at 10:00. The police found several witnesses who saw something suspicious on Sunday and have compiled a list of four suspects. The detective is now questioning the witnesses again and then will decide who the probable thief was.

WITNESS 2:

I was eating breakfast with Chris at the campus cafe when I saw a young guy run past with a computer. I think he was wearing jeans, but I'm not sure. He might have had a cap on. I didn't see his hair. I thought it was strange that someone would be running on campus with a computer. That's why I noticed him. Anyway, I told Chris to look, and he turned around to see. We were talking about last night's party at the time.

✂ -

SITUATION:

A computer and printer were stolen from the ESL office on Sunday at 10:00. The police found several witnesses who saw something suspicious on Sunday, and they have compiled a list of four suspects. The detective is now questioning the witnesses again and then will decide who the probable thief was.

WITNESS 3:

Well, I didn't see much. I was eating and talking to Sandy at the cafe. Actually, my back was to the sidewalk. Sandy said, "Hey, look at that!" so I turned around. I saw a guy running, and he was carrying something. I couldn't see what it was, but it seemed heavy. I only saw him from the back, but I can describe him. I have good eyes. He was wearing shorts and a blue T-shirt. His hair was dark—or maybe he had a dark cap on. He was about average height.

✂ -

SITUATION:

A computer and printer were stolen from the ESL office on Sunday at 10:00. The police found several witnesses who saw something suspicious on Sunday, and they have compiled a list of four suspects. The detective is now questioning the witnesses again and then will decide who the probable thief was.

SUSPECTS:

1. John Peters   office worker on campus, recently quit.
   Age: 30. Hair: brown. Height: 6 ft.

2. Dr. James Brown   professor in the history department.
   Age: 39. Hair: brown and gray. Wears glasses.
   Height: 5'7"

3. Paul Taylor   unemployed. Lives near campus.
   Age: 20. Hair: blond. Height: 6'1"

4. Ken Dey   student in the ESL department.
   Age: 22. Hair: black. Height: 5'9"

GAME 1

1 be	2 became	3 begin	4 caught	5 break
6 chose	7 cost	8 bent	9 broke	10 cut
11 catch	12 become	13 built	14 cut	15 cost
16 build	17 choose	18 was	19 bend	20 began

GAME 2

1 write	2 spoke	3 won	4 shook	5 rode
6 told	7 threw	8 sang	9 speak	10 ride
11 win	12 wear	13 said	14 wrote	15 sing
16 shake	17 say	18 wore	19 throw	20 tell

GAME 1

1 flew	2 drunk	3 known	4 torn	5 taught
6 caught	7 forgotten	8 flown	9 fell	10 caught
11 felt	12 taught	13 spoken	14 forgot	15 fallen
16 drank	17 felt	18 knew	19 spoke	20 tore

GAME 2

1 ate	2 laid	3 taken	4 lain	5 eaten
6 got	7 stolen	8 did	9 frozen	10 slid
11 sung	12 slid	13 lay	14 laid	15 stole
16 done	17 froze	18 gotten	19 took	20 sing

GAME 1

1	2	3	4	5
6	7	8	9	10
11	12	13	14	15
16	17	18	19	20

GAME 2

1	2	3	4	5
6	7	8	9	10
11	12	13	14	15
16	17	18	19	20

teach	catch	buy
grow	hear	bring
fight	shoot	see

be	bite	build
choose	cut	draw
fit	drive	feed

hide	hurt	keep
leave	let	lend
light	lose	hold

What did you eat for breakfast?	Where did you go after class yesterday?
How much did your grammar book cost?	What did you drink with lunch yesterday?
What did you buy recently at the grocery store?	What did you hear the teacher say?
Where did you leave your books?	Who did you see before class?
Who did you last send a letter to?	How late did you sleep this morning?
How much money did you spend on lunch yesterday?	What did you bring to school today?

Who did you recently send a package to?	What did you make for dinner yesterday?
Who was the last person you saw before class?	What did you lend a friend last week?
Who did you last fight with?	What did you break recently?
Where did you put your books when you got home from class yesterday?	Who did you sit next to in class today?
What did you recently lose?	What did you quit doing?
When did you last go swimming?	What did you read yesterday or today?
What did you cut out of the newspaper or magazine?	How much did you pay for your last haircut?

Fun with Grammar 51

was	blew	bought	cut	ate
found	went	hid	left	paid
ran	shook	FREE	spoke	took
thought	won	broke	caught	fought
did	fell	felt	got	said

said	got	felt	fell	did
fought	caught	broke	won	thought
ran	shook	FREE	spoke	took
paid	left	hid	went	found
was	blew	bought	cut	ate

ate	left	won	did	said
caught	went	was	found	shook
broke	got	FREE	paid	spoke
fought	fell	ran	thought	felt
took	blew	bought	cut	hid

		FREE		

You and your partners will write sentences to describe this picture, using the past progressive. Write as many as you can in ___ minutes.

Use the following verb phrases to ask questions using the present perfect. Try to get a yes *answer to each question. When you find someone who answers* yes, *write his/her name on the blank. Do not write the name if he/she answers* no.

1. arrive late to a movie _____

2. dream in English _____

3. be "stood up" _____

4. lose your homework _____

5. sleep in class _____

6. eat raw fish _____

7. go to traffic court _____

8. act crazy with friends _____

9. go on a "blind date" _____

10. meet someone famous _____

11. visit a country in Asia _____

12. fly over an ocean _____

13. get on the wrong bus or train _____

14. lose your ID _____

15. speak your own language in English class _____

What have you _____ *(eat)* this morning?	Who have you _____ *(speak)* to before class today?
What have you _____ *(forget)* to do?	What have you _____ *(think)* about doing after class?
Where have you _____ *(go)* shopping?	What have you _____ *(give)* a friend?
How much money have you _____ *(lend)* a friend?	What have you _____ *(send)* to your family recently?
What habit have you _____ *(quit)*?	How often have you _____ *(be)* to the movies this month?
What have you _____ *(tell)* a family member more than once?	What have you _____ *(lose)* recently?

How often have you ——————— (see) your family since you came to this school?

Who have you ——————— (tell) a secret to more than once?

What have you ——————— (drink) more than once today?

What have you ——————— (do) more than once today?

How many essays have you ——————— (write) in writing class?

How many people from your country have you ——————— (meet) in this class?

How often have you ——————— (buy) a soft drink in the last week?

What have you ——————— (begin) to do since coming to the United States?

What is the longest you have ——————— (sleep) since coming to this school?

How much money have you ——————— (spend) on lunch this past month?

What have you ——————— (break) more than once?

How have you ——————— (feel) this week?

Who have you ——————— (know) since you were a child?

Who have you ——————— (sit) next to in class more than once this week?

Where —————— *(you, study)* English before you —————— *(come)* to this school?

Who (if anyone) —————— *(you, know)* in this class when you —————— *(start)* to study here?

What —————— *(you, hear)* about this school before you —————— *(come)* here?

How many times —————— *(you, see)* a movie in English before you —————— *(come)* to this city?

What —————— *(you, already, do)* before you —————— *(leave)* home this morning?

What —————— *(you, already, eat)* before you —————— *(come)* to class?

When you —————— *(leave)* for class this morning, —————— *(the sun, come up)*?

Who —————— *(already, get up)* when you —————— *(leave)* home this morning?

What —————— *(you, never, see)* before you —————— *(go)* to a museum?

What —————— *(you, never, eat)* before you —————— *(go)* to a Mexican restaurant?

Where —————— *(you, be)* before you —————— *(get)* home yesterday?

Before you —————— *(go)* to bed last night, what —————— *(you, already, do)*?

Write your partner's answers in complete sentences.

1. What is something you have done more than once today?

   _____

2. What is something you have done more than five times in your life?

   _____

3. What is something you have never done, but would like to try?

   _____

4. What is something you have done only since coming to this school?

   _____

5. Who have you just spoken to?

   _____

6. What is something you had thought about the opposite sex before you talked to many of them?

   _____

7. Who is someone you wish you had seen before you left home to come here?

   _____

8. What is something you had already done before you entered high school?

   _____

9. Where had you traveled before you came to this school?

   _____

   _____

10. Where had you learned English before you came to this school?

    _____

✂ -

Student A had entered the class before the teacher (Student B) arrived.	Student A had eaten the entire meal before Student B returned from the restroom.
Student A had finished his/her homework before he/she called Student B.	Student A had already gotten ready for class before Student B woke up.
Student A had already washed the dishes by the time Student B arrived.	Student A had talked to the teacher (Student B) before entering the classroom.
Student A had already fed and walked the dog by the time Student B was ready to go.	The mother (Student A) had already changed the baby's diaper by the time the father (Student B) got up from watching TV.
Student A had already finished the race by the time Student B was halfway through.	Student A had already walked to the door by the time the doorbell rang.
Student A had already gotten a sunburn by the time his/her friend got to the beach.	Student A had already finished washing his/her car by the time Student B offered to help.

CHAPTER 3

Verbs: Future

3.1 FUTURE — Predictions

1. FORTUNE COOKIES*

Materials: One fortune cookie per student

Dynamic: Whole class

Time: 15 minutes

BLACK BLUE

Procedure:
1. Discuss with the class where they find predictions in the "real world." (Usual answers will include weather forecasts and fortune telling.) Ask if they can think of a restaurant where fortunes are used. Most of the time, at least one student will mention Chinese restaurants. Explain that the fortune cookies at Chinese restaurants sometimes contain fortunes, but sometimes may be just factual statements ("You are a good person").

2. Give each student a fortune cookie and have them look at their "fortunes" to see if the main verb form is either *to be* + *-ing* or *will* + simple form. If a student has one of these forms in his/her fortune, ask him/her to read it aloud to the class.

3. Because these fortunes are often difficult for a non-native speaker to understand, go over the meanings, perhaps asking the class what they think is meant.

   NOTE: *Fortune cookies can usually be found in large supermarkets in the Asian food aisle.*

*Suzanne W. Woodward's **Fortune Cookies** was originally published in *TESOL Journal*, Vol. 5, No. 3, Spring 1996, p. 31. Used with permission.

2. WRITE YOUR OWN FORTUNES

Materials: One slip of paper per student with the name of a classmate on it

Dynamic: Whole class

Time: 10 minutes

BLACK BLUE

Procedure:
1. Distribute the slips of paper. Tell the students they are going to write a fortune for the student whose name is on their paper. The fortunes may be silly or serious, but must contain one of the future forms studied in class.

2. Collect the slips. Redistribute the fortunes to the students whose names are on the papers.

3. Invite students to share their fortunes with the class, but do not <u>require</u> them to do so. If the students know each other well, the fortunes may be too personal to share with the rest of the class.

4. Have students check their fortunes to see if one of the correct forms was used. If not, have them try to rewrite the prediction, using a correct future form.

NOTE: *This is a good follow-up activity to Activity 1:* **Fortune Cookies,** *but it can be done alone by doing steps 1 and 2 of Activity 1 first.*

3. MAGIC 8 BALL

Materials: A 3″ x 5″ index card per student, Magic 8 Ball

Dynamic: Whole class

Time: 30 minutes

RED BLACK BLUE

Procedure:

1. Have students write two predictions for their classmates on their index cards—one using *will* and the other using *be going to.* Tell them to make the predictions general so that they can apply to anyone in the class. They can be serious or funny and should be positive. Put all the cards into a hat or bag.

2. Each student pulls a card. If a student draws the card he/she wrote, he/she replaces it and chooses another.

3. The students read one of the predictions on the card, turn it over, and on the back write one or more questions that might come before the prediction.

Example:	**Prediction:**	You will win a hundred dollars.
	Questions:	Will I be lucky in Las Vegas?
		Will I win the lottery this weekend?

4. Collect the cards again. Pull out the Magic 8 Ball and announce that Professor Grammar has a magic ball that can tell the future. Ask volunteers to pose a question to the Magic 8 Ball. Professor Grammar reads the ball's answer to the class. Everyone will want to question the ball at least once.

5. If time, they can read the second question for the second prediction.

NOTE: *The Magic 8 Ball is available in any toy store.*

SUGGESTION: *Instead of using a Magic 8 Ball, you can prepare some general answers on slips of paper, such as* yes, no, definitely, probably not, it's unclear at this time, *etc. When a student asks his/her question, Professor Grammar can reach into a bag and pull out a slip with the answer to the question.*

4. WHAT'S NEXT?

BLACK BLUE

Materials: Several different pictures representing
some activities

Dynamic: Small groups

Time: 30 minutes

Procedure:

1. Arrange students in groups of three or four, and give each group a picture. (Magazine advertisements are good for this activity.)

2. Tell the groups to look carefully at their pictures and decide what is happening or has happened. If various scenarios are possible, the group should settle on the most likely. Then, the students predict what they think will happen next to the people in the picture.

3. You may want each group to work together to write a short paragraph describing what they think will happen. Another way to close this activity is for each group to show its picture, describe the scene, and then give its predictions.

5. SONG

RED BLACK BLUE

Materials: Worksheet 22, or other song lyrics
Tape recorder and tape (optional)

Dynamic: Pairs

Time: 20 minutes

Procedure:

1. Choose a song with several lines that use future verbs. Type up the words, but eliminate the future forms. Instead, provide the simple form of the verb (see Worksheet 22).

2. Students work in pairs to fill in the blanks.

3. To check the answers, either go over the song together or play the song so students can check for themselves. (Explain that either *to be* + *-ing* or *will* + simple form is acceptable as long as it makes a prediction, so they should not change their answers from one form to the other when going over the words.)

6. ROLE PLAY

BLACK **BLUE**

Materials: None

Dynamic: Whole class/Pairs

Time: 45 minutes

Procedure:

1. Assign each student a role. In some cases, the students will work in pairs.

   Suggestions:
   Fortune teller (pairs)
   Weather forecaster
   Politician running for election
   Job applicant (pairs)
   Greenhouse (nursery) worker (pairs possible)
   Guest lecturers: pollution, environment, economy
   Graduation speaker
   Student talking about future plans

   Give students class time to prepare a short speech, or have them prepare a speech (1–3 minutes) for homework.

2. Students take turns giving their speeches/role plays to the class.

3. To keep the class's interest, try one of the following:

   a. Have the audience write down all the predictions they hear. This could be an individual activity, or a group activity where you allow the group members to compare notes briefly. The group or students with the most correctly recorded predictions "wins."

   b. For each role play/speech, assign one student to count the number of times a future form is used. Assign another to make a list of the predictions. The speaker decides if they are correct. Alternate these roles so everyone gets a chance to do at least one.

Variation: To incorporate writing, you may have the students write out their speeches or conversations for homework and hand them in before giving their oral presentations.

7. INTERVIEWS

RED **BLACK** **BLUE**

Materials: None

Dynamic: Pairs

Time: 30 minutes

Procedure:

1. Divide the class into pairs. The partners interview each other about their future plans—either immediate or long term.

Sample questions:

> What are you going to do after you finish this English program?
> Are you going to go to a university?
> When you return home, are you going to look for a job?
> When do you think you will get married?

2. Have each student give a short oral report to the class about his/her partner's future plans, or have each student write a paragraph about his/her partner's future plans.

NOTE: *You may prefer to use this activity to review prior plans, keeping in mind that often long-range "plans" are really predictions. You may want to discuss which of the future plans is really a prior plan (going to a university if the student has already filled in the paper work) and which are really predictions (I will look for a job when I return home).*

3.2 FUTURE — Willingness

1. ACCIDENT

Materials: Props for accident role play

Dynamic: Whole class

Time: 10 minutes

BLACK BLUE

Procedure:

1. Without telling the class, role play an accident in class. If more than one person is needed, "recruit" another instructor, a member of the class, or a student from another class.

2. Keep the "accident" simple, but be sure to include something the students may or may not be willing to help with.

    Suggestions:

    Spill water on tests: "Will anyone volunteer to ask the secretary for more (or get other copies off my desk, etc.)?"

    Arrange for an accomplice to slip on the floor and pretend to be injured: "Will someone help this person to the office?"

    Be sure to arrange in advance with anyone the students may go to for help.

3. Explain that the activity the students witnessed was not real. Go over what happened and discuss why students were or were not willing to get involved.

FUTURE — Prior Plan

1. MAKING AN APPOINTMENT

RED   BLACK   BLUE

Materials: Worksheet 23A (For variation, 23B and 23C)

Dynamic: Pairs

Time: 15–30 minutes

Procedure:

1. Divide the class into pairs. Give a copy of Worksheet 23A to each student. Student A is calling to make an appointment. Student B is a receptionist in a doctor's office. The students must refer to Worksheet 23A to see when they can schedule an appointment.

    Sample conversation:

    Student A: Hello. I need to make an appointment with the doctor.

    Student B: How about Monday at 3:30?

    Student A: No, I have a class every afternoon until 4 o'clock. Are there any appointments open in the morning?

    Student B: Can you come Wednesday at 9:00?

    Student A: No, I have a dentist appointment then. How about 12:30?

    Student B: I'm sorry, the doctor is at lunch between 12:00 and 1:00 every day. Can you come Thursday at 10:15?

    Student A: Yes, I'm free then.

Variation: Choose five students to be receptionists and station them around the classroom. Each has one of the <u>office</u> schedules in 23A, 23B, and 23C. The other students need to make appointments with all the receptionists. Each student making an appointment uses the <u>student</u> schedule in 23A. They form lines in front of the five receptionists and make appointments. To give all students a chance, you may want to impose a time limit. If a student has not made an appointment in that time, he/she goes to the back of the line or to a different receptionist. The size of the class will determine how many appointments each student can make.

2. This activity can stop when the first student has made all his/her appointments or when a specified time limit has been reached.

2. DAILY PLANNER

RED   BLACK   BLUE

Materials: Worksheet 24

Dynamic: Whole class

Time: 20 minutes

Procedure:

1.   Give each student a copy of Worksheet 24 and tell them to think of one thing that they are planning to do each day for the next week or half-week. They should write a short note on their planner (worksheet) indicating each activity.

Example: SUNDAY: visit my parents

2.   Each student tries to find another student to accompany him/her on each activity by asking, first, what they are doing at a specific time in the future and, second, if they are interested in doing the particular activity. You may want to write the following sample dialogues on the board.

> **Student A:**   Are you free on Sunday at 2 PM?
> **Student B:**   Yes, I'm free.
> **Student A:**   I'm visiting my parents at their farm. Would you like to come?
> **Student B:**   Yes, I'd like to.
>
> **Student A:**   I'm going to visit my parents at their farm on Sunday afternoon. Would you like to come?
> **Student B:**   No, I have other plans.
> **Student A:**   Well, let me know if you change your mind.
>
> **Student A:**   Are you free on Sunday at 2 PM?
> **Student B:**   Yes, I'm free.
> **Student A:**   I'm visiting my parents at their farm. Would you like to come?
> **Student B:**   I'm sorry, but I really don't like the country.

A student may refuse to accompany another because he/she is busy, is uninterested in the activity, or has another valid excuse.

3.   The students find a different person for each activity, thereby mingling with other students and practicing the structure as much as possible. They must write down the name of the student who agrees to accompany them on each activity.

4.   When they have a different name for each day, they are finished. It may not be possible for them to find students to accompany them on every activity. Therefore, you may want to set a time limit. Whoever has the most names at that point is the winner.

5. Follow up by asking students at random what they are doing at a specific time/date and with whom.

NOTE: *This variation on the previous activity,* **Making an Appointment,** *uses the present progressive to express future time.*

3. INTERVIEWS

RED   BLACK   BLUE

Materials:	None
Dynamic:	Pairs
Time:	30 minutes
Procedure:	1. Same as the interview activity listed in **Interviews** (3.1.7). This time, the students must focus on immediate plans. In their interviews, they should pick a specific time, such as "this evening," "tomorrow morning," or "this weekend." Follow the same procedure as in activity 3.1.7.

3.4   FUTURE — Predictions, Prior Plans, or Willingness

1. GOSSIP, GOSSIP, GOSSIP

RED   BLACK

Materials:	None
Dynamic:	Whole class
Time:	10 minutes
Procedure:	1. Arrange student desks in a circle, or have students stand in a circle. To the first student, the instructor whispers a sentence that contains at least one future form. Each student whispers to the next until the sentence reaches the last student.
	2. The last student writes what he/she heard on the board. The instructor also writes the first sentence to compare the differences. Discuss whether the future in the sentence on the board expresses a prediction, a prior plan, or willingness.
	3. Play a few more rounds if time allows. This time, let a student start the gossip.

2. FAIRY TALES

BLACK   BLUE

Materials: Worksheets 25A, 25B, and 25C
Worksheet 25D (optional)

Dynamic: Pairs

Time: 40 minutes

Procedure: 1.   Briefly discuss fairy tales with the class. Who are fairy tales for? What are some popular ones from their countries? Does the class know any that are popular in the United States/North America?

2.   Give half the class Worksheet 25A and the other half, Worksheet 25B. For homework, they should read the story and be ready to tell the story to their partner without reading from the paper. (You may want to allow them to use notes or to glance at the worksheet.)

3.   Form the class into pairs, one with Worksheet 25A and the other with Worksheet 25B. The students tell each other their fairy tale. The partners then work together to answer the questions on Worksheet 25C.

Variation: If the students are familiar with these two fairy tales, instead of giving them the worksheets, you may want to have them tell the stories on their own. This is a less controlled format because you will not be sure the students are using future forms in their retelling.

Follow-up: Read aloud short one-page fables, but eliminate the moral. Put the students in groups to discuss what they heard and to guess the moral. See Worksheet 25D for possibilities.

3.5   FUTURE IN TIME CLAUSES

1. SONG

Materials: Worksheet 26, or other song lyrics
Tape recorder and tape (optional)

RED   BLACK   BLUE

Dynamic: Pairs

Time: 20 minutes

Procedure: 1.   Arrange students in pairs or in groups of three. Give a copy of the song to each pair or group. Have the students work together to fill in the missing verb forms.

2.   Go over the answers together. If you have the music, play it and let the students check their own answers.

FUTURE PROGRESSIVE AND FUTURE TIME CLAUSES

1. SONG

BLUE

Materials: Worksheet 27A and 27B, or make your own
Tape recorder and music (optional)

Dynamic: Pairs

Time: 20 minutes

Procedure:
1. Put students in pairs or in groups of three. Give a copy of the song to each pair or group. Have the students fill in the missing verb forms and answer the questions on the worksheet.

2. Go over the answers together. If you have the music, play it and let the students check their own answers.

FUTURE PERFECT

1. LIFE EVENTS

BLACK   BLUE

Materials: None

Dynamic: Small groups

Time: 30 minutes

Procedure:
1. Divide the class into groups of three or four. Each group brainstorms a list of events that may happen to them in the future (get married, have children, get a degree, go to a university, finish the English program, return home, buy a new car, etc.).

2. Each student in the group works independently to make five sentences that use two of the items on the list. They may use an item more than once. For example, a student may decide to combine the items *get married* and *finish the English program* into a sentence such as *By the time I get married, I will have finished this English program*.

3. Each student reads his/her sentences to the group. The group decides if the sentences are grammatically correct. The group may

also want to comment on logic. (For example, do they want to accept *By the time I finish the ESL program, I will have gotten my BA degree* or *By the time I finish the ESL program, I will have returned to my country* as logical?)

"Some of These Days"*

I hope you'll never forget to remember me
when you hear . . .

REFRAIN:
Some of these days
You _____ me baby *(miss)*
Some of these days
You _____ so lonely *(be)*
You _____ my kissing *(miss)*
You _____ my hugging *(miss)*
You _____ me baby *(miss)*
When I'm far away
Well, I feel so lonely
For you only
Ah, but honey,
You had your way.
When you leave,
I know it _____ me *(grieve)*
You _____ me baby *(miss)*
When you're gone.

REFRAIN
Repeat lines starting with "Well, I feel so lonely . . ."

* by Shelton Brooks (1910)

Student	MON	TUES	WED	THURS	FRI
9 – 10	Writing class	Writing class	Writing class	Writing class	Writing class
10 – 11					
11 – 12		Reading class	11:30 Dentist	Reading class	
12 – 1	Lunch w/Ann				
1 – 2	Pick up film				
2 – 3		Meeting w/advisor			
3 – 4	Elective 3 – 4:30		Elective 3 – 4:30		Elective 3 – 4:30
4 – 5					

Doctor	MON	TUES	WED	THURS	FRI
9 – 10					
10 – 11		Hospital		Hospital	T. Duong
11 – 12					
12 – 1	Lunch	Lunch	Lunch	Lunch	Lunch
1 – 2					
2 – 3	Mrs. Graham		Meeting 2 – 3:30, Dr. Lee	S. Lopez	
3 – 4				T. Johnson	M. Goldman 3:30 – 4:30
4 – 5	Julieta Bejar				

Vet	MON	TUES	WED	THURS	FRI
9 – 10	P. Philips				
10 – 11				J. Clemens	
11 – 12					
12 – 1	Lunch	Lunch	Lunch	Lunch	Lunch
1 – 2	Surgery	Surgery	Surgery	Surgery	Surgery
2 – 3					
3 – 4		V. Ohama			C. Carstairs
4 – 5	S. Moon				

Counselor	MON	TUES	WED	THURS	FRI
9 – 10		Drop-in		Drop-in	
10 – 11					
11 – 12	Lunch	Lunch	Lunch	Lunch	Lunch
12 – 1					
1 – 2			Meeting w/Director		Meeting w/Advisory committee
2 – 3					
3 – 4					Doctor appt.
4 – 5	off	off	off	off	off

Dentist	MON	TUES	WED	THURS	FRI
9 – 10	J. Smith				CLOSED
10 – 11			R. Phillips		
11 – 12					
12 – 1					
1 – 2	Lunch	Lunch	Lunch	Lunch	
2 – 3				S. Case	
3 – 4			Conference		
4 – 5		Meeting			

Hair-dresser	MON	TUES	WED	THURS	FRI
9 – 10	CLOSED	M. Lee			
10 – 11					
11 – 12					Dominick
12 – 1			Alicia		Carolyn F.
1 – 2		Lunch	Lunch	Lunch	Lunch
2 – 3					
3 – 4			J. Peterson		
4 – 5					Florence

Worksheet 23D: BLANK APPOINTMENT SCHEDULES

	MON	TUES	WED	THURS	FRI
9 – 10					
10 – 11					
11 – 12					
12 – 1					
1 – 2					
2 – 3					
3 – 4					
4 – 5					

	MON	TUES	WED	THURS	FRI
9 – 10					
10 – 11					
11 – 12					
12 – 1					
1 – 2					
2 – 3					
3 – 4					
4 – 5					

WEEK OF _____	
MONDAY _____ _____ _____ _____	THURSDAY _____ _____ _____ _____
TUESDAY _____ _____ _____ _____	FRIDAY _____ _____ _____ _____
WEDNESDAY _____ _____ _____ _____	SATURDAY SUNDAY _____ _____ _____ _____

Once upon a time, a little red hen and her chick found a stalk of wheat. "With this stalk, we can grow wheat to make into bread," the hen told her chick. "Now, who will help us plant this wheat?"

"I won't," said the pig.

"I won't," said the duck.

"I won't," said the goat.

"Then my chick and I will plant it ourselves." And they did just that. After some time, the wheat grew, and it was time to harvest it.

"Who will help us harvest this wheat?" the hen asked.

"I won't," said the pig.

"I won't," said the duck.

"I won't," said the goat.

"Well, then we will have to do it ourselves." So the little red hen and her chick harvested all the wheat. "Now, who will help us grind this wheat into flour?"

"I won't," said the pig.

"I won't," said the duck.

"I won't," said the goat.

"Hmmm. Then I guess we will do it ourselves." After the wheat had been ground into flour, the little red hen asked if any of the others were willing to help make the bread. Again, she got the same responses from the pig, duck, and goat. So the little red hen and her chick worked hard to make the flour into bread.

The pig, duck, and goat could smell the bread cooking. "Mmmm. That smells good," they all said. "Is it ready?"

"Yes, it is," said the little red hen, taking the bread out of the oven. "Now, who will help us eat it?

"I will," said the pig.

"I will," said the duck.

"I will," said the goat.

"Oh, no you won't!" she cried. "You didn't help us plant the wheat, you didn't help us harvest the wheat, you didn't help us grind the wheat or make the bread. Now, my chick and I are going to eat it ourselves!!"

Once upon a time, three little pigs decided to build houses. The first little pig built his house out of straw because it was cheap and easy to use. Just when he had finished, a wolf came to his door.

"Little pig, little pig," he called. "Let me come in."

"Not by the hair of my chinny-chin-chin!"

"Then I'll huff, and I'll puff, and I'll blow your house in!" cried the wolf. And he did! The little pig ran to the second pig's house, which was built of twigs. The wolf followed him, but the little pig managed to get in before the wolf caught him.

"Little pigs, little pigs," he called. "Let me come in."

"Not by the hair of our chinny-chin-chins!"

"Then I'll huff, and I'll puff, and I'll blow your house in!" the wolf cried. And he did! The two little pigs ran to the third pig's house. The third pig had built his house out of brick, even though brick was more expensive and took longer to build with. He had just finished his house when his two friends ran up.

"Quick, inside!" they shouted. The three pigs ran inside and locked the door. Just then the wolf arrived.

"Little pigs, little pigs," he called. "Let me come in."

"Not by the hair of our chinny-chin-chins!"

"Then I'll huff, and I'll puff, and I'll blow your house in!" the wolf cried. He started to blow, but nothing happened to the house. He blew and blew, but the house was strong. Finally, the wolf gave up and went away. The little pigs were very happy.

"Come on," said the third pig. "I will show you how to build a house out of bricks." Soon, all three pigs had brick houses to protect them from the wolf.

Answer the following questions with your partner.

1. Which story or stories used some form of the future?

2. Did one (or more) of the stories use the future to express a prediction? If so, which one(s)? Give an example.

3. Did one (or more) of the stories use the future to express willingness? If so, which one(s)? Give an example.

4. Did one (or more) of the stories use the future to express prior plans? If so, which one(s)? Give an example.

5. Did any of the stories use the negative with the future? If so, which one(s)? Give an example.

6. For questions 3, 4, and 5, decide why a specific form of the future was used.

"The Quack Frog"

Once upon a time, an ugly old Frog came out of his home in the marshes. He proclaimed to the world that he was a learned physician, able to cure all diseases and ailments. However, among the crowd listening to the Frog was a Fox. He shouted, "How can you claim to be a healing doctor? Look at yourself! How can you claim to cure others when you can't cure your own crooked legs and blotched and wrinkled skin?"

Moral: Physician, heal thyself.

"The North Wind and the Sun"

A disagreement arose between the North Wind and the Sun. Each claimed that he was stronger than the other. Finally, they decided to try out their powers on an unsuspecting traveler to see who could blow off his cloak first. The North Wind went first. He gathered all his force and blew with all his might, but the harder he blew, the more closely the man wrapped his cloak around himself. Then it was the Sun's turn. He smiled down on the traveler with all his warmth. Soon, the traveler undid his cloak and walked away with the cloak draped loosely over his shoulders. The Sun then put his whole force to the task, beaming his hot rays onto the traveler. The traveler quickly shed his cloak and continued his journey, carrying the cloak.

Moral: Persuasion is better than force.

Fill in the blanks in the song, using the appropriate form of the verbs provided.

"When Johnny _____ (*Come*) Marching Home"

When Johnny _____ (*come*) marching home again,

Hurrah! Hurrah!

We _____ (*give*) him a hearty welcome then, Hurrah!

Hurrah!

The men _____ (*cheer*), the boys _____ (*shout*),

the ladies they _____ (*all, turn out*)

And we _____ (*all, feel*) gay when Johnny _____

(*come*) marching home.

Fill in the blanks in the song, using the appropriate form of the verbs provided. Choose from simple future, future progressive, or the simple present.

"She'll Be Comin' Round the Mountain"

She _____ *(come)* round the mountain when she _____ *(come)*

She _____ *(come)* round the mountain when she _____ *(come)*

She _____ *(come)* round the mountain,

She _____ *(come)* round the mountain,

She _____ *(come)* round the mountain when she _____ *(come)*.

She _____ *(drive)* six white horses when she _____ *(come)*

She _____ *(drive)* six white horses when she _____ *(come)*

She _____ *(drive)* six white horses,

She _____ *(drive)* six white horses,

She _____ *(drive)* six white horses when she _____ *(come)*.

Oh, we _____ *(all go)* out to meet her when she _____ *(come)*

Oh, we _____ *(all go)* out to meet her when she _____ *(come)*

Oh, we _____ *(all go)* out to meet her,

Oh, we _____ *(all go)* out to meet her,

Oh, we _____ *(all go)* out to meet her when she _____ *(come)*.

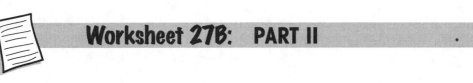

Answer the questions about the verbs you used in the song.

1. What form of the verb did you use in the first half of the sentences in the first two paragraphs? _____

2. Why did you choose this form? _____

   _____

3a. Did you use any different form in the first part of the sentences in the third paragraph? _____

   b. Explain your answer. _____

   _____

4a. What form of the verb did you use in the time clause? _____

   _____

   b. Give a reason for your answer. _____

   _____

CHAPTER 4

Verbs: Review

REVIEW OF PERFECT TENSES

1. TIME LINE

BLACK   BLUE

Materials: Board

Dynamic: Whole class

Time: 15 minutes

Procedure:

1. Draw a time line on the board.

2. Ask for a student volunteer to provide dates and facts about past events in his/her life. Write them on the time line.

3. Ask the class to predict what this student will do in the future. Write the suggestions on the time line.

    Example:

1995	1996	1997	1998	1999
finish hs	come to U.S.	now	return home	get married

4. With the help of the class, write two sentences based on the time line for each of the perfect tenses.

    Examples:

    a. Before John came to the United States, he had finished high school.

    b. He has been studying English since he came to the United States.

    c. He will have returned home by the time he gets married.

5. For homework, have the students make their own time line and write two sentences for each of the perfect tenses based on their time line.

    SUGGESTION: *Cash register tapes are inexpensive and make good time lines. Instead of doing a volunteer time line on the board, you can divide the class into groups and have each group construct a time line for one of its members. Then put the tapes on the walls and have another group make sentences using some other group's time line.*

REVIEW OF ALL VERB FORMS

1. SONG

Materials: Worksheet of lyrics based on models in Chapter 3

Tape and tape player (optional)

Dynamic: Pairs

Time: 20 minutes

RED   BLACK   BLUE

Procedure:

1. Prepare a handout for each student of song lyrics with verbs omitted (make sure to omit only verbs whose tenses/forms the students can figure out from context). Sometimes many different forms can work in the song.

2. Divide the class into pairs, and have each pair work on the song to fill in the missing verb forms.

3. Go over the answers together, or listen to a tape of the song to check answers. Be sure to explain where more than one answer is possible even if it is not the one in the song.

   NOTE: *Choose a song that has verb forms appropriate to your level. If you find a song that is appropriate for reviewing forms that you have covered but has one or two forms you have not studied, simply leave those in the song. Some good songs for this activity are "Rocky Raccoon" (Lennon and McCartney, sung by the Beatles) and "It Doesn't Matter Anymore" (Paul Anka).*

2. ERROR ANALYSIS DRAW

Materials: Worksheet 28A or 28B, cut into strips, or make your own

Dynamic: Teams

Time: 25 minutes

RED   BLACK   BLUE

Procedure:

1. Divide the class into two teams. Have them stand or sit on opposite sides of the room. If your class is large, you can divide the class into several teams.

2. A student from the first team comes to the front of the class and selects a strip. He or she reads the strip aloud and decides if the sentence is correct or incorrect. If it is incorrect, the student must correct it.

NOTE: *It is probably best not to let the team help, but if you are using small teams or want more interaction, you can have the team discuss the sentence. For scoring purposes, accept only the answer given by the student who selected the strip.*

3. If the sentence is correct and the student says so, the team receives a point. If the sentence is incorrect and the student correctly identifies it as such, the team receives a point. The team receives one more point for correcting it. If the student identifies a sentence as incorrect but fails to provide an accurate correction, the other team (or next team if you have more than two) can "steal" a point by correcting the sentence. That team then takes the next turn.

SUGGESTION: *Make your own strips so that the grammar covered accurately reflects the content of your course. Use the worksheet as a model only if it is appropriate for your class. Cash register tapes work well for make-your-own strips because they can be seen by everyone. They can be purchased at office supply stores or large variety stores.*

3. BOARD GAME

RED BLACK BLUE

Materials: Worksheet 29A (lower level) or
29B (higher levels)
Die for each team, one marker
for each student

Dynamic: Groups

Time: 20 minutes

Procedure:

1. Divide the class into teams of approximately four. Distribute a copy of the worksheet to each team.

2. Students roll to see who goes first. The students move their markers around the game board. When a player lands on a square with a sentence, he/she must correct the sentence. If the group judges the corrected answer to be accurate, the student may roll again. If not, the turn passes to the next student. The players should <u>not</u> discuss the correct answer when an incorrect answer has been given since another player may land on that same space and have a chance to give an answer.

3. Circulate among the groups to see how they are doing and to act as judge if the group cannot decide if an answer is correct. The first player in each group to reach the end is the winner.

4. MIXED-UP ANSWERS

Materials: Board

Dynamic: Teams

Time: 10 minutes

RED

Procedure:

1. Divide the class into two teams and have them line up on either side of the board.

2. On each side of the board write the same short answers, but in mixed-up order (so that a student on one team cannot simply look over and see where his/her counterpart is marking).

   Sample short answers:

Yes, I do.	Yes, I am.
No, he wasn't.	No, I didn't.
No, we didn't.	Yes, I do.
Yes, she is.	Yes, she is.
Yes, I am.	No, we didn't.
No, I didn't.	No, he wasn't.

3. The first student from each team comes to the board. Ask a question. The students try to circle the answer as quickly as possible. The first student to circle the correct answer gets a point for his/her team.

   Sample questions:

   Do you have a sister?
   Did you eat lunch today?
   Did we have class yesterday?
   Are you in level 2?
   Is John's sister married?
   Was Tom late for class today?

   NOTE: *The questions can be about your class or not. The students do not need to know if the answer is* yes *or* no. *They are looking for the correct <u>verb</u> <u>form</u> that answers the question. It is recommended that you do not have both* yes *and* no *answers (for example: "Yes, I do" and "No, I don't") that could be appropriate to a question. There should only be one possible answer for each question asked.*

Variation: Use tag board sentence strips attached to the board. Students check next to the strip; their marks can be erased without erasing the sentence, and you can reuse the strips in other classes.

5. SHORT ANSWERS

BLACK BLUE

Materials: Worksheet 30

Dynamic: Small groups

Time: 20 minutes

Procedure:

1. Divide the class into groups of three or four.

2. Give each group approximately 5 cards with short answers on them. Have the group work together to create appropriate questions for the answers.

   Example:

   > **Sample card:** Yes I did.
   > **Student question:** Did you eat breakfast this morning?

3. Have each group read aloud its questions and answers and have the other groups decide if they are good matches. Another way to go over the questions is to have each group read the questions they have created and have the other students provide the short answers. If the question matches the answer given to the group on the card, the group has done a good job of creating a question. (Either a *yes* or a *no* answer is acceptable.)

6. TIME CHART

BLACK BLUE

Materials: Worksheet 31

Dynamic: Pairs

Time: 15 minutes

Procedure:

1. Divide the class into pairs. Give each pair a copy of the worksheet. The students make sentences as directed, using the information in the chart.

2. When all pairs are finished, call some students to the board to write their sentences. The class decides whether they are correct. If not, correct the sentences.

7. DICE SHOOT

Materials: Dice of various colors (two different colors per pair)

Pencils, 3″ x 5″ cards

RED   BLACK   BLUE

Dynamic: Pairs

Time: 15 minutes

Procedure:

1. Have the same number of cards and dice as you have students. Head each card with the name of the color of one of the dice. Under the heading for one of the colors, number from one to six. Next to each of those numbers, write a subject. On the other card, write a different color, number from one to six and write six infinitives.

2. Divide the class into pairs. Give each pair two dice (in two different colors) and the cards corresponding to the colors.

3. Set a timer for three minutes.

4. One player in each pair rolls the dice. He/She then looks at the paper with the same color as that die and notes the subject that matches the number rolled. He/She next looks at the paper that matches the color of the second die. He/She selects the infinitive corresponding to the number rolled on the second die. Now he/she makes a sentence using the subject and infinitive, making sure the verb agrees with the subject. If the player is correct, he/she receives one point.

5. Repeat the process with the second student in the pair. The person in each pair with the most correct matches wins.

NOTE: *This can be used with any verb tense, but be sure to tell the class which tense they are expected to use.*

8. ERROR ANALYSIS

RED BLACK BLUE

Materials: Worksheet 32A or 32B

Dynamic: Pairs/Small groups

Time: 20 minutes

Procedure:

1. Arrange students in pairs or groups of three. Give each group a copy of the worksheet (Worksheet 32A for lower-level classes, Worksheet 32B for higher-level classes). Have the students find and correct the verb mistakes in the passages.

2. When the pairs or groups seem to be done, go over the worksheet together, explaining (or having the students explain) the reason for the changes.

   NOTE: *Refer to the Answer Key if you want to provide students with copies of the correct versions.*

She isn't happy here.

Yoko is in class now.

He don't eat lunch with us.

My cousin live very far away.

I never do eat Mexican food.

I am going to be in class tomorrow.

She has a big yellow dog with two spots.

What time go you to class everyday?

How many dogs does you have?

Is pretty your sister?

I often go to the movies.

Do you have a VCR?

Sam and his father was happy to see us.

Were your aunt a teacher?

I going to the grocery store after class today.

My brother sings right now.

My brother is home because he usually did his homework in the afternoon.

We hasn't been very lucky recently.

She will have gotten married before she is moving to New York.

My wife is seeing the doctor now.

The grass is green.

A pencil was made of lead and wood.

My husband and I was married since 1985.

The news are exciting these days.

I usually have eaten lunch before 1:00.

She is always yelling at me.

He hadn't met many famous people in Los Angeles before he leaves.

He had gotten married before he came here.

My uncle is working on a book.

It will rain tomorrow.

I have met your sister.

Chris does from Switzerland.

She is the laziest person I have never met.

I have eaten here many times.

START →		You has a book.	Is Mary sleep?	**GO AHEAD 3 SPACES**	She doesn't happy here. ↓
GO BACK 2 SPACES ↓	Does she has a sister?			I going to be in class tomorrow.	They studied at the library next Monday. ←
→ **ROLL AGAIN**	I did not walked to school.	I often goes to the movies.	Did he brought the money?	**GO AHEAD 4 SPACES**	She'll will go to the bank. ↓
↓	When she will arrive?		I will go to the zoo last weekend.		Why came you to class? ←
→	**GO AHEAD 2 SPACES**	Yoko was in class now.	**ROLL AGAIN**		Did Mary lives in New York? ↓
↓	She hasn't two brothers.	I sit in class right now.	**LOSE A TURN**	We doesn't have a car.	**ROLL AGAIN** ←
→	A bird is fyling because it has wings.	**GO BACK 1 SPACE**		She have a big yellow dog with two spots.	Rick is wearing jeans every day. ↓
LOSE A TURN ↓	It wears a dress.		I was sorry I break the dish.	He is going to the beach every day.	←
→	What time you eat dinner?		**GO AHEAD 3 SPACES**	**ROLL AGAIN**	Yes, he wasn't late. ↓
STOP! YOU REALLY KNOW YOUR VERBS!	I see you last night.	Mary and her sister has a cold.	**GO AHEAD 3 SPACES**		Thomas didn't likes turkey. ←

START →		I saw that movie five times.	I had eaten here many times.	**GO AHEAD 3 SPACES**	My dog barks when it rained. ↓
GO BACK 2 SPACES ↓	I know her before I met her at the party.		I bought groceries because I will make dinner.		He has gotten married before he came here. ←
→ **ROLL AGAIN**	My wife seeing the doctor now.	I usually has eaten lunch before 1:00.	The child have seen his mother leave.	**GO AHEAD 4 SPACES**	↓
↓	I was 20 years old— and you?		She is yelling at me last Tuesday.		**GO BACK 1 SPACE** ←
→	**GO AHEAD 2 SPACES**	I never eaten such strange food before.	It is rain tomorrow.		I am knowing you for 3 years. ↓
↓	I hasn't met your sister.	She was studying while I am eating.	**LOSE A TURN**	They has often been late for class.	**ROLL AGAIN** ←
→ Do you need help? I'm going to carry those boxes for you.	Lorenzo does from Italy.	**GO BACK 1 SPACE**		John has many girlfriends during his life.	I have eaten sushi before I went to Japan. ↓
LOSE A TURN ↓	I have caught a cold last night.		Lisa and her sister was walking to class today.	I am always brushing my teeth in the morning.	←
→ The earth was round.		**GO AHEAD 3 SPACES**	The store opening at 9 A.M.	I have met your fiancé yesterday.	**STOP! YOU REALLY KNOW YOUR VERBS!**

Yes, I have.	No, we haven't.
Yes, I did.	No, he didn't.
Yes, she had.	No, they hadn't.
Yes, we were.	No, she wasn't.
Yes, I had been.	No, it hadn't been.
Yes, he was.	No, it wasn't.
Yes, you did.	No, you weren't.
Yes, they had.	No, it hadn't.

TIME	ACTIVITY
6:30 A.M.	get up
7:00 A.M.	fix breakfast
7:45 A.M.	leave for school
9:00 A.M.	attend a math lecture
12:15 P.M.	talk to friends
12:30 P.M.	eat lunch
2:30 P.M.	study in the library
4:30 P.M.	leave for work

Using the chart above, write sentences using the verb tenses indicated below. You may write in any person, but make sure the verbs agree with your subject. Also, you may use two subjects in your sentence if you want.

1. (simple present) _____

2. (present perfect) _____

3. (past perfect) _____

4. (past progressive) _____

5. (future) _____

6. (future perfect) _____

Work with your group or partner to find all the mistakes involving verbs (tense, form, or agreement).

1. My brother don't like coconut. Can you believe it? I never met anyone else in my life who felt this way. It seem very strange to me. What was there about coconut that he don't like? It seemed very inoffensive to me. Perhaps, he says he don't like it in order to get attention. When he refused to eat a coconut cookie or cake with coconut frosting, he gets a lot of attention and people try to figure out why he disliked it so much. Of course, my brother always will deny this, but I think that was the real reason.

2. When I first move here 10 years ago, it gets cold in December and January. In fact, the first two years, we have a freeze which killed all of my outdoor plants. As a result, I decide not to try to grow anything else. Now, however, it is staying pretty warm all winter. In fact, just the other day I wear shorts and a T-shirt. The sun shone and I felt as if it were summer! I can't resist calling my family and friends back home to brag about the good weather here.

3. Last week my brother-in-law was taking me to the desert about 45 minutes away and we stay there a couple of days. One of the reasons why we went there is to shoot rifles just for fun. He sets up some cans and bottles for targets and shot at them. He also lets me shoot his rifle. It is the first time I am shooting a gun and I feel very scared. Even though I can see how much he enjoy target practice, I thought gun ownership should be limited.

Work with your group or partner to find all the mistakes involving verbs (tense, form, or agreement).

1. I first learn about this English program from a teacher at my school back home. Surprisingly, it isn't my English teacher, but rather my history teacher. He attends this program when he was a university student. He told me how good this school is and what an interesting city this is. However, he warns me that he has been a student here many years ago and that sometimes things are changing. I have noticed some changes, but basically, I had found this to be a good program with friendly teachers. I also enjoyed living in this city.

2. One of the most important decisions in life is deciding on a job. I first come to this country without knowing any English. Therefore, I have a hard time finding a job. I applied everywhere, but no one call me for a job. For that reason, I had attended college and take some classes that help me to have a good career. Now I have almost gotten my AA degree. After I am attending college for one year, I applied at a shoe store, and they hire me right away. My plans are to transfer to the university; after that, I can easily found a better job.

3. My son became a "snackaholic." There was a time when he eats three big meals a day. Now, he only want to snack. Popcorn, cookies, candy, soft drinks: these is his favorite foods. He has seemed to want to eat constantly, but only sweets or chips. What has happened to my good little eater? Could it be that he follows the example of his parents? I guessed we better look at our own eating habits!

CHAPTER 5

Questions

These games and activities concentrate on the practice of question word order in verb tenses. Although the worksheets may feature just one tense, you can adapt them for other tenses, or as a review for all verb forms. See Chapters One and Two for other games and/or activities that also use questions as part of the activity.

5.1 YES/NO QUESTIONS

1. SHORT ANSWERS 1

RED   BLACK   BLUE

Materials: Worksheet 33A or 33B, or your own strips with answers

Dynamic: Pairs/Small groups

Time: 15 minutes

Procedure:

1. Arrange students in pairs or groups of three or four. Give each group a strip with short answers on them. Have the students work together to write questions for the answers.

    NOTE: *If you are using a worksheet, choose the one appropriate to your level. Preferably, use the worksheets as models for making your own.*

2. Have each group read the questions and answers aloud and let the rest of the group judge whether the questions are appropriate.

2. SHORT ANSWERS 2

Materials: None

Dynamic: Pairs/Small groups

Time: 25 minutes

BLACK   BLUE

Procedure:

1. Divide the class into pairs or groups of three or four. Have each group write five short answers on a piece of paper. You can either limit the answers to certain verb tenses or let students use any tense for review.

2. Each group exchanges papers with another group. Each group then creates questions for the answers provided by the other group.

3. Return the papers to their originators and have the group or pair that created the answers now check that the questions written by the other group or pair are good matches for their answers.

3. ARE YOU THE ONE?

Materials: Worksheet 34A or 34B

Dynamic: Whole class

Time: 20 minutes

RED   BLACK   BLUE

Procedure:

1. Distribute a copy of the worksheet to each student. Tell them to circulate, asking questions as in the model for each of the phrases.

Example:	**Worksheet:**	plays volleyball
	Student A:	Do you play volleyball?
	Student B:	Yes, I do.

2. When another student responds *yes,* the student asking the question writes the responding student's name on the blank. If the student answers *no,* the questioner continues until he/she finds someone who answers *yes.*

3. When a student completes the worksheet, he/she sits down, but should be prepared to answer other students' questions.

4. Go over as many of the questions/answers as time allows.

NOTE: *You can limit answers to only one* yes *answer per student. This avoids students pairing up and just talking to one or two other students. Or you may want to allow students to write a classmate's name as many times as that student answers* yes.

4. HUMAN BINGO

Materials: Worksheet 35A

Dynamic: Whole class

Time: 20 minutes

RED   BLACK   BLUE

NOTE: *Worksheet 35A contains some items in the present perfect, so it should be used only with intermediate/advanced classes. By adapting the worksheet to eliminate the present perfect, you can use this game in beginning classes. Use the blank Worksheet 35B to create your own game. At the higher levels especially, you may want to use the blank to create a game that is more interesting for your students by using "real" information about them.*

Procedure:

1. Copy a handout for each student. Worksheet 35A is for reviewing all verb forms. To limit this activity to one verb tense, reword the phrases so that the questions are in that tense and use Worksheet 35B.

2. Review question formation, if necessary, so the students are able to form questions from the prompts.

3. Tell students to circulate, asking their classmates questions as indicated by the prompts. If a student answers *yes,* the student asking the question writes that student's name after the prompt. If the student answers *no,* the questioner continues asking until he/she finds someone who answers *yes.*

4. As in Bingo, there are several ways to win.

   a. The first student who gets five names in a row wins.

   b. The first student who fills in the four corners wins.

   c. The first student who completes the board wins.

   d. The first student who makes a cross wins (third row down and third row across).

   e. Use any other variation you choose.

5. After a winner is found, go over the tense used and why (could be fact or habit) and some of the answers ("Who speaks Spanish?" "Who has more than one pet?").

   SUGGESTION: *This is a great game to play at any holiday time. Fill in the blank worksheet with prompts related to the holiday and whatever tense you're working on at the time.*

5. TWENTY QUESTIONS 1

Materials: None

Dynamic: Whole class

Time: 10 minutes

RED   BLACK   BLUE

Procedure:
1. Choose a category (famous people, occupations, food, animals, etc.)

2. Choose one student to answer questions from the rest of the class. Show the student a word on a piece of paper (what he or she is). The word should be an object or person. Have this student sit in front of the class. Instruct this student to answer only *yes* or *no* to any question asked of him/her.

3. Instruct the class to ask only *yes/no* questions. Their purpose is to discover the identity of the student in front of the class. The class is allowed only 20 questions. If they can guess the student's identity before or by the twentieth question, the class wins. If they do not guess correctly, the student wins. (Although this is based on the popular "Twenty Questions" game, you may want to actually vary the number of questions the class can ask. Be sure to make the number clear before the activity begins.)

Variation: To make the game more challenging, especially at the higher levels, you may want to omit step 1 so that the students use up some of their questions determining the category.

6. TWENTY QUESTIONS 2

Materials: Small pictures

Dynamic: Whole class

Time: 15 minutes

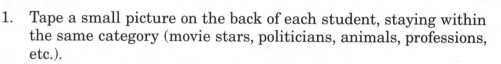

RED   BLACK   BLUE

Procedure:

1. Tape a small picture on the back of each student, staying within the same category (movie stars, politicians, animals, professions, etc.).

2. The students circulate and ask each other *yes/no* questions to discover "who" or "what" they are. The responding students look at the picture on the back of the questioners before answering. Circulate around the class to help out if the students are not sure of the answer. Instruct the students that they can answer "I don't know" if they are unsure and you are not available to ask. In the example below, the first two questions can be answered with *yes* or *no* just by looking at the picture. The other two require that the student being questioned know the identity of the person in the picture. The following questions could be used with a famous-person picture:

   Examples: Am I a woman?
   Do I have blond hair?
   Did I win an award?
   Have I been in more than one movie this year?

   If using a different category such as professions, the following type of questions may be asked:

   Do I work in a hospital?
   Am I wearing a uniform?
   Do I work in an office?

3. For a competition, the first student to discover his/her identity wins. If it is not a competition, set a time limit and try to have as many students discover their identities as possible. When a student discovers his/her identity, be sure that he/she continues to answer questions for those students who are still guessing.

INFORMATION QUESTIONS

1. BOARD GAME

BLACK   BLUE

Materials: Worksheet 36
One die per group, one marker for each student

Dynamic: Groups

Time: 20 minutes

Procedure:
1. Divide the class into groups of four. Give each group one die, one game board, and a marker for each student in the group.

2. The students roll the die and move around the game board by making questions for the answers on the board. The other students in the group judge whether the questions are appropriate and grammatically correct. Be sure to circulate to settle any disputes or questions that arise.

3. The first student in each group who reaches the end is the winner.

2. THE NEWLYWED GAME

BLACK   BLUE

Materials: 4 or 5 large pieces of paper for each student volunteer

Dynamic: Whole class

Time: 40 minutes

Procedure:
1. Ask for volunteers or nominations from the class to form four sets of "newlyweds." There will be four "husbands" and four "wives." Choose a theme, such as *food, work, weekends,* or *relatives,* to give the couples a focus in preparing their "marriage."

2. If your theme is food, tell the "husbands" that you are going to ask them questions about the eating habits of their "wives." Then send each "husband" and "wife" pair to a different part of the room to exchange information. Stress that only the "husband" needs to get information from the wife at this stage. The "wife" doesn't need to know about the eating habits of the "husband."

3. Have the remaining students come up with a list of questions (based on the theme) that will be directed to the "husbands."

Possible questions:

> What does your wife put in her coffee?
> What is her favorite fruit?
> What food does your wife hate?
> Where does she like to go for dinner?
> How does she like her eggs/steak cooked?

If there is time, have the class think of a prize, such as an all-expenses-paid week in Hawaii.

5. When you have four or five questions and the "husbands" have had about 10 minutes to get the necessary information, recombine. Have the "husbands" and "wives" sit on opposite sides of the room, facing each other. Write the couples' names on the board and ask for a volunteer scorekeeper. Have another volunteer be the announcer; give the announcer the questions.

6. The announcer reads the questions slowly and carefully to the couples. Both "husbands" and "wives" write down their answers. (Other students watch to make sure there is no eye-contact or hand signals between them.)

7. When all the questions have been asked and the answers written, the announcer reads the questions again, but this time the couples show what they have written. The scorekeeper gives points if the answers match. The winning couple gets the prize.

8. Switch roles. Choose a new theme and have the "wives" get information from the "husbands." Repeat the steps. (At this point, you may want to choose new "couples.")

3. YOU'RE THE REPORTER

Materials: One newspaper article for each student

Dynamic: Pairs

Time: 40 minutes

BLUE

Procedure:

1. Either provide a newspaper article for each student, or ask students to bring one to class (a previous night's homework assignment). If you have time, distribute old news magazines which students can use to find articles. You may want to suggest an approximate size for these articles.

2. Have students read the article and write five to eight *Wh*-questions based on it.

3. Divide the class into pairs. Have the partners check each other's questions for grammatical accuracy. Then the partners trade articles and answer the questions by reviewing the material in the news articles.

4. A BUSINESS FOR YOUR TOWN

Materials: Pencils and paper

Dynamic: Groups

Time: 45 minutes

BLUE

Procedure:

1. Discuss with the class what types of businesses there are in your area and what types of businesses students might like to set up.

2. Divide the class into groups of approximately four. Tell the groups that they are going to research and design a new business for their town. To determine whether the business will be successful, they must design a simple survey (5–10 questions) that will give them the necessary information about the kind of business that they choose to set up.

3. Help the students come up with *Wh-* questions for their survey. The following questions could be used for a shoe store.

   > What kind of shoes do you wear?
   > How many pairs of shoes do you have?
   > How much do you spend on a pair of shoes (on average)?
   > What color shoes do you like?
   > Where do you buy your shoes?
   > How many people are there in your family?

4. Students should write simple questionnaires and make copies for each group member. (You may need to do this.) Each member should do at least five interviews with people in the community. (You may want to assign this step for homework.)

5. After interviewing community members, students regroup and compare results. Results can be compiled in the form of a bar graph. They can then make an educated decision about whether the "business" will fail or succeed. The groups then present their results to the class in a mini-presentation.

INFORMATION QUESTIONS AND/OR YES/NO QUESTIONS

1. QUESTION ORDER

RED   BLACK

Materials: Cards or strips of paper

Dynamic: Groups

Time: 10 minutes

Procedure: 1. Prepare a list of questions for this activity. Make questions with enough words so that each student will have one card.

Example: Where has he already traveled?

Cards or strips:

Where	has	he	already	traveled

2. Arrange students in groups corresponding to the number of words in each question. Give each group one cut-up question.

3. Have the group put the words into correct question order. When they have finished, call each group to the front of the class and have the students stand in order, holding the cards. (If a student is absent on the day of this activity and you have an extra card, simply have a student hold up two cards.) The rest of the class judges if the order is correct.

NOTE: *This activity can be used at any level. Just prepare questions that cover the tenses/structures that you want to review. If you want to use punctuation, include that on a card also.*

2. WHAT'S THE QUESTION 1?

RED   BLACK   BLUE

Materials: Board

Dynamic: Small groups

Time: 20 minutes

Procedure: 1. Write a list of answers about yourself on the board. Divide the class into groups of approximately three. Students are to write logical and grammatical questions that correspond to your answers. Accept any question that fits the answer. For example, if you write "1995" on the board, you would have to accept questions such as *When were you married? When did you move here? When did you begin teaching?* The questions can be humorous as long as they match the answers.

Example:	**Answer:**	Las Vegas
	Questions:	Where are you from?
		Where did you go on vacation?
		Where did you live before you moved here?
		Where were you arrested?

	Answer:	20
	Questions:	How old are you?
		How old were you when you got married?
		How many sweaters do you own?
		How many years have you been teaching?

2. After all groups have finished, go around and have each group read its question for each answer.

3. If you are playing as a competition, give each group a point if the question is grammatically correct. In the first example above, all groups would get one point. But if a question is grammatically incorrect, such as *How old is you?*, do not give them a point. Tell them it doesn't matter what the "real" question is as long as it is grammatical, although students usually want to know if they are correct (unless they are being purposely funny). To satisfy their curiosity, you could give one point for a grammatical question and then another point (or 1/2 point) to the group(s) that have the "real" question.

Sample answers:	1. Linda.	5. Yes, once.
	2. Buffalo, N.Y.	6. Next month.
	3. Two.	7. Since 1987.
	4. Yes, I do.	

NOTES: *I usually use 10 answers, but that is up to you. Also, if you plan to give extra points for the "real" question, put on the board only the information that you are willing to share about yourself.*

While it is more interesting to play this game at intermediate and advanced levels with a variety of verb tenses, it can be played at the beginning level if you write answers that generate questions using only the verb forms the students have studied. For variety, you can incorporate frequency adverbs and modals.

As a follow-up, have students write short answers about themselves on a piece of paper, then exchange papers with a partner who will devise questions. Last, the students exchange papers again and discuss the accuracy of the questions—first grammatically, and then factually.

3. WHAT'S THE QUESTION 2?

RED

Materials: Worksheets 37A and 37B

Dynamic: Pairs

Time: 20 minutes

Procedure:

1. Arrange students in pairs and give one student Worksheet 37A and the other Worksheet 37B. They should work separately to write the appropriate question for each answer. The questions must correspond to the underlined word. For example, given the answer *Kathy worked yesterday*, the correct question is *When did Kathy work?* Such questions as *Where did Kathy work?* or *Did Kathy work?* would not be acceptable.

2. The partners exchange papers and check each other's questions. They also help each other rewrite any questions not worded correctly.

4. QUESTION AND ANSWER PRACTICE

RED   BLACK   BLUE

Materials: Notecards

Dynamic: Whole class

Time: 15 minutes

Procedure:

1. Before class, write one notecard per student. Each notecard should have a subject (person) and a time expression.

   Examples:

She / every day	You / in the morning	The president / every week
Your children / weekends	The teacher / on Fridays	My friends and I / on Saturday nights

2. Have students sit in a circle. Hand out the notecards and give everyone a minute or two to think about the question they will ask, using the information on their notecard. For example, if a notecard says "Your friends / last night," possible questions include *What did your friends do last night?* and *Did your friends do the homework last night?* Any grammatical question is acceptable as long as it uses the words on the card.

3. After giving everyone a minute or two, choose one student to begin. That student chooses any other student in the class and asks his/her question. The asker must address the answerer by name and ask the question. The answerer replies in any logical

way, using the correct tense. The asker then accepts the answer if correct, or asks for clarification if he/she detects an error. (You may need to facilitate here when you are the only one who detects an error.) The answerer then becomes the asker and chooses another student in the class to direct his/her question to.

Variations: This activity can be used to practice only one tense at a time, or it can be used as a review of many tenses. It becomes a real listening activity when students are reviewing several tenses and must listen for clues to past, present, or future.

Students can also be given an answer card. On the answer card is only a verb in the simple tense. The student answering has to use that verb in his/her answer in the appropriate tense.

5. ANSWERING ADS

Materials: Several "for sale" ads from a newspaper

Dynamic: Pairs

Time: 30 minutes

BLACK   BLUE

Procedure:
1. Group students in pairs and give Partner A one ad, Partner B a different ad. Car or apartment ads work well. The students take turns role playing telephone conversations based on the ads. For example, Partner A calls Partner B and asks questions about his/her ad.

   How old is your car?
   What color is it?
   Are there many miles on it?

2. Student B supplies answers based on the information in the ad. If some information is missing, instruct students to give a reasonable answer. For example, if student A asks, "What color is your car?" and the ad doesn't mention color, Student B makes up an answer.

3. Reverse roles, with Student B calling Student A to inquire about his/her ad.

   NOTE: *Each student in a pair needs a different ad, but all Student As can have the same ad, and all Student Bs a different one. That is, you will need only two ads and copy the number you need for your class. If you want the student pairs to act out their role playing for the class, you may want to provide a different ad for each student. This way, all conversations will be different when they are presented to the class.*

TAG QUESTIONS

1. TAG QUESTIONS

BLACK

Materials: Worksheet 38

Dynamic: Whole class

Time: 20 minutes

Procedure:

1. Give each student a copy of the worksheet. Direct the students to fill in the missing tag questions.

2. The students then circulate, asking their classmates the questions. When they receive a *yes* answer, they write the student's name on the line.

3. If you do this as a competition, the first student who finishes is the winner. Otherwise, after all students have finished or a certain period of time has passed, ask students at random to give answers.

Example:

> **Instructor:** Who was absent from school yesterday, Maria?
> **Maria:** Yoko was absent from class.

Worksheet 33A: SHORT ANSWERS (PRESENT/SIMPLE PAST)

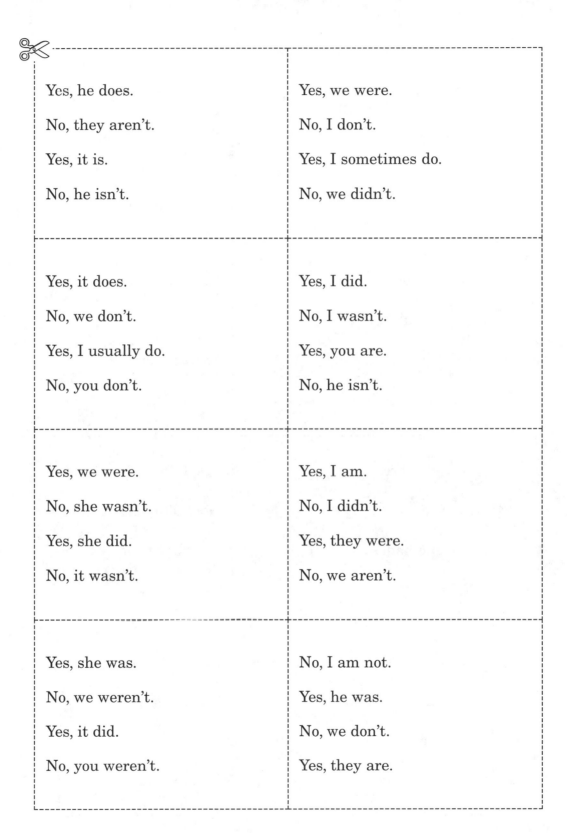

Yes, he does.

No, they aren't.

Yes, it is.

No, he isn't.

Yes, we were.

No, I don't.

Yes, I sometimes do.

No, we didn't.

Yes, it does.

No, we don't.

Yes, I usually do.

No, you don't.

Yes, I did.

No, I wasn't.

Yes, you are.

No, he isn't.

Yes, we were.

No, she wasn't.

Yes, she did.

No, it wasn't.

Yes, I am.

No, I didn't.

Yes, they were.

No, we aren't.

Yes, she was.

No, we weren't.

Yes, it did.

No, you weren't.

No, I am not.

Yes, he was.

No, we don't.

Yes, they are.

Yes, he does.	Yes, we were.
No, they weren't.	No, I haven't.
Yes, it has.	Yes, I sometimes do.
No, he hadn't.	No, we didn't.
Yes, it does.	Yes, I do.
No, we didn't.	No, I wasn't.
Yes, I usually have.	Yes, you are.
No, you hadn't.	No, he hasn't.
Yes, we were.	Yes, I am.
No, she didn't.	No, I didn't.
Yes, she had.	Yes, they have.
No, it isn't.	No, we had not.
Yes, she was.	No, I am not.
No, we haven't.	Yes, he has.
Yes, it does.	No, we don't.
No, I hadn't.	Yes, they did.

Ask your classmates questions using the phrases. When you get a yes answer, write your classmate's name in the blank across from the phrase. If you get a no answer, continue asking classmates the same question until someone gives you a yes answer.

plays volleyball	
speaks three languages	
likes cats more than dogs	
has traveled to Europe	
likes to speak English	
watches TV every day	
takes the bus to school	
has a last name that begins with the same letter as yours	
likes to go to the movies	
is afraid of snakes	

Ask your classmates questions using the phrases. When you get a yes *answer, write your classmate's name in the blank across from the phrase. If you get a* no *answer, continue asking classmates the same question until someone gives you a* yes *answer.*

has been to Disneyland	
speaks more than two languages	
had a headache last week	
is going shopping this weekend	
is older than you are	
has gone to more than one movie this month	
was late to class this week	
has a first name that begins with the same letter as yours	
had graduated from high school or college before coming to this school	
will go to college	

has been to Hollywood	eats at fast-food restaurants more than three times a week	has more than one pet	was active in sports in high school	had a toothache in the last year
is single	listens to music while studying	speaks Spanish	is a party animal	has gotten a speeding ticket
has had a job	knows how to use a computer	has gone water skiing	has seen a tourist attraction in Europe	has a younger brother
has gone bungee jumping	has blue eyes	has met someone famous	knows what the limbo is	can name two U.S. presidents
has seen the Grand Canyon	can drive a stick-shift car	has four living grandparents	was late for class this week	forgot to brush teeth this morning

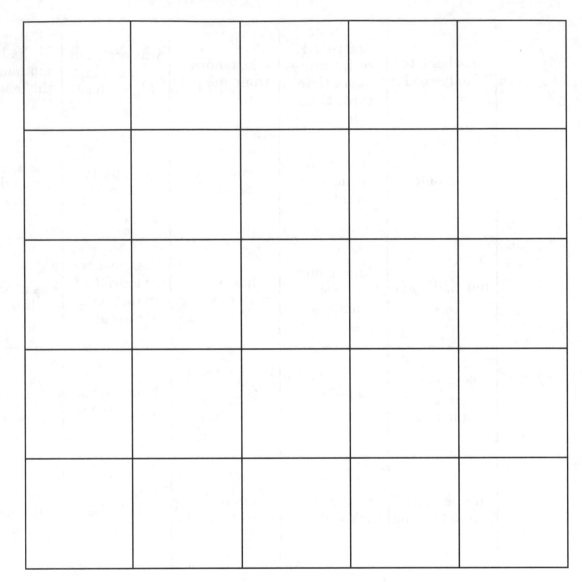

Worksheet 36: BOARD GAME

START ➡	My rent is due on Thursday.	I failed the test.	I ran out of gas, and I don't have any money with me.	My sister lives in Wyoming. ⬇
I love to swim. ⬇	We're going to Disneyland because my friend has never been there.	I need to borrow some money for lunch.	I had a doctor's appointment at 10:30.	I got my hair cut. ⬅
➡ I'm going to the movies tomorrow.	I have freckles on my nose.	I have three cats and a dog.	His name is Matthew.	I gained a lot of weight over the holidays. ⬇
She poked me in the eye. ⬇	I love horses.	My family lives far from here.	I'm worried about my sister. She's never been this late before.	He's crying because another kid pushed him. ⬅
➡ She's my mother.	He's going bald.	I look just like my grandmother.	He twisted his ankle and couldn't go on the ski trip.	My shoes are worn out. ⬇
I have some free time later today. ⬇	I'm planning to graduate in the fall.	The water in the bathtub is overflowing.	There's a fire truck out front.	That man just grabbed my purse! ⬅
➡ I just bought a new Mustang convertible.	I've had a headache all day.	This book belongs to my best friend.	I just couldn't resist.	**THE END**

Write a question for each of the answers. Use a question word that corresponds to the underlined parts of the sentence.

Example: ___*When did Kathy work?*___   Kathy worked <u>yesterday</u>.

1. _____   John watched <u>T.V.</u>

2. _____   Mary studied <u>in the library</u>.

3. _____   She was talking to <u>Debbie</u>.

4. _____   The movie began <u>at 7:30</u>.

5. _____   Ali went to the dentist <u>because he had a cavity</u>.

6. _____   My watch cost <u>$35.00</u>.

7. _____   I bought <u>three bags of ice</u>.

8. _____   They missed the party <u>because they had a flat tire</u>.

9. _____   I am going to the zoo <u>today</u>.

10. _____   Akiko saw <u>a movie</u> last night.

Write a question for each of the answers. Use a question word that corresponds to the underlined parts of the sentence.

Example: _When did Kathy work?_   Kathy worked <u>yesterday.</u>

1. _____   Jeremy played <u>baseball</u>.

2. _____   José rode his bike <u>to school</u>.

3. _____   I was writing a letter to <u>my mother</u>.

4. _____   Class begins at <u>8:00</u>.

5. _____   Ken stayed home last night <u>because he didn't have enough money for the movie</u>.

6. _____   Kenji has <u>three sisters</u>.

7. _____   I spent <u>$300.00</u> on gifts for my family.

8. _____   My parents were angry <u>because I didn't leave any gas in the car</u>.

9. _____   Mohammed is going to visit me <u>next week</u>.

10. _____   Yuko bought <u>a new coat</u> at the mall.

Write the missing tag questions following the statements. When you finish, ask classmates the questions until you find someone who answers yes. *Write that student's name in the space before the questions.*

_____ 1. You were absent from school yesterday,

_____ ?

_____ 2. You know at least three languages,

_____ ?

_____ 3. You will visit your relatives when you return home,

_____ ?

_____ 4. You had a job in your country,

_____ ?

_____ 5. You're thinking of getting married next year,

_____ ?

_____ 6. People should be more careful when they drive,

_____ ?

_____ 7. You live with a roommate,

_____ ?

_____ 8. You can ski, _____ ?

_____ 9. You have been in this city for more than three weeks,

_____ ?

_____ 10. You will travel after this school term ends,

_____ ?

© 1997 Prentice Hall Regents. Duplication for classroom use is permitted.

CHAPTER 6

NOUNS

SINGULAR-PLURAL

1. FILL-IN CHART

RED   BLACK   BLUE

Materials: Worksheet 39A, 39B, or 39C

Dynamic: Pairs

Time: 20 minutes

Procedure:

1. Have students work together in pairs to complete the worksheet, using the worksheet appropriate to their level. (39A is for the lowest level.)

2. Check each pair's worksheet as they finish. The first pair to complete the chart successfully wins. If some answers are incorrect, you can either indicate the incorrect answers or tell them how many are incorrect. The game then continues until one pair has all correct answers.

2. RELAY

Materials: Board, 2 markers or pieces of chalk

Dynamic: Teams

Time: 10 minutes

RED   BLACK

Procedure:

1. Divide the class into two teams and have each line up on the opposite side of the room.

2. On the board, make two lists of the same singular nouns, but in different order. (Variation: list the plural forms.)

3. Give the first person in line a piece of chalk or marker (depending on your board type). He/She goes to the board and writes the correct plural form of one word, then passes his/her marker to the next person in line. Each student can write only one plural form, but may correct as many incorrect forms on the board as he/she wants.

4. When you call "Time!" the team with the most correct answers wins.

3. MOUSE STORY

Materials:	Worksheet 40
Dynamic:	Pairs
Time:	20 minutes
Procedure:	1. Divide the class into pairs, and give each pair a copy of the worksheet.
	2. The students read the story and change the underlined nouns to the plural form if necessary. Be sure they understand that some of the underlined nouns will not need to be changed.
	3. Go over the answers when pairs have finished.
Variation 1:	If this game is a competition, tell the students to call you over as soon as they finish. The first pair who has all the answers correct, wins. If a pair calls you over but has mistakes, the game proceeds until a winning paper is found.
Variation 2:	You may want to use this story in other ways. After you have checked the answers, you can divide the class into small groups and have them practice retelling the story in their group without using the worksheet, and then tell the story to you. The group that most closely retells the story "wins."
Variation 3:	For oral practice, have the pairs role play the story. They will be practicing the singular/plural forms as they act out the story. Choose one pair (or ask for volunteers) to present its role play to the class.

4. TIC TAC TOE

Materials:	Worksheet 41, board
Dynamic:	Teams
Time:	10 minutes
Procedure:	1. Make a tic tac toe grid on the board with singular (or plural) forms of nouns. Divide the class into two teams.
	2. The teams take turns coming to the board and writing in one plural (or singular) form under the word of their choice. If a student from team X writes a correct form, he/she then marks a large X over that space. When team O writes a correct response, it marks a large O over the space.
	3. The first team that succeeds in having three of its marks in a row is the winner.

NOTE: *You may want to discuss blocking strategy, but usually students can figure it out themselves or are limited to choosing a blank with a word whose form they are sure of.*

FOLLOW-UP: *Divide the class into groups of three and give each group a copy of the worksheet. There are three games on the worksheet. Two students will be the players (X and O), and the third student is the judge who may have his/her book open to check the answers. In the second and third games, the students alternate roles, so that each student gets to play two games and is a judge in a third game.*

5. CONCENTRATION

Materials:	Board
Dynamic:	Groups
Time:	20 minutes

RED BLACK

Procedure:

1. Draw a blank grid with only numbers on the board (see below). Divide the class into teams of about five.

2. Each team takes turns calling out two numbers, trying to match a singular and a plural form. As the number is called, write in the word that corresponds to the number from your filled-in grid. Caution the teams to wait until you write the word before they call out a second number.

3. If a team makes a match, leave the answers on the board and draw an "X" through them. The team then takes another turn. If the team does not make a match, erase the two words.

4. Team members may talk together, but remind them that this is also a memory game, so no writing is allowed.

NOTE: *You can use any size grid, but be sure to have an even number of spaces. You can use this game to review plural spelling rules (as in the example below), irregular plural forms, or a combination.*

On the board:

1	2	3	4	5
6	7	8	9	10
11	12	13	14	15
16	17	18	19	20

On the instructor's paper:

1 match	2 dishes	3 country	4 glass	5 radios
6 monkey	7 toy	8 baby	9 countries	10 babies
11 potato	12 glasses	13 matches	14 leaves	15 toys
16 potatoes	17 dish	18 monkeys	19 radio	20 leaf

6. BALL TOSS

RED   BLACK

Materials: Any soft ball or beanbag

Dynamic: Whole class

Time: 5 minutes

Procedure:

1. Have students sit or stand in a circle. Decide if you want them to provide the singular or the plural form when they catch the ball.

2. Begin the game by tossing the ball to a student and saying a noun. If you said a singular noun, the student catching the ball must provide the plural form. That student then throws the ball to another student and says a new noun.

Example:	**Instructor:**	city
	Student A:	cities
		mouse
	Student B:	mice
		child
	Student C:	children
		radio, etc.

6.2 NOUNS AND ADJECTIVES

1. PICTURE SENTENCES

RED   BLACK

Materials: Large magazine pictures

Dynamic: Pairs

Time: 15 minutes

Procedure:

1. Give each pair of students a magazine picture (pictures from picture dictionaries may work well also). The picture should have several objects in it. Have the pairs write 5–10 sentences about the picture, using an adjective and a noun in each sentence.

2. When the pairs have finished, have the students in each pair take turns holding up their picture and reading out their sentences.

6.3 AGREEMENT

1. ERROR ANALYSIS

RED BLACK BLUE

Materials: Worksheet 42A or 42B

Dynamic: Small groups

Time: 25 minutes

Procedure:
1. Divide students into small groups of approximately three. Give each group a copy of the worksheet appropriate to your class level.

2. Instruct the members of each group to work together to find the errors indicated after each paragraph.

3. Students exchange papers with another group. Go over the answers to make sure each group found the errors indicated and can correct them.

6.4 COUNT-NONCOUNT NOUNS

1. SCAVENGER HUNT 1

RED BLACK

Materials: Magazines to share in class

Dynamic: Small groups

Time: 15 minutes

Procedure:
1. Arrange the class into groups of three or four. Give each group several magazines to cut up. (You may want to assign students to bring in magazines in advance, or provide them yourself.)

2. Have the groups look for noncount nouns and cut out pictures containing as many of them as they can find in the time provided. The group that finds the most correct pictures wins. (That is, if a group cuts out a picture of a table, for example, that picture cannot be counted.)

Variation: Assign a certain number of count and noncount nouns (perhaps 10 of each) and a time limit. The group that finds the most of each, wins.

> **SUGGESTION:** *Instead of giving magazines to each group, you can keep the magazines on a front desk or in another central location. Each group can take two. When a group finishes with a magazine, the students return it to the table and exchange it for another. Instead of cutting out the pictures, the group can list the objects they found on a paper.*

2. SCAVENGER HUNT 2 (Categories)

RED   BLACK

Materials: Magazines to share in class

Dynamic: Small groups

Time: 15 minutes

Procedure:
1. Arrange students in groups of three or four. Give each group several magazines to cut up (or make lists from). (Either have students bring in magazines as a previous homework assignment or provide them yourself.)

2. Assign a category of noncount nouns (liquids, abstracts, weather, meat, whole groups, etc.) and a specific time limit. The group with the most pictures of objects in the stated category at the end of the time period, wins.

Variation: Give each group a different category. At the end of the time period, each group reads out its list (or pictures), perhaps writing the items on the board. The class decides if they are appropriate to the category. The group with the most acceptable answers wins.

3. NAME THAT NOUN

RED   BLACK   BLUE

Materials: Objects brought in by students

Dynamic: Whole class

Time: 15 minutes

Procedure:
1. The day before, tell students to bring in two objects from home—one a count noun and one a noncount noun. Encourage them to find unusual items.

2. Collect the objects and distribute them around the class with a number for each.

3. Have the students walk around, looking at the objects. On a paper, they write what noun they think each number indicates and whether it is count or noncount. They can write only one noun for each number (so if two apples and a pear have the same number, they must write "fruit").

4. Go over the answers and have students check how many they got correct.

   SUGGESTION: *Bring in your own objects to use as noncount nouns because these will be more difficult for students to find.*

4. GRAMMAR'S WILD

BLUE

Materials: Colored 3″ x 5″ and 5″ x 7″ cards

Dynamic: Teams

Time: 10 minutes

Procedure:

1. Write a noun on each 3″ x 5″ card. Include count and noncount nouns, and nouns that can be either. Write the headings *Count, Noncount,* and *Both* on the 5″ x 7″ cards. Divide the class into teams.

2. Give each team a set of noun cards and the three heading cards. (To make it easier for you to reuse, use different-colored sets of cards.) Each team must sort their cards into the appropriate categories of count, noncount, or both.

3. The team that sorts the cards correctly and finishes first is the winner.

5. WHAT'S IN YOUR REFRIGERATOR/KITCHEN?

BLUE

Materials: None

Dynamic: Pairs

Time: 30 minutes

Procedure:

1. Review expressions of quantity if necessary.

2. Divide the class into pairs. Have each pair make one sentence containing each expression of quantity you have studied, using the different foods they have in their own refrigerator or kitchen. They can use a page in their grammar book, or you can give them a list. This is a list of some suggested expressions of quantity.

a couple of	*a number of*	*lots of*	*one*
a few	*all*	*many*	*plenty of*
a little	*both*	*most*	*several*
a great deal of	*each*	*much*	*some*
a lot of	*every*	*no*	

3. Check the sentences as each pair finishes. (To check the sentences, one pair reads its sentences to another pair.) The pair that finishes first with all correct sentences wins.

   SUGGESTION: *You can expand this activity to topics other than the refrigerator, such as other rooms in the house or other buildings.*

  **ARTICLES**

1. SCAVENGER HUNT 3

RED   BLACK

Materials: Magazines for students to share

Dynamic: Small groups

Time: 15 minutes

Procedure: 1. Divide the students into groups of three or four. Give each group several magazines to cut up. (You can assign students to bring in magazines in advance, or provide them yourself. Or, as in the previous scavenger hunt activities, you may want to stack magazines on a front desk and let students trade in magazines when they are through. This provides for better circulation of the magazines. Set a limit that each group can have at any one time.)

2. Have the groups look for nouns that take the article *a* or the article *an*. You may want to assign a certain number (find 10 of each). The students can either cut out the pictures in the time provided, or make a list of the objects they find. Or make the game competitive by seeing which group can find the most pictures that correctly depict the items in the time specified.

Examples of pictures: a book   an apple
                            a cat   an elephant

2. ARTICLE PASS-ALONG

BLACK   BLUE

Materials: Worksheet 43

Dynamic: Groups

Time: 15 minutes

Procedure: 1. Divide the class into groups of four or five. Give each group a copy of the worksheet.

2. Assign a time limit and have the students in each group work together to fill in the missing articles. Have the groups correct each other's papers as you go over them aloud.

Variation: Divide the class into large groups or, if you have a small class, do the game as a whole-class activity. Give each student a copy of the handout. Have students write their names on the page and fill in as many articles as possible in the time allowed. When you say "Pass," they pass the paper to the next student. They can also correct any errors they see. Continue until most or all of the blanks have been filled in. Have students correct the last paper they ended up with (unless it is their own).

3. ERROR ANALYSIS DRAW

Materials: Worksheet 44 or make your own

Dynamic: Teams

Time: 20 minutes

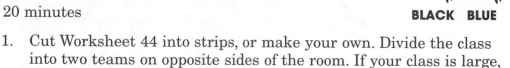

BLACK   BLUE

Procedure:

1. Cut Worksheet 44 into strips, or make your own. Divide the class into two teams on opposite sides of the room. If your class is large, you can divide the class into several teams.

2. A student from the first team comes to the front of the class and selects a strip, reads the strip aloud, and decides if the sentence is correct. If it is incorrect, the student must correct it.

   NOTE: *Generally it is better not to let the team help, but if you are using small teams or want more interaction, you can have the team discuss the sentence. However, for scoring purposes, accept only the answer given by the student who drew the strip.*

   SCORING: *If the sentence is correct and the student says so, the team receives one point.*

   If the sentence is incorrect and the student correctly identifies it as such, the team receives one point. The team receives one more point for correcting it.

   If the student/team identifies a sentence as incorrect but fails to provide an accurate correction, the other team (or next team if you have more than two) can "steal" a point by correcting the sentence. That team then goes on to draw its own sentence.

   SUGGESTION: *Make your own strips so that the grammar reflects the content of your course. Use the worksheet as a model only if it is appropriate for your class.*

Write the correct plural form for each word. Call your instructor to check when you have completed the chart.

SINGULAR	PLURAL
city	
key	
tomato	
radio	
mouse	
house	
man	
pan	
fish	
wish	
foot	
boot	
mother	
brother	
this	
kiss	
that	
hat	
life	
line	
fox	
lock	

Write the correct plural form for each word. Call your instructor to check when you have completed the chart.

SINGULAR	PLURAL
kiss	
this	
that	
hat	
mouse	
house	
man	
pan	
boot	
foot	
tooth	
booth	
zoo	
potato	
goose	
sheep	
cactus	
class	
shell	
shelf	
box	

Write the correct plural form for each word. Call your instructor to check when you have completed the chart.

SINGULAR	PLURAL
box	
ox	
hero	
piano	
auto	
chief	
thief	
louse	
house	
tooth	
booth	
this	
kiss	
bat	
that	
root	
boot	
man	
ban	
blouse	
goose	

Change the underlined nouns to their plural forms if necessary.

A town mouse and a country mouse were <u>friend</u>, so the country mouse
$\underset{1}{}$
invited his <u>friend</u> to his home in the field. The town mouse came, and they
$\underset{2}{}$
sat down to a dinner of <u>root</u> and <u>vegetable</u>. The town mouse was not
$\underset{3}{}$ $\underset{4}{}$
impressed by this <u>dinner</u>. He said, "You live no better than the <u>ant</u> and
$\underset{5}{}$ $\underset{6}{}$
other <u>insect</u> here. You must come and see all the <u>thing</u> you can eat at my
$\underset{7}{}$ $\underset{8}{}$
<u>house</u>." The town mouse then took the country mouse back to town with
$\underset{9}{}$
him. The town mouse showed the country mouse the kitchen full of <u>cookie</u>,
$\underset{10}{}$
<u>pastry</u>, <u>apple</u>, <u>roll</u>, and other food. They were just about to eat when two
$\underset{11}{}$ $\underset{12}{}$ $\underset{13}{}$
<u>child</u> came running into the kitchen and scared the two <u>mouse</u> away. They
$\underset{14}{}$ $\underset{15}{}$
hid and waited for these <u>kid</u> to leave. They tried to eat again, but this time
$\underset{16}{}$
they were scared away by a <u>woman</u> working in the kitchen. Finally, the
$\underset{17}{}$
country mouse said, "You may have many <u>luxury</u> here, but I prefer my
$\underset{18}{}$
home where I can have a simple dinner in peace!"

1. _____
2. _____
3. _____
4. _____
5. _____
6. _____
7. _____
8. _____
9. _____

10. _____
11. _____
12. _____
13. _____
14. _____
15. _____
16. _____
17. _____
18. _____

mouse	child	fish
fish	tooth	man
foot	man	goose

house	knife	fox
tomato	book	brush
zero	party	zoo

rose	shelf	girl
baby	banana	city
puppy	tray	island

A.   Clothes can tell a lot about a person, but we can't judge a person by the clothes they wears. In my country, a lot of peoples judges a person by what name brand of clothes they wears. A lot of times, peoples talks about what clothes their friends wears or says some peoples wears inappropriate clothes to high school.

7 subject-verb–agreement errors   3 number-agreement errors

B.   Now I'm in California where it is warm all through the year and where there's many beautiful beach. When you take a walk on the beach, you see people wearing baggy clothes—at least two size larger than what they should be wearing. This people are surfers. Personally, I believe that the reason surfers wears baggy clothes are they always has wetsuits on in order to be ready for waves.

4 subject-verb–agreement errors   3 number-agreement errors

C.   We have some important decision to make in our lives. We can't run away from them and needs to choose what is best for us. The three most important decisions for me are where to study, choice of jobs, and whom to marry. All of them is important, but perhaps marriage is the most important ones. We has to choose whether we will marry or not. If we doesn't marry, it mean that we will not have a family—including our own children. The decision about whom we'll marry are difficult to make also. In conclusions, we can't predict what will happen and how our lives will be influenced by those decision, but we has to decide even if it turn out bad.

7 subject-verb–agreement errors   5 number-agreement errors

D.   There is a lot of important thing in a lifetime. The most important thing for a young people is to get a good educations. A good education help you to get a good job later on. You needs a good job to earn enough money to live comfortably. It is not as important to have a really high-paying job as it is to be happy in your choices of occupation. Also, everyone need to settle down by having a families because it is important in order for civilization to continue. However, being happy with oneself is truly the most important thing in life.

4 subject-verb–agreement errors   5 number-agreement errors

A. I has lived in Poland most of my life, and there is a places that I remembers very well. It is a short, dark streets with building on both side. The buildings are very tall—at least four floor. There are an entrance, but no exit from these street. The windows looks dirty, but it is only shadow and window coverings that makes them look dark. Most people keep them clean and nice. I thinks about these place often because I spent most of my lives there with many good friend.

6 subject-verb–agreement errors   8 number-agreement errors

B. Explorers has lived in almost all times and in almost every countries. There is many interesting books written and lots of adventure movie made about them. We can see that an explorer's life is not just interesting, but it is also dangerous. In my opinion, explorers should be strong and brave, smart and experienced, and also has a sense of adventure.

3 subject-verb–agreement errors   2 number-agreement errors

C. All the government of democratic nations makes laws according to the necessity of the social life of the country at the moments the law is enacted. After many year, some of that laws becomes inadequate, and there are an attempt by citizen to change them. This is what is happening in the U.S. now regarding gun control. In my opinion, a law that control guns is necessary because it reduce slaughters, gun accidents and violence in general.

5 subject-verb–agreement errors   5 number-agreement errors

D. Dreams—these interesting topic have been on people's minds for a long time. Everybody have the ability to dream in one way or another. Some peoples even says that dreaming is a sign that we are sleeping the perfect sleep. Throughout time, it have always been a top priorities to figure out the nature of dreams. Although our knowledge of dreams are still in a primitive stage, we has already managed to divide them into category. The majority of people will agree that nightmares, daydreams and visions are the most common types of dream.

6 subject-verb–agreement errors   5 number-agreement errors

Fill in the blanks with the appropriate article: a, an, the, *or* 0.

1. _____ yellow dog that belongs to my brother is _____ old dog.

2. Does Yasuyuki drive _____ truck or _____ car?

3. My sister's boyfriend works at _____ restaurant across from _____ school he attends.

4. My new watch is made of _____ gold.

5. When Martha heard _____ terrible news, she was filled with _____ sadness.

6. _____ women generally live longer than _____ men.

7. Many people return to _____ college after working for several years.

8. The teacher said, "You may take _____ break if you have finished _____ rest of _____ test."

9. I'm going to _____ market on Hill Street. Can I get you anything?

10. After Thanksgiving weekend, you would probably agree that _____ football is _____ most popular sport in North America.

11. I hope to get _____ degree in _____ computer science by _____ end of this year.

12. What is more important to you— _____ good health or _____ money?

13. If _____ telephone in the kitchen rings, will you pick it up?

14. _____ radio had _____ biggest influence on _____ people until _____ invention of _____ television.

15. One reason Rafael bought his house is that _____ backyard is a good place for his kids to play.

16. What is _____ quickest way to get to _____ mall?

Japanese eye contact between women and a men is impolite.

Eyes, hands, and entire body help express what we want to say.

When people meet for the first time, they shake hands.

Gestures are used by many people such as a teacher and policemen.

If a guy and a girl are sitting together on a sofa and talking about something, and suddenly the girl is moving and tossing her hair, this signals her interest in the guy.

When we are talking, we like to see the people's eyes.

Body language is part of our system of communication.

The gestures mentioned earlier are also important to interpret nonverbal communication.

The misinterpretation of nonverbal signals can cause the serious problems between cultures.

The way a person stands or sits can reflect his self-image.

This example reminds me of the memories of the past 24 years.

People can tell by the wrinkles on others' faces what they have done in the past.

CHAPTER 7

Pronouns

7.1 PRONOUNS

- Concentration
- Possessives
- Mixed-up Answers
- Fill in the Blanks
- Songs
- Crossword
- What's the Answer?

7.1 PRONOUNS

1. CONCENTRATION

Materials:	Board and markers or chalk
Dynamic:	Groups
Time:	25 minutes
Procedure:	

RED   BLACK

1. Draw a blank grid on the board. Keep a copy of the filled-in grid on a piece of paper. Divide the class into groups of four or five.

2. Each team takes turns calling out two numbers, trying to make a match between subject and object pronouns, or subject and possessive pronouns, etc. Tell the students before the game begins what they are expected to match. As the team calls out the numbers, write the word that corresponds to that square on the board.

3. If the words are a match, draw a line through the words, but leave them on the grid, and give that team a point and an extra turn. If it is not a match, erase the words.

4. This is a memory game, so no one may write during the game. Team members may talk together to make a match, but only one student should call out the numbers.

On the board:

1	2	3	4	5
6	7	8	9	10
11	12	13	14	15

Your paper copy:

1 I	2 ours	3 theirs	4 you	5 they
6 she	7 we	8 X	9 its	10 he
11 it	12 mine	13 yours	14 hers	15 his

2. POSSESSIVES

Materials:	Worksheet 45
Dynamic:	Teams
Time:	10 minutes
Procedure:	

RED   BLACK

1. Divide the class into two teams and have them stand in lines.

2. Using the worksheet, read a sentence to the first student in Team 1. The student must change the possessive adjective and noun to a possessive pronoun.

   Example: This is my pen. $\longrightarrow$ This is mine.

3. If the student answers correctly, he/she scores a point for the team. In either case, the student goes to the end of the line. Read the next sentence to the first student on Team 2.

4. The team with the most points at the end of the game wins.

3. MIXED-UP ANSWERS

RED

Materials: Board, two pieces of chalk or markers

Dynamic: Teams

Time: 10 minutes

Procedure:

1. Divide the class into two teams and have them form two lines on either side of the board.

2. Divide the board in half and write the same short answers on each side, but not in the same order. It does not matter if you write a *yes* or a *no* answer for a question, but you should not write both. If you ask a question such as "Is Jim home?," you should have either "Yes, he is" or "No, he isn't"—but not both.

Example:	Yes, he is.	Yes, we are.
	No, she doesn't.	No, it isn't.
	No, we don't.	No, she doesn't.
	Yes, we are.	Yes, he is.
	Yes, they are.	No, we don't.
	No, it isn't.	Yes, they are.

   Have the first two students in line come to the board. Read out a question.

3. Since the focus of this activity is pronouns, do not use pronouns in your questions. Use nouns that the students need to match with the correct pronoun in the answer. Also be sure you do not read questions in the order of the answers on either side of the board. The students need to search for the correct answers.

   Example questions for the above answers:

         a. Is your father retired?
         b. Does Madonna live in Chicago?
         c. Do you and your sister live together?
         d. Are you and your family happy here?
         e. Are all your relatives still in Japan?
         f. Is that your dog?

4. Stress that speed is important. The first student who checks the correct answer gets a point for his/her team.

5. You can write as many answers as you want on the board. Again, make sure there is only one correct response to your questions. You may want to keep all the questions in the same tense, or you can mix tenses, which will allow you more answers. Since the focus is on pronouns, it does not matter what tense you use, as long as it is one your class knows.

NOTE: *To make this activity more relevant to your class, try to use the names of students in the class in your questions where possible.*

4. FILL IN THE BLANKS

RED   BLACK

Materials:	Worksheets 46A and 46B
Dynamic:	Pairs
Time:	10 minutes
Procedure:	1. Use the worksheets or create your own story. Divide the class into pairs and give each pair one of the worksheets. Have the students fill in the blanks in the story with the correct pronouns.

2. When all pairs have finished, go over the story together.

SUGGESTION: *For stories, use fairy tales, fables, summaries of stories the students are reading in other classes, summaries of TV shows or movies, or make up your own.*

5. SONGS

Materials:	Worksheet 47A or 47B or other song lyrics Tape player and recorded song (optional)
Dynamic:	Pairs
Time:	15 minutes
Procedure:	1. Make copies of song lyrics with the pronouns deleted. You may want to put a list of pronouns above the song, as in Worksheet 47A.

2. If it is clear what the pronoun should be from the text, have the students work in pairs to provide missing pronouns. Then play the song for the students to check their work.

3. If it is not clear what the pronoun should be (if the answer could be *she* or *he*), do this activity as a listening activity. The students fill in the blanks individually as they listen to the song. Then, with a partner, they check their answers and discuss why the pronouns they chose are appropriate. (Even though they listened to the song, sometimes it is not easy to hear what the pronoun was—*he*, *she*, *we* can all sound alike, but the context should make the choice clear.) Go over the lyrics as a class.

SUGGESTION: *Although you will probably want to use lyrics for which you have the music, another song that works well for this activity is "Running Scared" (Roy Orbison).*

6. CROSSWORD

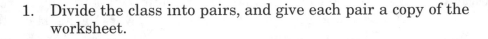

Materials:	Worksheet 48
Dynamic:	Pairs
Time:	10 minutes

RED   BLACK

Procedure:
1. Divide the class into pairs, and give each pair a copy of the worksheet.

2. The first pair that successfully completes the crossword wins.

7. WHAT'S THE ANSWER?

Materials:	Worksheet 49
Dynamic:	Pairs
Time:	15 minutes

RED   BLACK

Procedure:
1. Divide the class into pairs and give each pair a copy of the worksheet. The students choose the correct pronoun forms. Once they choose, the instructions on the worksheet direct them where to go next.

2. The first pair to finish the worksheet successfully wins.

1. I have your books.

2. Is she your baby?

3. Do you have my dictionary?

4. That new car is their car.

5. This is your jacket; it isn't my jacket.

6. This is my test paper.

7. Did you bring his ID?

8. Those aren't our tickets. We have our tickets.

9. Did you see her project?

10. My purse is leather; her purse is straw.

11. Your car is nice, but our car is nicer.

12. The winning science project is my project.

13. I like your sweater better than my sweater.

14. His experience was worse than her experience.

15. May I borrow your pencil? I broke my pencil.

16. Those brownies are their brownies.

17. The books on the table are their books.

18. I sold my computer.

19. That cocker spaniel is our dog.

20. Their shoes are outside.

A GROUP OF FRIENDS

I have a friend named John who is a student. John has two brothers. _____ older brother, Tad, now lives in San Francisco. _____ is a beautiful city, as you know. I met _____ (the two brothers) when _____ were all working at the mall after school. John and Tad's younger brother, Paul, lives in Austin, Texas. _____ is a swinging, single guy with two girlfriends. One girlfriend is a singer, and _____ sings every night with _____ twin sister. The other girlfriend lives in an apartment with _____ pet dog. _____ is a huge German shepherd. This dog likes to go camping with _____ , so _____ take _____ with them every chance _____ get. _____ is pretty much a "people" dog. By that, I mean _____ doesn't like to be left alone. Now that _____ know a little bit about John, _____ two brothers, and _____ , read on to find out more about _____ .

NUISANCE

Once upon a time, there was a tomcat named Nuisance. _____

lived with a wonderful woman named Lisa, but for some reason,

_____ seemed to like everyone but _____. The harder Lisa

tried to please _____, the more Nuisance thought of things

_____ could do to annoy _____. One day Lisa's friend

brought over a beautiful hanging plant. _____ hung _____ in

_____ bedroom window. Then the two friends went out to dinner.

When _____ returned, _____ found the plant on the floor.

"What happened to _____?" asked _____ friend, but Lisa

knew, and _____ do too, don't _____? That Nuisance!

Another time, _____ ran away and was gone for three months. Lisa

asked the people in the apartment building to help search for _____.

_____ all agreed to help, but no one found Nuisance. Just when

_____ had given up hope, _____ turned up. Nuisance spent

_____ whole life doing things like this to Lisa, but she always

forgave _____.

Choose a pronoun from the list to fill in each blank as you listen.

Subject pronouns		Object pronouns		Possessive adjectives	
I	it	me	it	my	its
you	we	you	us	your	our
he	they	him	them	his	their
she		her		her	

"He Stopped Loving Her Today"

_____ said _____ 'll love _____ 'till _____ die.

_____ told _____ , " _____ 'll forget in time."

As the years went slowly by,

_____ still preyed upon _____ mind.

He kept _____ picture on _____ wall
And went half crazy now and then.

But _____ still loved _____ through it all,

Hoping _____ 'd come back again.

Kept some letters by _____ bed
Dated nineteen-sixty two.

_____ had underlined in red

Every single " _____ love _____ ."

_____ went to see _____ just today.

But _____ didn't see no tears.
All dressed up to go away.

First time _____ 'd seen _____ smile in years.

REFRAIN:

_____ stopped loving _____ today.

They placed a wreath upon _____ door.

And soon _____ 'll carry _____ away,

_____ stopped loving _____ today.

_____ came to see _____ one last time,

_____ all wondered if _____ would.

And _____ kept running through _____ mind

This time, _____ 's over _____ for good.

REFRAIN

Fill in the blanks with the appropriate pronoun or adjective.

"The Erie Canal"

I've got a mule, _____ name is Sal,

Fifteen miles on the Erie Canal.

_____'s a good ol' worker and a good ol' pal,

Fifteen miles on the Erie Canal.

_____'ve hauled some barges in our day,

Filled with lumber, coal and hay.

And _____ know every inch of the way

From Albany to Buffalo.

REFRAIN:

Low bridge, everybody down!

Low bridge, for _____'re coming to a town!

And _____'ll always know _____ neighbor,

_____'ll always know _____ pal,

If _____'ve ever navigated on the Erie Canal.

_____ better get along on our way, ol' gal,

Fifteen miles on the Erie Canal.

'Cause _____ bet _____ life

_____'d never part with Sal,

Fifteen miles on the Erie Canal.

Get up there, mule, here comes a lock

_____'ll make Rome about six o'clock,

One more trip and back _____'ll go,

Right back home to Buffalo.

REFRAIN

Fill in the blanks with an appropriate pronoun.

"Red River Valley"

From this valley they say you are going,

We will miss _____ bright eyes and sweet smile,

For _____ say _____ are taking the sunshine,

That brightens _____ pathway awhile.

REFRAIN

Come and sit by _____ side if _____ love me,

Do not hasten to bid me adieu,

But remember the Red River Valley

And the girl that has loved _____ so true.

Won't _____ think of the valley _____'re leaving?

Oh, how lonely, how sad _____ will be,

Oh, think of the fond heart _____'re breaking,

And the grief _____ are causing _____ .

REFRAIN

From this valley _____ say _____ are going,

When _____ go, may _____ darling go, too?

Would _____ leave _____ behind unprotected?

When _____ loves no other but _____ ?

REFRAIN

I have promised _____ , darling, that never

Will a word from _____ lips cause _____ pain;

And _____ life, _____ will be _____ forever

If _____ only will love _____ again.

REFRAIN

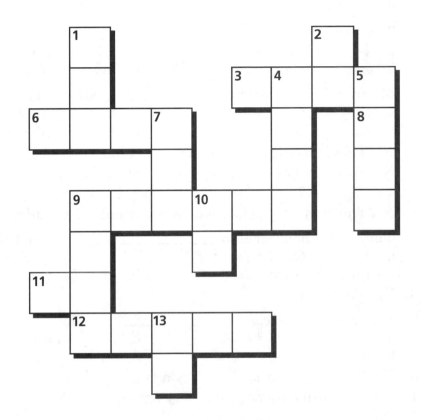

ACROSS

3. Third person plural object pronoun.

6. That book belongs to us. It is _____ .

8. Subject pronoun that corresponds to *me*.

9. Third person plural possessive pronoun.

11. Object pronoun that corresponds to *I*.

12. If it belongs to you, it is _____ .

DOWN

1. "Where do _____ live?"

2. Refers to my brother.

4. Goes along with *she*.

5. If it belongs to me, it's _____ .

7. Subject pronoun that goes along with *her*.

9. As a subject, refers to my brother and sister.

10. Neutral pronoun.

13. If we want something, we'll ask you to give it to _____ .

With your partner, choose the best answer and follow the instructions for your choice.

1. That book is _____ .
   a. I   *Go to # 3*   c. mine   *Go to # 8*
   b. me   *Go to # 16*   d. my   *Go to # 4*

2. My friends are thoughtful. _____ always ask how I feel.
   a. they   *Go to # 5*   c. him   *Go to # 16*
   b. them   *Go to # 16*   d. he   *Go to # 11*

3. No. This is a subject pronoun. Try again.

4. No. This is a possessive adjective. Try again.

5. Yes. Go to # 7.

6. No. The subject is neither male nor female. Try again.

7. John had a headache, so _____ stayed home today.
   a. I   *Go to # 18*   c. her   *Go to # 16*
   b. they   *Go to # 10*   d. he   *Go to # 14*

8. Yes. Go to # 2.

9. See that book? Please give _____ to me.
   a. him   *Go to # 6*   c. her   *Go to # 6*
   b. it   *Go to # 19*   d. them   *Go to # 10*

10. No. The subject is singular. Try again.

11. No. The verb does not agree. Try again.

12. Do _____ know my name?
    a. he   *Go to # 11*   c. I   *Go to # 21*
    b. you   *Go to # 23*   d. she   *Go to # 11*

13. No. This is an object pronoun, but it does not make any sense here. Try again.

14. Yes. Go to # 9.

15. Yes. Fruit is neither masculine nor feminine. Go to # 22.

16. No. This is an object pronoun. Try again.

17. **YES!** You really know your pronouns! You have finished the quiz correctly.

18. No. This pronoun does not agree with the subject. Try again.

19. Yes. Go to # 12.

20. Eat fruit. _____ is good for you.
    a. it   *Go to # 15*   c. they   *Go to # 11*
    b. its   *Go to # 4*   d. he   *Go to # 6*

21. Grammatically OK, but a strange question to ask. Try again.

22. My sister asked to borrow my sweater, so I gave it to _____ .
    a. it   *Go to # 13*   c. she   *Go to # 3*
    b. her   *Go to # 17*   d. me   *Go to # 13*

23. Yes. Go to # 20.

CHAPTER 8

Prepositions

8.1 PREPOSITIONS OF TIME AND PLACE

1. MAGAZINE SEARCH

RED   BLACK

Materials: Magazines to share in groups

Dynamic: Small groups

Time: 15 minutes

Procedure:

1. On the board, write a list of prepositions of place that the students have studied. Divide the students into groups of three or four and give each group several magazines. You may want to ask students to bring in their own. If you are supplying them, be sure that they have full-page ads or other large pictures.

2. Give the groups a time limit and have them search through their magazines to find a picture that contains situations illustrating prepositions of place.

3. When the time is up, each group goes to the front of the class, holds up its picture, and explains (in sentences) the contents of the picture, using prepositions of place.

   Example: The dog is under the table.
   The table is next to the man.
   The table is in front of the window.

4. The group that found a picture allowing them to correctly use the most prepositions of place from the list on the board wins.

   NOTE: *With an intermediate group, choose a wider range of prepositions that they have already reviewed.*

2. SCAVENGER HUNT

Materials: Worksheet 50, objects filled in
Various objects provided by instructor

Dynamic: Pairs

Time: 20 minutes

RED

Procedure:

1. Before students come into the classroom, distribute various objects around the room, placing them in visible positions that students can describe using their prepositions of place. List the objects on the worksheet.

2. Divide the class into pairs and give each pair a copy of the worksheet.

3. The students look around the room for each object listed on the worksheet and write a complete sentence describing its location. The first group to finish brings their worksheet to you to be checked. If the answers are correct, that group wins.

3. PREPOSITIONAL CHAIN DRILL

RED   BLACK

Materials: None

Dynamic: Whole class

Time: 10 minutes

Procedure:

1. Review prepositions of place.

2. Take a small object, such as a pen, and do something with it, then describe your action. (Put the pen on the desk and say, "I put the pen on the desk.")

3. Give the pen to a student and ask him/her, "What did I do with the pen?"

4. The student answers and then does something different with the object that involves a different preposition of place.

5. The student then passes the object to the next student and asks, "What did we do with the pen?" That student repeats what the teacher did and what the first student did with the object. The second student then does something different with the object before passing it to the third student.

    Example:

Teacher:	I put the pen on the desk. What did I do with the pen?
Alfredo:	You put the pen on the desk. *(to the next student, Damian)* I put the pen above my head. What did we do with the pen?
Damian:	The teacher put the pen on the desk. Alfredo put the pen above his head. I put the pen under my book. *(to the next student)* What did we do with the pen? etc.

6. This activity continues until no one can do something different with the pen that can be described using a preposition of place.

    NOTE: *You may want to write the prepositions that have been used on the board to help the students remember.*

Variation: Give each student a card to use with a preposition of place on it.

4. ERROR ANALYSIS

RED

Materials: Worksheet 51 or other similar picture

Dynamic: Pairs

Time: 20 minutes

Procedure:

1. Divide the class into pairs. Give each pair a copy of the worksheet or other similar picture.

   NOTE: *If you are using your own picture, also give the pairs several sentences you have written about the picture, as on the worksheet. Some sentences should be accurate, and others incorrect.*

2. The pairs read the sentences about the picture and decide if they are correct or incorrect in their preposition usage. If they are incorrect, they must correct them.

3. When a pair is finished, check their work. If this is a competition, the first pair to finish the worksheet correctly wins. If using this activity as a review activity, go over the answers together when everyone has finished.

   SUGGESTION: *As a follow-up activity, have each pair write 10 True/False sentences with which to challenge another pair.*

5. PREPOSITION BEE

RED   BLACK

Materials: Worksheet 52A or 52B for instructor's use

Dynamic: Teams

Time: 10 minutes

Procedure:

1. Divide the class into two teams. Have them line up along opposite walls, or arrange their desks in two lines.

2. The first student from Team A steps to the front of the class. Read a sentence, omitting the preposition. The student must fill in the blank. Several answers will probably be possible; give the team a point for any appropriate answer.

3. Alternate students from the two teams until everyone has had a turn or you are out of time. The team with the most points wins.

   SUGGESTION: *Instead of reading the sentences, use an overhead and reveal one sentence at a time. This avoids repetition and helps the students to focus on the sentence.*

   NOTE: *You may want to make your own sentences based on the prepositions your class has covered. This activity could also be done at a higher level with sentences using phrasal verbs.*

8.2 PHRASAL VERBS

1. CONCENTRATION

Materials: Board, instructor's grid

Dynamic: Groups

Time: 25 minutes

BLACK BLUE

Procedure:

1. Draw a grid on the board with just the numbers. On a paper, your grid will have the answers written in.

   NOTE: *In the example below, the phrasal verbs have been taken from the list in* Fundamentals of English Grammar. *Several of the verbs in the chart below can take more than one particle, but the list is usually limited to one or two combinations. It is important to choose combinations you have studied and to limit entries so that three or even four matches are not possible. If you have studied more than one combination (such as* ask out, ask over, *and* ask around*) and you want to review them using this activity, you will need to use some particles more than once. That way, the students will be able to make matches such as* ask out, drop out, *and so on. This chart is intended only as a model to help you explain the game; your own chart will be geared to the lessons in your class.*

   On the board:

1	2	3	4	5
6	7	8	9	10
11	12	13	14	15
16	17	18	19	20

   Instructor's grid:

1 ask	2 back	3 drop	4 up	5 through
6 around	7 out	8 off	9 down	10 fill
11 in	12 get	13 write	14 start	15 throw
16 over	17 away	18 put	19 fool	20 call

2. Divide the class into groups of about five. Tell them that this is a memory game and no writing is allowed. Explain that they are looking for matches and will get a point for each match. They can confer as a team, but you will accept an answer only from the student whose turn it is. They can call out two numbers together the first time since no one knows where any of the words are. In subsequent turns, they should wait for you to write the first answer before they call out their second number.

3. As the first student calls out numbers, write the words that correspond to these numbers in the blanks. Ask the class if it is a match. If not, erase the words. If so, leave them there and cross them out (see below).

On the board:

1	2	3	4 ~~up~~	5
6 ~~around~~	7	8	9	10
11	12	13	14	15
16	17	18	19 ~~fool~~	20 ~~call~~

Variation: Instead of matching the verb with an appropriate preposition, you can set up the grid to review meaning. Your instructor's grid might then look like this model. Follow the same rules for the game above.

Instructor's grid:

1 call back	2 give back	3 stop sleeping	4 stop a machine/ light	5 get through with
6 return	7 invent	8 return a call	9 start a machine/ light	10 throw out
11 make up	12 shut off	13 be careful	14 put off	15 discard
16 wake up	17 postpone	18 turn on	19 watch out for	20 finish

2. TIC TAC TOE

Materials: Board, Worksheet 53 (optional)

Dynamic: Teams

Time: 10 minutes

BLACK BLUE

Procedure:
1. Draw a tic tac toe grid on the board with the first word of the phrasal verbs written in. Divide the class into two groups.

2. A student from Team X comes to the board and writes in the corresponding particle for the verb he/she selects. If correct, he/she draws his/her mark in the square (an X). (You may choose to accept only combinations you have studied in class or that are listed in the students' books, or you may decide to accept any correct combination. Whichever you decide to accept, make your decision clear to the students before playing the game.)

3. A student from Team O then comes to the board and does the same. If an answer is incorrect, the student cannot draw his/her mark and erases the answer. The next player on the other team may choose that same square or another square.

4. The first team with three marks in a row wins.

   NOTE: *You will probably want to explain game strategy such as blocking, but often the student's choice is based on which verb he/she knows.*

5. As a follow-up, divide the class into groups of three and use the worksheet. One student is X, one is O, and the other is in charge and can have his/her book open to the verb page to judge whether an answer is correct. After the first game, the students should rotate roles so that the judge is now one of the players. Continue until all students have had a chance to be the judge. As you will see, some of the verbs on the handout take several different prepositions. As long as the students make an acceptable phrasal verb, the answer is correct.

   NOTE: *The items on the worksheet come from the list in* Fundamentals of English Grammar. *If this worksheet is not appropriate to your class, modify it.*

Variation: On the grid on the board (or on a modified worksheet), fill in the squares with both parts of phrasal verbs. When a student selects a certain square, he/she must use the phrasal verb in a complete sentence which demonstrates understanding of the meaning. If the sentence is correct, the student puts his/her team's mark in that square.

   Example:

ask out	do over	fill up
get off	give up	try on
turn off	make up	hang up

A student from Team X chooses "give up." The student then makes a sentence orally: *I couldn't understand the assignment, so I gave up.* The sentence must reflect the student's understanding of the meaning of the phrasal verb. A sentence such as *I gave up* or *Don't give up* is not acceptable. If a sentence is accepted as being correct, the student writes an X over the square. A student from Team O then chooses a square and makes a meaningful sentence using that phrasal verb. Alternate turns until one team has three in a row or the game is a draw.

3. PREPOSITION BEE

*See the directions for the **Preposition Bee** on page 162. Use Worksheet 54 or a similar list of your own sentences.*

4. BEAT THE CLOCK

BLUE

Materials: 3" x 5" cards (see sample)

Dynamic: Teams

Time: 30 minutes

Procedure:

1. Put a sentence using a phrasal verb on one side of as many index cards as you need. Review and discuss phrasal verbs. Have the students create sentences or dialogues and practice orally.

2. Divide the class into two teams, A and B. Arrange the teams so that Team A's desks are directly across from (and touching) Team B's desks. If using tables, have Team A sit on one side and Team B on the other side.

3. Show the students the front of a card. The first student (A or B) who answers with a phrasal verb that correctly replaces the verb on the card gets a point for his/her team. If that student can then use the phrasal verb in a sentence with the correct tense, his/her team gets an extra point.

   Example:

Card:	I *raised* my children in Ohio.
Student response:	*bring up*
	I *brought* my children *up* in Ohio.

   Sample cards:

FRONT	BACK
I **raised** my children in Ohio.	bring up
I **met** John **by chance** at the mall.	run into
Tell Jill to **return** my call.	call back
Please be sure to **arrive** for the test at exactly 8:00.	show up

166

5. "UP" VERBS

BLACK   BLUE

Materials: 3″ x 5″ cards

Dynamic: Pairs/Small groups

Time: 20 minutes

Procedure:

1. Write one verb on each card. Choose some verbs that can also be phrasal verbs with *up*.

   Examples: *ask* (can't be used with *up*)
   check (can be used with *up*)
   cross (can't be used with *up*)
   get (can be used with *up*)

2. Divide the class into pairs or groups of three or four. Give each group a stack of verb cards.

3. Tell the students to divide the cards into two piles: verbs with *up*/verbs without *up*.

4. When all the *up* verbs are found, have the students take turns explaining the meaning of each phrasal verb to the other students in the group.

Variation: Make three identical sets of vocabulary cards. Divide the class into three teams. Tell the students to find the *up* verbs. The team that finds the most *up* verbs wins. Each correct *up* verb is worth one point. For each incorrect *up* verb, subtract one point from the total score. Use the same procedure for any phrasal verb pattern (for example, *out, away, through,* etc.).

6. PHRASAL CHALLENGE

BLACK   BLUE

Materials: None

Dynamic: Pairs

Time: 30 minutes

Procedure:

1. Divide the class into pairs. Tell the pairs to write down eight phrasal verbs and their meanings that they think the rest of the class will not know.

2. After they are finished, join two pairs and have the first pair challenge the other pair. Each pair takes turns reading the phrasal verbs from their list and having their opponents state the meaning of each phrasal verb and use it in a sentence.

3. If the opponents answer correctly, they get a point. The pair with the most points wins.

4. For homework, have the students use the phrasal verbs that they missed in correct sentences.

7. STORY TIME

Materials: 3″ x 5″ cards, writing paper

Dynamic: Small groups

Time: 40 minutes

BLACK   BLUE

Procedure:

1. Divide the class into groups of three, and give each group five 3″ x 5″ cards.

2. Each group writes down a different phrasal verb on each of their index cards. You may want to let them use the lists in their books. Have them write the definition of each phrasal verb on the back.

3. Have the groups quiz each other as to meaning by showing only the front of the card to another group.

4. Next, each group makes a sentence orally for each phrasal verb. Rotate the cards again until each group has seen every card and can make a logical sentence. Monitor the groups during this phase.

5. When the students have a good grasp of the definitions, return their original phrasal verb cards to them. Each group now writes a paragraph using all of their phrasal verbs.

6. When the students have finished, rotate their papers clockwise and the 3″ x 5″ cards counterclockwise. (Each group will have another group's story and a new set of cards.)

7. Each group reads the paragraph and adds a second paragraph, using their new group of phrasal-verb cards.

8. Have them repeat steps 6 and 7. Each group should now have a three-paragraph story.

9. Return the original story to each group. Tell the students to look it over and make any changes they think are necessary. Have one student from each group read the story to the class. Collect the stories for a final teacher correction.

8. CLASS SURVEY

BLACK   BLUE

Materials: 3″ x 5″ cards in four different colors
list of difficult phrasal verbs
sheets of newsprint and markers (optional)

Dynamic: Groups

Time: 40 minutes

Procedure:

1. Choose four themes and for each theme make up a set of questions, using the phrasal verbs that you want to practice. (You may want to have the students compile a list.)

   Examples:

   Family:
   Do you *take after* your father or your mother?
   Did you *grow up* in a large family or a small family?
   Do you *get along* well *with* your brothers and sisters?
   Are you *named after* anyone in your family?

   School:
   Do you *go over* your notes after class?
   Do you try to *get out of* doing your homework?
   Do you ever have trouble *keeping up with* the assignments?
   What is an important grammar point that you have to *look out for*?

2. Write one set of questions on one yellow card, one set of questions on one green card, etc.

3. Divide the class into groups. (Four groups of four works well, but five groups of five or three groups of three also works. Put extra students into existing groups to work as pairs.)

4. Tell the students that they are going to do some investigation into the society of the classroom by doing a survey. Give each group a set of same-color cards and a theme: The Yellow Group—Family; The Green Group—Friends, etc. Give the question card to the group leader and a blank card to each of the other members.

5. The group members copy the questions from the group leader's card on their own cards so that each has a card with the same questions. They may add questions of their own if they wish or if there is extra time. *Any additional questions must include a phrasal verb.*

6. When each member has an identical set of questions, the teams stand up and form new groups with one member of each color. (If there are extras of one or two colors, they can work as partners within the group.)

7. In their new groups, the students take turns interviewing each group member. The yellows ask their questions first and record the data, then greens, then blues, etc. Everyone asks everyone else in the group his/her questions.

8. The students reform their original same-color groups, summarize their findings, and present them to the entire class. If time permits, have the groups prepare a visual on newsprint in the form of a pie chart, a graph, a list of statistics, or another type of visual. The posters can be part of the presentation and later be put up around the board.

NOTE: *To save time, write out the duplicate cards yourself on colored index cards or copy one set of questions on different-colored paper. This will take the place of step 5. Collect the cards and reuse them in later classes.*

SUGGESTION: *This activity works well with preposition combinations instead of phrasal verbs.*

Examples:

Best Friends:
What do you *look for* in a best friend?
Is your best friend *patient with* you?
Do you ever *hide* anything *from* your best friend?
Do you ever *argue with* your best friend?

Work:
Are you *content with* your job?
Do you *look forward to* going to work?
Do you *forget about* your job when you leave at the end of the day?
Does your boss ever *take advantage of* you by having you do extra work?

With a partner, find the objects on the list. They are all located somewhere in the classroom. Then write a complete sentence that includes a prepositional phrase to describe each object's location.

Objects:

1.   6.

2.   7.

3.   8.

4.   9.

5.   10.

Locations:

1. _____

2. _____

3. _____

4. _____

5. _____

6. _____

7. _____

8. _____

9. _____

10. _____

Worksheet 51: ERROR ANALYSIS

With your partner, decide whether the sentences desribing the picture are correct or incorrect. If they are incorrect, correct them.

___ 1. The bird is on the umbrella.

___ 2. The sandwiches are behind the salad.

___ 3. The spatula is on the man's hand.

___ 4. The hammock is between a tree and a pole.

___ 5. The dog is under the table.

___ 6. The cat is under the table.

___ 7. The baby is beside the father.

___ 8. The hot dogs are next to the plates.

___ 9. The chairs are under the table.

___10. The grill is in front of the man.

1. What time do you get up _____ the morning?

2. She is sitting _____ me.

3. The roof is _____ our classroom.

4. I have a doctor's appointment _____ 10:30.

5. Scott was born _____ June.

6. Do you have any money _____ your wallet?

7. I am standing _____ Sarah and Alison.

8. I'll meet you _____ the library this afternoon.

9. Our classroom is _____ the office.

10. Before the test begins, please put your books _____ the table.

11. Keiko attends class _____ 9:00 _____ 2:30.

12. What time does it get dark _____ night?

13. I'll be _____ my office after class if you want to talk to me.

14. Please keep your notes _____ your notebook.

15. I'm always cold because there is a ceiling fan directly _____ my desk.

16. When it's cold, I wear a sweater _____ my shirt.

17. Hugo works out in the gym _____ Saturday.

18. Where's my pencil? I don't see it, but it must be _____ here somewhere.

19. The back seat is _____ the driver's seat in a car.

20. I'm going _____ to take my dog for a walk.

21. The children pressed their noses _____ the glass to see what was inside the store.

1. I'll meet you _____ 4:00, give or take 15 minutes.

2. Mary was walking _____ from her car when I saw her.

3. It's raining; you'd better put a coat _____ your dress.

4. Marco was walking _____ the river when he fell in.

5. He set the vase _____ the table.

6. The basketball went _____ the hoop.

7. The sign warned people not to lean _____ the newly painted wall.

8. My partner's eyes kept closing _____ the entire presentation. It was so embarrassing!

9. Shut the computer _____ if you are the last to leave.

10. Max is _____ Mexico, but he has lived here for 10 years.

11. You can't get Jasmine's attention when she is _____ a group of her friends.

12. There were many accidents _____ the big storm last week.

13. The glass fell _____ her hands _____ the floor.

14. Because of my allergies, the doctor told me I would have to go _____ chocolate.

15. My house is located _____ the city limits.

16. Your final essays are due _____ May 27.

17. Jordan was born _____ the last day of July.

18. I sat in the middle seat, _____ Luci and Claudia.

19. Because of all the trees, I can't see what is _____ those buildings.

20. Dogs must be _____ their yards or on a leash.

21. Is there any holiday that is celebrated _____ the world?

pay	hand	look
put	try	wake
make	shut	run

do	figure	grow
find	fill	tear
ask	call	drop

write	watch	pick
look	keep	hang
hang	give	fill

1. I first asked my girlfriend _____ on a date two years ago.

2. I had a message to call you _____ .

3. Rumi gave _____ on her math homework because she couldn't figure _____ the problems.

4. My handwriting was so messy that my teacher told me to do my homework _____ .

5. Ali is very easy-going; he gets _____ _____ everyone.

6. If the classroom gets too hot, take _____ your sweatshirts and sweaters.

7. Watch _____! There's a big pothole in the road.

8. The copy machine ran _____ _____ paper, so I couldn't make you copies.

9. I need an alarm clock to wake _____ .

10. They are tearing _____ the old building on the corner.

11. I'll lend you the money if you promise to pay me _____ .

12. Before our teacher hands _____ our tests, she always tells us to put our books _____ .

13. Yuji is not a serious student; he is always fooling _____ in class.

14. I know this class is difficult, but try to get _____ it.

15. Hitoshi grew _____ in a small town in Japan.

16. Cassio hung _____ the phone before I could ask him about the homework.

17. I like to buy clothes, but I hate trying them _____ .

18. If you don't know how to spell a word, look it _____ in the dictionary.

19. Elena lost her essay and had to start _____ .

20. I ran _____ my former teacher in the parking lot today. I hadn't seen him in three years.

CHAPTER

9

Adjectives

9.1 IDENTIFYING ADJECTIVES

- Scavenger Hunt
- Opposites Book
- Opposite-Adjective Bingo
- Adjective Charades
- What Does It Remind You Of?

9.2 ADJECTIVES IN SENTENCE CONTEXT

- Match the Description
- Description
- Make a Sentence
- What's in the Bag?
- Pass It On
- On-the-Spot Reports

IDENTIFYING ADJECTIVES

1. SCAVENGER HUNT

RED

Materials: Magazines to share

Dynamic: Groups

Time: 15 minutes

Procedure:

1. On the board, write a list of items you want the students to find a picture of. Each item should include an adjective and noun.

   Examples:
a happy person	an angry person
a sad person	an unusual person
a crying baby	a crazy person

2. Divide the class into groups of three or four and give each group a couple of magazines (or assign each student to bring in a magazine as the previous night's homework). Another method of distributing magazines is to keep a pile of magazines on a table and restrict each group to two magazines at a time. In order to get a new magazine, they must trade in one of their two. In this way, the students are not limited to one or two magazines that may not have good pictures in them, but at the same time, they cannot "hog" a pile of magazines.

3. The students cut out the pictures so they can show them to the other groups. You may want them to paste the pictures on paper, hold them up, or arrange them on their desks or a table. The students would then circulate to look at them.

4. You may want the groups to vote on which picture is the best example for each item. These could then be put together on a poster.

2. OPPOSITES BOOK

RED

Materials: Magazines or catalogs, construction paper

Dynamic: Individuals/Pairs

Time: 30 minutes

Procedure:

1. Have students bring in magazines or catalogs to cut up in class. Be sure there are plenty for them to use. In their magazines, students look for pictures of opposites, cut them out, and paste each picture on a separate page. They then label the picture with the adjective it depicts. (One page might have a picture of someone who is angry, and the next page have someone looking happy, for example.)

2. When they have found as many opposites as possible or when time is up, the students staple the pages together into an "Opposites Book."

3. The students can then exchange books to look at the pictures other students have found to depict opposite adjectives.

   SUGGESTION: *You can give the students free rein to choose the opposite adjectives they want, or you can give them a list to find. The students can easily find pictures of these adjectives.*

   comfortable/uncomfortable   common/uncommon
   bad/good   happy/sad
   healthy/sick   important/unimportant
   interesting/uninteresting (boring) beautiful/ugly
   necessary/unnecessary   clean/dirty
   pleasant/unpleasant   polite/impolite
   big/small   cheap/expensive
   cold/hot   dangerous/safe
   dark/light   dry/wet
   empty/full   fast/slow
   fat/thin   hard/soft
   heavy/light   long/short
   messy/neat   modern/old-fashioned
   noisy/quiet   old/young
   sour/sweet   strong/weak

Variation: By labeling the pictures, the students create a study book for themselves. For a more interactive activity, before they label the pictures, the students can exchange books with a classmate and have the classmate try to supply the adjectives.

3. OPPOSITE-ADJECTIVE BINGO

Materials: A bingo board (Worksheet 55A, 55B, or 55C) for each student, markers

Dynamic: Whole class

RED

Time: 15 minutes

Procedure:
1. Give each student a bingo board and markers to cover the words (paper squares, tiles, beans, etc.). You may want to give them time to look over the words on the board. Explain that when you call out an adjective, they are to look for and cover up that adjective's <u>opposite</u>. For example, if you call out "hard," the students cover up "soft."

2. The first person who covers five adjectives in a row is the winner. Check the answers. If the student has made a mistake, continue the game. (For variation, you could allow four corners or a cross, etc.)

Variations: Give everyone the same board so they will all hit bingo at the same time. Or make your own from the blank board (Worksheet 55D). You might also give the students blank boards and write a list of adjectives on the board. The students then choose from that list to fill in their boards in any order they want. Since the words you call off will be related to the words you write on the board, the students cannot write in their own adjectives.

4. ADJECTIVE CHARADES

Materials: Worksheet 56, cut up

Dynamic: Teams

Time: 20 minutes

RED

Procedure:

1. Cut Worksheet 56 into pieces and keep them in a hat, box, or bag. Divide the class into teams.

2. A student from the first team draws a slip with an adjective on it and must act out the adjective for his/her teammates. Set a time limit. If the team does not guess it, the other team (or teams) has a chance to "steal" the answer.

3. Give a point to the team if it guesses correctly in the time limit, or to the team that steals the answer. Play then passes to the next team. Continue until all slips have been played or until the time limit is reached.

5. WHAT DOES IT REMIND YOU OF?

Materials: Worksheet 57

Dynamic: Groups

Time: 20 minutes

RED

Procedure:

1. Divide the students into groups of four. Give each student a copy of the handout and have everyone fill in the chart under "you" with a place, person, or thing that the adjectives remind him/her of.

2. Have each student take turns asking the other three members of the group what the adjectives remind them of. The students then record this information on their charts.

3. Compare charts as a class by asking who had the same ideas in their group, who gave an unusual or funny answer, etc.

ADJECTIVES IN SENTENCE CONTEXT

1. MATCH THE DESCRIPTION

RED   BLACK

Materials: Worksheets 58A and 58B or your own cards

Dynamic: Whole class

Time: 30 minutes

Procedure:

1. Give each student two cards: one with a description of themselves (Worksheet 58A, cut up) and the other of a description of the classmate they are supposed to find (Worksheet 58B, cut up). Each student assumes the identity of his/her description from Worksheet 58A.

2. The students may not look at anyone's A card. They must circulate and ask each other questions based on the description of the person they are looking for.

   Example: If John's B card says "Find someone who is tall and thin and wearing a basketball uniform," John must ask other students questions to find that person. ("Are you tall?" "What are you wearing?")

   At the same time, the other students will be asking questions to match their B cards. John should be prepared to look at his A card to answer questions addressed to him even when he is finished asking questions.

3. When a match is made, the student with the B card takes the other student's A card. The students do not sit down until they have both given up their A card and received another student's A card.

4. When everyone has finished, you can ask some questions: "Who is tall and wearing a basketball uniform?" "Who has short curly blond hair?" "Who is handicapped?"

Variation: For a less complicated game, keep the B cards but use small pictures from a magazine instead of A cards. When a match is made, the person with the description card takes the picture card.

2. DESCRIPTION

RED

Materials: None

Dynamic: Whole class

Time: 15 minutes

Procedure:

1. Have each student write a one-sentence description of a classmate on a piece of paper, using at least one adjective in the description.

   Example: She has long curly hair.
   He is wearing a black leather jacket.
   She has on a colorful T-shirt.

2. The students take turns reading the descriptions aloud. The rest of the class tries to guess who is being described.

   NOTE: *Because students are competing to guess the identity of their classmates, caution them not to be too general (not "She is wearing dark blue jeans" if most of the class is wearing dark blue jeans) or too specific (not "She is wearing a T-shirt with a purple-and-yellow-striped zebra on it."). Descriptions that are too general result in a simple guessing game. Descriptions that are too specific take the fun out of the game.*

3. MAKE A SENTENCE

RED

Materials: Worksheet 59

Dynamic: Groups

Time: 20 minutes

Procedure:

1. Arrange the class in groups of approximately four. Give the cards from one cut-up worksheet to each group, face down. Tell the students to deal out five cards per person and keep the others face down in a pile.

2. The students take turns choosing a card either from the pile or from another student's hand, and then discarding. The object is to make a complete sentence with an adjective in it.

3. When one of the players has a complete sentence in his/her hand, he/she displays the sentence in order. All the cards in the student's hand must be used to make the sentence. If it is accepted by the group (you can intervene as ultimate judge), the game is over and that student is the winner. If the sentence does not make sense, is not grammatically constructed, or contains no adjective, the student picks up his/her cards and the play resumes.

While the words on the worksheet are arranged into four-word sentences, it is possible for the students to come up with other possibilities using the words on the worksheet. As long as the students are able to produce a logical sentence of the correct length, accept their answer.

NOTE: *If you are making your own cards instead of or in addition to using the worksheet, be sure all sentences are of equal length.*

4. WHAT'S IN THE BAG?

Materials:	5–12 small paper bags items for the bags
Dynamic:	Pairs/Whole class
Time:	20 minutes

RED BLACK BLUE

Procedure:

1. Place one item in each bag. You may want to use multiple pieces of one item, such as seven cotton balls or a handful of pot pourri. Suggested items:

cooked pasta	dry, broken pasta	pot pourri
cotton balls	flour	soil
croutons	paper clips	

2. Put a list of adjectives on the board. The words will depend on the level of your class. For example:

   Beginner: *round, hard, soft, long, small, large*
   Intermediate: *sharp, sandy, sweet-smelling, sour, flexible*
   Advanced: *sticky, rubbery, pliable, brittle, pungent, odorous*

3. Using an adjective order chart such as the one in *Basic English Grammar*, have students generate words from each adjective category (opinion adjectives, colors, sizes, etc.). Introduce new words in each of these categories and write them on the board.

4. Arrange students into pairs and assign each pair a number. Have each pair write its number on the outside of its bag.

5. The students feel the contents of the bag and then write adjectives on the outside of the bag describing what they feel. Ask students to draw from the words on the board.

6. Students pass the bags around so everyone can experience the contents of each bag. Then have the pairs generate a sentence using adjectives to describe the contents of the bag they are holding.

7. From the description, the other students try to guess the contents of the bag. You can have the other pairs call out their guesses, or for a competition, have each pair write down its guesses, exchange papers, and show the class the contents to correct the papers.

5. PASS IT ON

RED   BLACK

Materials:	None, or Worksheet 60
Dynamic:	Whole class
Time:	15 minutes
Procedure:	1. Choose five students (or ask for volunteers) to leave the room.

2. Before they go, explain to the class that you will send the five students out and then call them back one at a time. You will tell the first student a short story and then, when the second student comes in, the first student will tell him/her what you have just said. Continue until they get to the fifth student. You should try to talk at a normal rate that your students can understand, perhaps even a little faster. Do not purposely slow down to tell the story.

3. Have the five students leave the room. Follow the steps explained in step 2.

4. You can make up your own story or use an example from the worksheet. If you make your own story, be sure to include plenty of adjectives.

5. The class (and you) will judge how well the story got passed along.

6. To play again, select five different students and a different story to pass along.

   NOTE: *The other students in the class should not coach or help the students who make errors in content when relaying the stories. This should be stated before doing the activity.*

   SUGGESTION: *For fun, tape record both the first and final versions of the story. Then play them back for the whole class.*

6. ON-THE-SPOT REPORTS

RED   BLACK

Materials:	None
Dynamic:	Pairs/Small groups
Time:	20 minutes
Procedure:	1. Before class, ask a student to help you participate in a role play (or choose two students to do the role play). Bring in different types, colors, and patterns of clothing. The two actors "disguise" themselves with the clothes. One of the actors is the "thief" and the other, the "victim." (If you are taking one of the roles, you might want to play the thief.)

2. At the beginning of class, the "victim" comes in and walks in front of the class (perhaps as if looking for a place to sit or going out an opposite door—it depends on your classroom). The "victim" has a purse or backpack or some other article for the "thief" to steal. The "thief" rushes in behind the "victim" and grabs the agreed-upon article. Both exit, with the "victim" now chasing the "thief."

3. The two actors remove their "costumes" and leave them out of sight of the rest of the students.

4. Arrange the students in pairs or small groups and have them prepare "statements" for the police. The statements describe what they witnessed, details about what the "thief" was wearing, and a description of the stolen object.

5. Read the statements aloud or have students read them aloud so the class can agree on the best report of the incident. You can also show the clothes and see which group came closest.

happy	calm	cheap	intelligent	round
soft	difficult	sweet	sharp	light
cold	interesting	**FREE**	funny	large
new	dry	dirty	empty	short
loud	cool	attractive	slow	smooth

smooth	slow	attractive	cool	loud
short	empty	dirty	dry	sharp
large	funny	**FREE**	interesting	cold
light	cheap	sweet	difficult	soft
round	intelligent	new	calm	happy

happy	cheap	round	difficult	new
cold	funny	sharp	dirty	short
cool	slow	**FREE**	calm	soft
sweet	intelligent	light	interesting	large
dry	empty	loud	attractive	smooth

		FREE		

Worksheet 56: ADJECTIVE CHARADES

sad	wild	tired
lazy	sour	heavy
hot	bored	serious
small	wet	clean
full	tall	quiet
warm	ugly	fast
attractive	funny	crazy

a. *For each adjective, write in a place, thing, or person that that adjective reminds you of.*

b. *Now, ask the members of your group and write in their answers.*

ADJECTIVE	YOU	STUDENT 1	STUDENT 2	STUDENT 3
beautiful				
cheap				
boring				
ugly				
noisy				
dangerous				
huge				
tiny				
expensive				
relaxing				

You are tall and thin and are wearing a basketball uniform.	You have short, curly blond hair.	You are wearing a striped suit with a red tie.
You have a thin mustache and dark hair.	You are tall and are wearing a jogging outfit.	You have long blond hair.
You have a dark beard and dark hair.	You are wearing ski gloves.	You are wearing long black gloves.
You are wearing a short leather skirt.	You are wearing a miniskirt which has black polka dots.	You are wearing a blue jogging outfit.
You have short, curly blond hair and a mustache.	You are handicapped and are sitting in a wheelchair.	You are sitting in a rocking chair with a colorful blanket on your lap.
You are wearing dark glasses and a leather jacket.	You are holding a small, ugly dog.	You are walking a dangerous-looking dog.
You are wearing glasses and a hat.	You are sitting next to a white, long-haired cat.	You are holding a tiger-striped cat.

Worksheet 58B: MATCH THE DESCRIPTION

Find someone who is holding a tiger-striped cat.	Find someone who is sitting next to a long-haired cat.	Find someone wearing glasses and a hat.
Find someone wearing sunglasses and a leather jacket.	Find someone holding a small, ugly dog.	Find someone walking a dangerous-looking dog.
Find someone who is sitting in a rocker with a brightly colored blanket on his/her lap.	Find someone who is handicapped and sitting in a wheelchair.	Find someone with a mustache and short, curly blond hair.
Find someone who has a thin mustache and dark hair.	Find someone wearing a black polka-dotted miniskirt.	Find someone wearing a blue jogging outfit.
Find someone wearing long black evening gloves.	Find someone wearing a striped suit and red tie.	Find someone who is tall, thin, and wearing a uniform.
Find someone who is wearing a short leather skirt.	Find someone who is tall and wearing a jogging outfit.	Find someone with long blond hair.
Find someone who has short, curly blond hair.	Find someone with a dark beard.	Find someone wearing ski gloves.

a	lemon	tastes
sour	this	desk
feels	smooth	that
garbage	smells	bad
bungee	jumping	looks
dangerous	she's	a
pretty	girl	good
health	is	important
dogs	make	good
pets	silver	coins
are	rare	most
cats	are	furry

Worksheet 60: PASS IT ON

1. Yesterday, I was waiting for the elevator in a big department store. When the door opened, I was so surprised to see a lady wearing a long purple fur coat, carrying a reddish-brown monkey. As they got off, the monkey tipped his little straw hat to me.

2. I was extremely hungry yesterday, so I called a new take-out place. I ordered two chocolate shakes, three large bags of fries, and a family-size vegetarian pizza. The service was so slow that by the time my order arrived, I had lost my humongous appetite and couldn't eat a thing.

3. Last night I woke up suddenly when I saw some strange, bright lights in my yard. I ran through the wet grass to see what was happening. I heard a loud motor and looked up to see a shiny silver spaceship with pulsing lights. I couldn't move and watched as the spaceship slowly landed. The round door opened, and suddenly I heard piercing sirens and ringing bells. I turned to run and then . . . I woke up and shut off my alarm clock!

CHAPTER
10

Modals

10.1 MODALS

- Dialogue Advice
- Line-Ups
- What Can I Do with It? (Using *can*)
- Are You the One? (Using *can*)
- Stop Me, Please!
- Role Play
- Class Rules

10.2 PAST PROGRESSIVE MODALS

- Knock at the Door

10.3 REVIEW

- Board Game
- Riddles
- Modal Madness

10.1 MODALS

1. DIALOGUE ADVICE

Materials:	None
Dynamic:	Teams
Time:	10 minutes
Procedure:	1. Divide the class in half, and have the students form two lines on either side of the classroom. The first student in each line then comes to the center of the room.
	2. The two students converse with each other as in the examples, with one student stating a problem, and the other giving advice.

Examples:

Student A: What's wrong?
Student B: I have a headache.
Student A: You should go home and take some aspirin.

Student A: What's the matter?
Student B: I have to take my driver's license test, but my car isn't working.
Student A: You should try to postpone the test.

4. The two students then go to the ends of their respective lines, and the next two students converse. Continue the play until all students have had a chance, or until you reach a certain time limit.

NOTE: *You may want to give the class a topic, such as health, family matters, or transportation, or leave the conversation open-ended.*

2. LINE-UPS

Materials:	Worksheet 61
Dynamic:	Whole class
Time:	20 minutes
Procedure:	1. Copy the worksheets (using two colors of paper) and cut them into individual cards so that you have one card for each student, or make your own 3″ x 5″ cards in two colors. (Using two colors makes it easier to give directions and see that everyone is where he/she should be.) You will need only one worksheet if you have 12 or fewer students.

2. Call all students holding one color card to the front of the class and have them form a line. This is the question line. The other students come forward and stand in front of a student in the question line.

3. The students in the question line read the questions on their cards to the classmates in front of them. The students in the answer line must give advice. After answering a question, the students in the answer line move to the next position. The students in the question line do not move. Continue until the students in the answer line are back where they started (they have given advice to all the students in the question line). Now the students change positions. The students who answered questions are now the question line. They take out their cards to ask questions, and the opposite students answer.

4. As a follow-up, ask each student to summarize the kind of advice he/she received. In a lower class, you might just ask each student for one piece of advice he/she received.

3. WHAT CAN I DO WITH IT? (Using *can*)

Materials: None

Dynamic: Whole class

Time: 10 minutes

RED   BLACK   BLUE

Procedure:

1. Explain that a volunteer will leave the room. While this student is gone, you will give the class a word. When the volunteer returns, he/she will try to guess the word from class clues. The students will give clues using "can."

2. When everyone understands the game, ask for a volunteer to leave. Write a word on the board and solicit clues from the class.

   Example: **Word:** eggs
   Clues: You can find them on a farm.
   You can cook them.
   They can break if you drop them.

   If you want, go over strategy, such as using more general clues first and saving very specific ones (such as "They can be found under chickens") until last.

3. When you have solicited approximately five clues, erase the words on the board and call the volunteer back in. The class members take turns giving their "can" clues. The volunteer tries to beat the class by guessing the word before all the clues are given.

   SUGGESTED WORDS: *eggs, fish, aspirin, gloves, paper clips, bicycle, thermometer, turn signal*

4. ARE YOU THE ONE? (Using *can*)

RED   BLACK   BLUE

Materials: Worksheet 62

Dynamic: Whole class

Time: 20 minutes

Procedure:

1. Give every student a copy of the worksheet.

2. The object is for students to find someone who can give them a *yes* answer to each question. When they get a *yes* they write that student's name in the space. If they get a *no* answer, they continue to search for someone who will say *yes*.

3. Go over some of the answers as a closure.

   NOTE: *This same idea can be used with* **Human Bingo**. *See Chapter Five for sample worksheets of both* **Are You the One?** *and* **Human Bingo**.

5. STOP ME, PLEASE!

BLACK   BLUE

Materials: Bottles to use as props

Dynamic: Whole class

Time: 10 minutes

NOTE: *This short warm-up or review activity involves the entire class, but takes only 5–10 minutes.*

Procedure:

1. Begin by telling the class they can speak to you using negative modals only. On the board, list several possibilities, such as

   You don't have to . . .
   You must not . . .
   You don't need to . . .
   You should not . . .

2. Set up a group of small bottles in front of you. On one, attach a skull and crossbones picture, or write the word *poison* on an easy-to-see label.

3. Tell the students that you need to put eyedrops in your eye (or take some aspirin, etc.), but you don't have your contact lenses in, so you can't see very well.

4. Pick up the bottle with the poison label, saying "This must be the right bottle!," and act as if you are going to use it. If no one tries to stop you, draw out the activity a little longer before finally asking if anyone has something to say to you. (You might say "Is this the right bottle?" "Can anyone help me? I can't read the label." or "Do you think this is the right one?")

6. ROLE PLAY

RED   BLACK   BLUE

Materials: Worksheet 63

Dynamic: Pairs

Time: 20 minutes

Procedure:
1. Put students into pairs, and give each pair a card from the cut-up worksheet.

2. The pairs read their situation and plan a role play. They must use some modals in their role play, but are not limited to any in particular.

3. Check with the pairs to see how they are doing. When everyone is prepared, the pairs come to the front and role play their situations. The class states what situation is being portrayed.

7. CLASS RULES

RED   BLACK   BLUE

Materials: None

Dynamic: Small groups

Time: 10 minutes

Procedure:
1. Divide the class into groups of three or four.

2. The groups are to make a list of rules for the class that are fair for both students and teacher. Encourage them to use modals and the future.

3. A member of each group writes the group's rules on the board. As a class, decide which rules they would all accept.

PAST PROGRESSIVE MODALS

1. KNOCK AT THE DOOR

BLUE

Materials: 3″ x 5″ cards

Dynamic: Pairs

Time: 20 minutes

Procedure:
1. Model two or three **Knock at the Door** situations.

Examples:

Teacher: I knocked at my friend's door at 6:30 this morning. He came to the door with a razor in his hand, wearing half a beard and half a mustache.

Student: He must have been shaving.

Teacher: I knocked at my friend's door at 10:30 last night. She came to the door with the TV remote control in her hand, and I could hear loud music in the background.

Student: She must not have been studying for the big grammar test we have today.

2. Put students in pairs and have each pair write 3–5 **Knock at the Door** situations on their index cards.

3. Circulate and circle the two best situations on each card. Have the student pairs share them with the class.

SUGGESTION: *Instead of step 3, the pairs can pick their two favorite situations to share with the class.*

REVIEW

1. BOARD GAME

Materials: Worksheets 64A, 64B, and 64C
One die per group, one marker per student

Dynamic: Groups

Time: 20 minutes

RED   BLACK   BLUE

Procedure:

1. Divide the class into groups of approximately four. Give each group a copy of the worksheet appropriate to the class level and a die, plus one marker for each student in the group.

2. The students take turns rolling the die and moving the indicated number of spaces. They follow the directions on the space they land on. If they land on a blank space, they stop and wait for their next turn.

3. The first student in each group to reach the end is the winner.

NOTE: *Instead of using the worksheets, you may want to make your own to review the forms you have covered in class.*

2. RIDDLES

RED   BLACK   BLUE

Materials: None

Dynamic: Pairs

Time: 15 minutes

Procedure:

1. After working with modals of advice, possibility, and obligation, write the following riddle on the board and see if students can answer the question.

> She can listen to music or watch a movie.
> She must have a ticket.
> She doesn't have to stay in her seat.
> She must not smoke.
> She should relax and enjoy herself.
> Where is she?   *In an airplane.*

2. Have the students work in pairs and use the above structure to make riddles of their own. They can conclude with the questions *Where is she/he?* or *Who is she/he?* (with professions).

3. You can use the completed riddles in several ways.

   a. Collect the riddles, check for mistakes, and redistribute them to new pairs. The pairs discuss the riddle and write their answer on the paper before checking with the writers.

   b. Have each pair read their riddle aloud, and have the whole class guess the answer.

   c. Have each pair write their riddle on the board or tape it to the wall. The other students circulate, read, and write their guesses.

4. The riddles can then lead into a discussion of errors or of the different answers that came up as a result of the activity.

3. MODAL MADNESS

BLACK   BLUE

Materials: Worksheets 65A, 65B, and 65C
Dice and markers

Dynamic: Small groups

Time: 45 minutes

Procedure:

1. Arrange students in groups of three or four. Give each group a game board, situation sheets, answer key, and die, plus one marker per student.

2. The first student rolls the die, moves his/her marker the appropriate number of spaces, and reads aloud the situation from Worksheet 65C that corresponds to the numbered space.

3. The student then follows the directions, using an appropriate modal.

   Example:

   Student A lands on block 14. The instructions read:

   One of your partners is homesick. Make a possible suggestion to help him/her.

   Student A replies: You could call your family more often.

4. Other students in the group check the answer key to see if the modal used is acceptable. If it was correct, the student waits for his/her next turn, then goes again. If it was incorrect, the student misses his/her next turn.

5. If a student lands on a number that has already been done, he/she automatically advances to the next "new" (previously unused) number.

6. If a student lands on FREE CHOICE, he/she can choose any situation number.

7. The winning student or team is the first one to land on MODAL HEAVEN. (The numbers on the playing board are repeated to provide for maximum practice.)

My girlfriend/boyfriend is going to make dinner for me, and she/he is an awful cook! What should I say?

There's some money left on a table after everyone leaves class. What should I do?

If I arrive at class 30 minutes late, should I go in?

I just met my sister's new boyfriend. He's very impolite, and I don't like him. What should I say to her?

I didn't pass my test today. What should I do?

My boyfriend/girlfriend just broke up with me. What should I do?

It's very cold today. What should I wear?

I want a pet, but I don't know what kind to get. What kind of pet do you recommend?

I didn't have time to eat breakfast this morning. Now I'm in class, and my stomach is growling. What should I do?

My friend wants me to go to a party, but I'm very tired and I don't know the other guests. Should I go?

I just won a lot of money in Las Vegas! How should I spend my money?

My car always breaks down on the highway. What should I do?

I feel sick, but we are about to take a test. What should I do?

I have a headache. What should I take?

I left my books on the bus. What should I do?

I did my homework, but my dog chewed it up. I don't think the teacher will believe me. What should I do?

I lost a library book. What should I do?

I feel very sick, but I don't have a doctor. What should I do?

I have a toothache. What should I do?

I ruined my sister's favorite shirt by getting ink on it. Should I tell her?

Your sister tells you she just had a fight with her husband and asks for your advice. What should you say?

You forgot your boyfriend/ girlfriend's birthday, and now he/she is outside your door. What should you do?

You are having lunch with an old friend from school when your jealous boyfriend/girlfriend walks in. What should you do?

Your car runs out of gas at 2:00 A.M., and you have no money with you. What should you do?

Make questions of the phrases, using can. *If a student answers* yes, *write his/her name on the line. If a student answers* no, *continue looking for a yes answer.*

1. play the piano _____

2. use chopsticks _____

3. identify the president of the
   United States _____

4. snowski _____

5. make a strawberry shortcake _____

6. speak Japanese _____

7. use a computer _____

8. arrange flowers _____

9. sing your national anthem _____

10. give directions to the library _____

Book a room in a hotel.	Ask someone to go on a date with you.
Persuade someone to lend you money.	Ask someone to return something he/she has taken.
Get a noisy neighbor to be quiet.	Ask for directions to somewhere.
Explain to a police officer why you were speeding.	Explain to one of your parents how the big dent got on the family car.
Convince your friend to go to the movie you have chosen.	Explain to the teacher why you don't have your homework.
Make a reservation for a large group at an expensive restaurant.	Explain how you want your hair cut.

START →		Talk about something you can do well.	What is something you could do when you were little that you can't do now?	ROLL AGAIN	GO BACK 4 SPACES ↓
Describe something you know how to do that your partners do not. ↓	LOSE A TURN		What should you do this weekend?	What do adults have to do that children do not have to do?	←
→ GO BACK 3 SPACES		What did your parents tell you that you must do?	GO AHEAD 3 SPACES	What must you do to get a driver's license?	What would you like to see in the United States? ↓
What kind of weather might we have tomorrow? ↓	ROLL AGAIN		What must you do to get into a university?	What will you do after class?	What can a millionaire do that you cannot do? ←
→	What might you do when you finish this English program?	LOSE A TURN	What can you do that a family member cannot do?		GO AHEAD 1 SPACE ↓
What should you stop doing? ↓		Where would you like to have lunch today?		ROLL AGAIN	←
→ What do students have to do?		What are you going to be able to do next year?	LOSE A TURN	What can a magician do?	YOU WIN!!!!

	What is something a parent ought to tell a child?	ROLL AGAIN		Describe some activity that you can do well.	What is something you had better do tonight?
START →					
LOSE A TURN		What can you find in a deli?	What could you do in your country but not here?	GO BACK 4 SPACES	What is something you must not say in class?
	GO AHEAD 2 SPACES	What could you do if you had a car?		Discuss something you have got to do soon.	
What might you do if a dog starts to chase you?		What must you do to get a good grade?	ROLL AGAIN	What is something children must not do?	
GO BACK 2 SPACES	What will you do next summer?	What does a teacher not have to do?	LOSE A TURN		What is something a millionaire does not have to do?
What is something you must not ask an American?		What can you do very well?	What should you do to lose weight?	What can you do to avoid a traffic ticket?	
GO BACK 5 SPACES	What shouldn't you eat?		ROLL AGAIN	How many countries can you name?	YOU WIN!!!!

START →		What may I borrow from you?	What are you supposed to do for your family?	**ROLL AGAIN**	What can you do by yourself? ↓
What are you used to doing? ↓	**LOSE A TURN**	What could you do if you do not understand your teacher?	What is something you might do if it rains?		Where are you to be at 8:00 tomorrow?
→ **GO AHEAD 3 SPACES**	What would you rather do than study?			What did you use to do as a child?	**GO BACK 2 SPACES** ↓
↓	What must your best friend be doing right now?	What is something you must not talk about?	**LOSE A TURN**		What is something you might not do ever?
→ **GO AHEAD 4 SPACES**			What must a doctor have?		How many languages can you speak? ↓
What is an adult supposed to do? ↓	What does a pet owner have to do?	**ROLL AGAIN**	**GO AHEAD 2 SPACES**	What can you tell your best friend but no one else?	
→ Whose advice should you listen to?	Where can you find people to speak English?		How much money have you been able to save this year?	What must a person bring to your country?	↓
YOU WIN!!!!		**GO BACK 4 SPACES**		What is something a person ought to know before visiting your country?	Would you rather see a movie or watch a video?

© 1997 Prentice Hall Regents. Duplication for classroom use is permitted.

ANSWER KEY:

1. would, will, could, can
2. may, could, can, would you mind
3. would, will, could, can, would you mind
4. must, have to, have got to
5. must not
6. do not have to
7. should, ought to, had better
8. had better
9. should have (or should not have) + past participle
10. should have (or should not have) + past participle
11. be supposed to
12. be supposed to, be to
13. let's, why don't, shall I/we
14. could
15. must be
16. may be, might be, could be
17. had to
18. can, be able to
19. could, was able to
20. couldn't be, can't be
21. must not be
22. may not be, might not be
23a. must have + past participle
23b. may have, might have, could have + past participle
24. must have + past participle
25. may have, might have, could have + past participle
26. should, ought to
27. may, might, could
28. used to + verb
29. be used to
30. would
31. would rather

START		FREE CHOICE	5	4	3	FREE CHOICE
1		6		FINISH! MODAL HEAVEN		2
2		7				1
3		8		28		31
4		9		27		30
5		10		26		29
6		11		25		28
7		12		24		27
8		13		23		26
9		14		22		25
10		15		21		24
11		16		20		23
12		17		19		22
13		FREE CHOICE	18	FREE CHOICE		21
14						20
FREE CHOICE	15	16	17	18	19	FREE CHOICE

Situations

1. Invite one of your partners to go to a specific restaurant for lunch.

2. Make a polite request to take an extra turn in this game. Use "I" as the subject.

3. Politely request that one of your partners run to a nearby coffee shop to get you a cup of coffee.

4. Tell one of your partners three things that are necessary for you to do.

5. Prohibit one of your partners from cheating in this game.

6. Tell all of your partners that it's not necessary to stand and applaud when your grammar teacher enters the room. (But if they want to get an A, it's a good idea.)

7. Give one of your partners some advice: he/she has been invited on a date by a teacher of the opposite sex. (The teacher is attractive, and your partner likes him/her.)

8. Give one of your partners some very strong advice: if he/she doesn't like grammar class, but likes the rest of the program, . . .

9. One of your partners didn't go to bed early enough last night because he/she went to a disco. He/She is yawning in class today. Tell him/her that it was a mistake to go to bed so late.

10. One of your partners went jogging on the beach and lost his/her car keys. Tell him/her it was a mistake to have the keys in his/her pocket.

11. In North American classrooms, students are expected to actively participate. Tell your partners this.

12. The teacher strongly expects the students to arrive for class on time, with their homework finished. Tell your partners.

13. Suggest to your partners that you all play hookey from your next class.

14. One of your partners is homesick. Make a possible suggestion to help him/her.

15. Your favorite classmate isn't in class today. You are 95 percent sure you know the reason. Tell your partners.

16. What time is it in your home country? Tell your partners what your family/friends are perhaps doing right now. (You are less than 50 percent certain.)

17. Tell three things that were necessary for you to do before you left your hometown.

18. Tell three things you have the ability to do well.

19. Tell three things you had the ability to do well when you were younger.

20. Tell what you think one of the people you live with is *not* doing right now. You are 99 percent sure.

21. Same as #20, but you are 95 percent certain.

22. Same as #20, but you are less than 50 percent certain.

23. Bad luck! You have to follow both these instructions to continue the game:

    > Your classmate had a car accident last week. Why do you think it happened?
    > You are 95 percent sure.
    > You are less than 50 percent certain.

24. Your teacher was 45 minutes late for class yesterday. Why? (You are 95 percent certain.)

25. Same as #24, but you are less than 50 percent sure.

26. You are 90 percent sure your friend will do well on the midterm exam. Tell him/her.

27. You are less than 50 percent sure that you will win money when you gamble in Las Vegas next weekend. Tell your partners.

28. One of your classmates came to class late every day for the first four weeks of class, but now he/she is always on time. Tell your partners about this past activity that is no longer true.

29. Tell what people in your family are accustomed to eating for breakfast.

30. Before you came to this school, you went dancing every weekend with your friends. Tell your partners about this repeated action from the past.

31. Tell your partners which you prefer: coming to grammar class to see your wonderful, charming teacher or going to the beach to watch the sunset with your friends.

CHAPTER

11

Passive Voice

PASSIVE VOICE

1. AT THE MOVIES

BLUE

Materials: Short excerpt from video
Worksheet based on video (see sample Worksheet 66)

Dynamic: Small groups

Time: 40 minutes

Procedure:

1. Select either a short video (no more than 30 minutes) or an excerpt from a longer video. Use about 10 minutes of an action-packed scene. Go over vocabulary that the students will need in order to understand the video and to write their sentences. I recommend including this on the worksheet.

2. Go over the questions on the worksheet so the students know in advance what to look for when you show the video. Use a variety of tenses in your questions.

   Examples:

   > What happened to the balloon?
   > What had already happened to the man before he entered the cave?
   > What do you think will happen to the woman next?

   Be sure the students understand that they must reply in the passive. They cannot answer, "The balloon flew away," to the first question (above). They must answer with a response such as "The balloon was taken by the gang of boys." Students have a tendency to answer in the active voice for a question in the future, so you may want to solicit some responses in the passive or have the students brainstorm answers to the questions in groups.

3. Show the video. Let the students take notes if they want.

4. Arrange the students in groups of three or four to discuss the video and try to form answers to the questions.

5. For homework, have the students write out the answers to the questions, using only the passive voice.

   NOTE: *Worksheet 66, intended as an example, is based on approximately 10 minutes near the beginning of* Raiders of the Lost Ark, *from the time Indiana Jones enters the cave until he flies off in the airplane. Pick a short segment of a video with a lot of action, one that lends itself to writing passive sentences.*

2. BUSY PICTURES

Materials: Picture for each student (see Worksheets 67A & 67B for examples)

Dynamic: Individuals/Groups

Time: 25 minutes

BLACK   BLUE

Procedure:

1. Choose a picture with a lot of activity. Be sure that students will be able to generate some passive sentences about the picture you have chosen. A funny or strange picture works well. Good sources for pictures are magazine ads, certain comics, and pictures from lower-level writing books.

2. Have students write a specific number of sentences in the passive based on the picture. Have an advanced class write a paragraph that contains both passive and active sentences. Tell them not to limit themselves to what they see in the picture. Encourage them to stretch their imagination and be creative. The funnier and more outrageous the situations or sentences, the more fun the activity will be. Give them some help to get started. For example:

   > Last weekend I was at a very elegant restaurant where the food was being served by a sophisticated-looking waitress when . . .

   > I had dinner with my girlfriend's parents for the first time. As the menu selections were being discussed, I leaned back to drink my water and suddenly . . .

   If you are asking for a paragraph, make sure the students understand that it is impossible to write every sentence in the passive, so their paragraphs will be a mixture of passive and active sentences. You may want to tell them approximately how many passive sentences you would like them to produce.

3. Collect and correct the students' sentences, then prepare an error analysis page focusing on mistakes in the passive taken from their writing (see Worksheet 67B). Different types of mistakes may be included, such as

   > The waitress is brought the meal.

   > The menu are being discussed by the women.

   > The meal is being serving.

4. Before handing back the students' work, arrange the students in small groups and have them try to correct the errors on the error analysis page. The individual students can use these corrections to help with their own papers when they are returned.

3. MATCH

Materials: Worksheet 68

Dynamic: Pairs/Small groups

Time: 20 minutes

BLUE

Procedure:
1. Arrange students in pairs or groups of three or four, and give a copy of the worksheet to each group.

2. The students are to choose two related words on the worksheet and make a passive sentence using them. They will have to supply their own verbs and other words.

Words chosen: **children**, *Aladdin*
Possible sentence: *Aladdin* is loved by children.
Words chosen: **dog, bone**
Possible sentence: Bones are eaten by dogs.

3. As a follow-up the next day, you might make a worksheet of inappropriate passive sentences. The students would correct the sentences and explain what was wrong: the sentences are illogical, silly, do not have correct subject/verb agreement, or do not use the passive.

4. STORYTIME

Materials: Worksheet 69

Dynamic: Small groups

Time: 30 minutes

BLUE

Procedure:
1. Arrange students in groups of three or four. Give each group a copy of the worksheet.

2. Direct students to read the short summaries on the worksheet and then write four sentences based on the readings, using the passive voice.

Sample responses, Worksheet 69, story 1:

Lucy was fooled by her boyfriend, who was dressed as a woman.
Lucy is attracted to her disguised boyfriend.
Kevin and Mac are taken out to public places by Lucy.
Dates were arranged for the two men dressed as women.

NOTE: *You can use summaries of soap operas (as in the handout), movies, TV shows, stories the students are reading in their reading classes, fairy tales, or fables, or make up your own.*

PARTICIPIAL ADJECTIVES

1. REVIEWS

BLUE

Materials:	Worksheet 70
Dynamic:	Pairs
Time:	15 minutes
Procedure:	1. To review participial adjectives, use the worksheet or make a similar one of your own, based on a current TV show or movie.
	2. Have students work in pairs (one worksheet per pair) to fill in the blanks with the appropriate form of one of the verbs listed.
	3. Go over the worksheet as a class and discuss the reasons for the answers.

2. PICTURES

BLACK   BLUE

Materials:	A large picture for each pair
Dynamic:	Pairs
Time:	10 minutes
Procedure:	1. Put students into pairs. Give each pair a picture and a verb to use. A good source of pictures is full-page ads in magazines.
	2. The partners make a sentence based on their picture, using a participial adjective form of the verb they have been assigned.

Examples:

> Use a picture of a man watching TV. Assigned verb: *bore*
> The man is bored by the programs on TV. or
> The TV programs are very boring.

Be sure to assign a verb that can be logically used with the picture. Sometimes different forms can be used, but other times only one form is logical.

3. Each pair shows their picture to the class and reads their sentence.

Answer the questions about the movie excerpt you just watched. Use the vocabulary words below to help you. Be sure to answer in complete sentences, using the passive.

boulder	flatten	idol	replace	spear	stones
chase	follow	Indians	sand	spiders	surround
exchange	hole	opening	skeleton	squash	whip

1. What was placed in the bag by Indiana Jones?

2. What was Indiana's helper frightened by?

3. What had happened to the other scientist (skeleton) earlier?

4. What happened to the idol?

5. What almost happened to Indiana Jones when he tried to get under the door?

6. What had already happened to the helper when Indiana reached him?

7. What happened to Indiana next?

8. What happened to Indiana when he got outside the cave?

9. What happened to the idol outside the cave?

10. What happened to Indiana when he tried to escape?

11. What was Indiana scared by in the plane?

12. What do you think will happen to Indiana next?

Write a paragraph describing the scene below. Use the passive voice as appropriate.

The following sentences all have problems related to the passive voice. Find the mistakes and correct them.

1. The bald man was being read a menu.

2. The man was poured the water.

3. The waitress is being carried by a tray.

4. The waiter is set by the table.

5. The silverware have been placed on a table by a waiter.

6. The menus is being read by two women.

7. The order was wrote by the waiter.

8. The rolls has already been set on the table.

9. A drink is being drunk by a glass.

10. An order is being listened by the waiter.

© 1997 Prentice Hall Regents. Duplication for classroom use is permitted.

Choose two words from the lists on the top or bottom of the page. Make a logical sentence using these two words and the passive voice. You have more words than you need to make 10 sentences.

| new bank | The President | scholarship | ESL/EFL |
| bone | my construction company | mouse | speech |

1. _____

2. _____

3. _____

4. _____

5. _____

6. _____

7. _____

8. _____

9. _____

10. _____

| children | foreign students | *Aladdin* | dog |
| tests | cat | athletes | teachers |

1. *General Hospital*

    Lucy has become very involved with Madame Maya, a psychic. Kevin, Lucy's boyfriend, is concerned about the relationship and feels that Madame Maya is trying to get money from Lucy. To find out what goes on at the meetings, which are for women only, Kevin and his friend Mac disguise themselves as women and attend. Lucy feels strangely attracted to Norma, who is Kevin in disguise. Finally she realizes that Norma and Eve are really Kevin and Mac. To teach them a lesson, she decides to have them go out in public with her and Madame Maya and tries to arrange dates for Kevin and Mac in their disguise as women. Of course, Kevin and Mac feel very embarrassed, but they can't admit who they really are.

    a. _____

    b. _____

    c. _____

    d. _____

2. *General Hospital*

    Lois, Brenda, and Sonny are partners in L & B Records. Because of legal problems, Sonny needs to sell his share of the company. He decides not to sell to Lois' husband, Ned, whom he dislikes. Instead, Sonny sells his share to Edward, Ned's grandfather (a business tycoon). Edward doesn't like the fact that Ned sings part time for L & B. He wants Ned to work full time for Edward's company. In order to gain control, Edward lies to Brenda about some papers he says she must sign immediately. Brenda tries to reach Lois, who is out of town with Ned on business, to talk about Edward's papers. Edward pressures Brenda who, because she can't find Lois, signs the papers. Later, she finds out she has signed over her share of the business to Edward and that Edward now owns the majority share of the company.

    a. _____

    b. _____

    c. _____

    d. _____

Fill in the blanks with a participial adjective form of one of the verbs in the list. Some of the words will be used more than once.

confuse	embarrass	frighten	shock
depress	excite	humiliate	surround
disgust	fascinate	interest	

A Walk in the Clouds is an _____ movie starring Keanu Reeves. The movie takes place after World War II in the wine country of California. The characters are _____ by beautiful scenery. Keanu's character is married to a woman he met before he went overseas. They don't really know each other, nor are they _____ in the same things. He is a traveling salesman, and on his first trip after returning home he meets a _____ woman on the train. Every time he runs into her, he gets into trouble. She is _____ to have caused him so many problems, but he notices that she is very _____ , and finally she tells him that she is pregnant and unmarried. This is an especially _____ position to be in because her parents are very strict and will be _____ by this news. She is very _____ and doesn't know what to do. Keanu's character offers to pose as her husband, who will then have a fight with her and leave the _____ woman. Her family, however, will believe she is married and that the husband is a _____ person. They will feel sorry for her. Before the two can carry out this somewhat _____ plan, they start to really fall in love. Watch the movie to find out the _____ ending!

CHAPTER 12

Gerunds and Infinitives

12.1 PREPOSITION COMBINATIONS

1. CONCENTRATION

BLACK   BLUE

Materials: Board and chalk or markers

Dynamic: Groups

Time: 20 minutes

Procedure:

1. Draw a blank grid on the board with just the numbers in the spaces. Prepare a concentration grid with all words filled in for your use. Below is a possible example. Some prepositions will have to be repeated.

1 interested	2 on	3 apologized	4 insist	5 for
6 to	7 afraid	8 thank you	9 instead	10 about
11 for	12 excited	13 in	14 start	15 in
16 of	17 to	18 accustomed	19 fool	20 of

2. Divide the class into groups of four or five. The groups take turns calling out two numbers as they try to make a match. As they call out the numbers, write the corresponding word in the appropriate square on the board. If they make a match, give the group a point and cross out the two words, but leave them on the board. If the words are not a match, erase the words and go to the next group. When a group makes a match, it gets an extra turn.

3. When all matches have been made, the group with the most points wins.

NOTE: *The groups can discuss among themselves the numbers they want to call out, but cannot write down any numbers and words. Although they can talk together, you will accept an answer only from the student in the group you call upon.*

2. TIC TAC TOE

Materials: Board and chalk or markers
Worksheet 71 for variation game

Dynamic: Teams

Time: 10 minutes

Procedure:

1. Draw a tic tac toe grid on the board and fill in verbs or expressions that take prepositions, as indicated on the next page. Divide the class into two teams.

be used	stop me	be responsible
insist	be capable	look forward
object	talk	be remembered

2. The object is to fill in the preposition that follows each verb. A player on the first team goes to the board and fills in the word in the square of his/her choice, then sits down. The first player from the opposing team goes to the board. He/she has the choice of either completing another word or correcting what he/she thinks is someone else's incorrect completion. The first team with three correct answers in a row, any direction, is the winner.

Variation: Divide the class into groups of three. You can become the third person in a group of two, or, if one student is left over, make one team of four. Two students are the players in a group of three, and the third student is the judge, who may have his/her grammar book open to the list of preposition combinations. He/she decides if a player has filled in the correct word. (In a group of four there are two judges.) Distribute one worksheet to each group.

After the first game, the students change roles so the judge becomes a player. Continue until all students have had a chance to be the judge.

3. RELAYS

Materials: Board and chalk or markers

Dynamic: Teams

Time: 10 minutes

BLACK   BLUE

Procedure:
1. On the board, make lists of verbs and/or expressions that require a preposition. The two lists include the same words, but are arranged in different order.

Example:

interested	responsible
dream	insist
apologize	apologize
believe	interested
crazy	worry
responsible	dream
worry	believe
insist	crazy

2. Divide the students into two teams and have them line up on either side of the board. One member from each team comes to the board and adds the correct preposition to one of the words on the board. The students then quickly pass their chalk to the next

student in line. Succeeding players can either choose another word to add a preposition to or correct any incorrect answer written by one of his/her teammates.

3. The first team to finish the list with all answers correct is the winner.

12.2 INFINITIVES WITH *TOO/ENOUGH*

1. FIND OUT ABOUT A CLASSMATE

RED   BLACK   BLUE

Materials: Worksheet 72 or similar 3″ x 5″ cards

Dynamic: Whole class

Time: 20 minutes

Procedure: 1. Cut Worksheet 72 into cards and fill in the name of a student from the class in each blank, or make similar cards. Distribute a card to each student, making sure that he/she does not receive the card with his/her own name on it.

2. Each student finds the classmate whose name is in the question on his/her card. The students ask and receive an answer to their questions and respond to the question being asked of them by the classmate who has the card with their name on it. (This will most likely not be the same person. Carlos may have the card with Rosa's name on it, while Rosa has the card with Young's name on it. This means Rosa will have to answer Carlos' question and ask Young a question.)

> **Example card:** What is *Keiko* too short to do?
> **Student A asks Keiko:** What are you too short to do?
> **Keiko's answer:** I am too short to play basketball.

3. If they question another student but no one has asked a question of them, they should sit down and wait for a classmate to approach them with a question. This will avoid too much congestion in the classroom. If you have a large room, however, you may want the students to continue standing until they have both asked and answered a question.

4. When all students have finished, call on each student to read his/her question and provide the answer in a complete sentence.

> **Student A's response to instructor:**
> What is Keiko too short to do?
> She is too short to play basketball.

1. MATCH GAME

Materials: Worksheet 73 (two pages)

Dynamic: Groups

Time: 20 minutes

BLACK   BLUE

Procedure:

1. Cut Worksheet 73 into cards, or make similar cards. Divide the class into groups of four. Distribute an even number of cards to each group. (If you have a large class, you will want to make up more cards.) Each group should receive at least eight. This may mean giving one or two groups one pair more than another (some groups may receive six cards while others receive eight) or eliminating extra cards from play.

2. Each group makes as many matches as possible. The matches must be grammatically correct and logical. (It is sometimes possible for a group not to make <u>any</u> matches initially, although that is rare.)

3. When a group can make no more matches, it goes to other groups to look for a trade. Important: Students cannot just take a card from a group; they must trade. A group does not have to trade a card just because another group wants it. Usually, two students stay with the matches to make trades, while the other two go to different groups to see if they can make trades. Usually the students split up the unmatched cards: the students staying to make trades keep some, and the students looking for matches take others.

4. When one group has made all its matches and the students think they are correct, the game stops. One group member (or members taking turns) reads out the matches. The other groups vote to accept or reject each match. A match can be rejected because it is not grammatical or not logical.

5. If all matches are accepted, the game is over and that team wins. If some matches were rejected, the play continues until another group feels it has made all its matches and they are accepted.

VERB + INFINITIVE OR GERUND
(Difference in meaning)

1. EXAMPLES

BLUE

Materials:	Worksheets 74A and B
Dynamic:	Pairs
Time:	30 minutes
Procedure:	1. Give each student a copy of both worksheets.

2. Have the students work with a partner to match the meanings to the sentences in Worksheet 74A. When everyone has finished, go over the worksheet. See which pair has the most correct answers. Ask the students at random to explain why they chose the answers they did.

3. Have the pairs do Worksheet 74B. Call on several pairs for each question. This way, there will be a variety of answers and, in case one pair uses the incorrect form, several correct versions will have been provided.

2. WHICH IS IT?

BLUE

Materials:	Worksheet 75
Dynamic:	Small groups
Time:	15 minutes
Procedure:	1. Arrange students in groups of three or four and give each group one copy of the worksheet.

2. Read the following questions to the class one at a time. The students should decide together in their groups which choice on the worksheet to circle.

   1. In which case have gas prices risen too high for John?

   2. In which case is Mary thinking back about what she did earlier that day?

   3. In which case have I already told you something before I began the sentence?

   4. In which case was the air conditioner only one of the options Thu tried?

   5. In which case did Kim have a responsibility to do something?

231

3. Go over the correct answers by assigning one set of sentences to each group. Have the group act out the two sentences so that the answer to the question is obvious to all.

12.5 GERUND OR INFINITIVE?

1. COCKTAIL PARTY

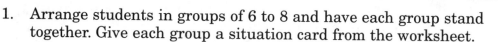

Materials: Worksheet 76

Dynamic: Groups

Time: 15 minutes

BLACK BLUE

Procedure:
1. Arrange students in groups of 6 to 8 and have each group stand together. Give each group a situation card from the worksheet.

2. As in a party setting (but with a time limit), students mingle by asking questions or making statements and suggestions about the situation. They must use verbs followed by infinitives or gerunds whenever possible.

3. A different situation may be given to the group after a few minutes of talking.

4. As a follow-up activity on the same day, students can write the questions or statements on the board that they remember from the party interaction.

2. WHICH ONE DO I USE?

Materials: Three different colors of 4″ x 6″ cards
(red, blue, yellow, for example)
Writing paper

Dynamic: Large groups

Time: 30 minutes

BLACK BLUE

Procedure:
1. Review charts and rules for gerunds and infinitives as needed. Divide students into three groups, ideally of three or four students. (A larger class will have larger groups.) Give each group one of the sets of cards.

2. The red-card holders write down verbs followed by gerunds. The blue-card holders write down verbs followed by infinitives. The yellow-card holders write down verbs followed by a (pro)noun and infinitive. Each group writes a sentence for each verb on its cards, then quizzes each other orally, using the cards.

3. Switch the colored cards from group to group. Each group reads the cards and corrects each other's sentences.

4. After each group has practiced with all the cards, divide the class into pairs. Give each pair six cards (two red, two blue, two yellow) and have the pair write a dialog, using all six cards.

5. Put two pairs together and have one pair read its dialog to the other pair.

6. Put the students into new groups of approximately four. Have them write a story (on the writing paper) using at least five gerunds/infinitives. Every time they use a gerund or infinitive, they write both forms down and let the reader choose.

    Example: Once upon a time, there was a student who admitted to *to steal/stealing* a book. He stole it because he couldn't <u>afford</u> *to buy/buying* it. The . . .

7. Last, the groups exchange papers so that each group reads another group's story and circles the correct form each time there is a choice.

3. GO + GERUND

BLACK   BLUE

Materials: 3″ x 5″ cards or Worksheet 77

Dynamic: Whole class

Time: 20 minutes

Procedure:

1. Pantomime several familiar *go* + gerund activities (for example, go fishing, go surfing, etc.). Have students guess the activity being pantomimed.

2. Give each student a card with a common *go* + gerund activity written on it (Worksheet 77, cut up, or your own). Whisper explanations or give alternative cards to students who are unsure of/reluctant to perform their assigned activity.

3. One by one, students pantomime their activities for the class. A student volunteer writes the activity on the board as it is guessed.

Variation: Have pairs of students make up short lists of related vocabulary for each *go* + gerund activity (*tent, sleeping bag, grizzly bear,* etc., for *go camping*).

REVIEW

1. LINE-UPS

Materials: Worksheet 78

Dynamic: Whole class

Time: 20 minutes

BLUE

Procedure:

1. Copy one page of Worksheet 78 on one color paper and use a different color for the second page, or make your own questions on two different colors of 3″ x 5″ cards. Give one card to each student. Have all the students with the same color card come to the front of the class and form a line; have the other students come up and stand before one of the students in the question line.

2. Explain that the students in the question line are going to ask their question of the students in the answer line, using either *doing* or to *do* in the blanks in their questions (You may want to write these two forms on the board as a reminder.)

3. When everyone has answered the person in front of them, the answer line moves down one person and answers those questions, continuing until they have answered all the questions. Then the students change positions so that the students in the answer line are now asking the questions, using their cards. Everyone in the question line should have the same color card.

4. Students should be able to check each other. For example, if a student asks, "What do you want me **to do**?" he/she is expecting the answer to contain the infinitive. Circulate among the lines to settle any disagreements and make sure the students are proceeding properly.

5. After everyone has finished, you might ask for a sampling of answers from each student.

2. RELAYS

Materials: Board

Dynamic: Teams

Time: 5 minutes

BLACK BLUE

Procedure:

1. On the board, make lists of verbs and/or expressions that are followed by either a gerund or an infinitive. The lists contain the same words, but vary the order of the words in the lists.

Examples:	permit me	instead of
	quit	need
	go +	permit me
	miss	hope
	hope	go +
	instead of	avoid
	avoid	miss
	need	quit

2. Divide the students into two teams and have the teams line up on either side of the board. The game is a relay race between the teams, who must identify whether the words are followed by a gerund (G) or an infinitive (I) (alternative designations: *doing* for a gerund, *to do* for an infinitive). At your signal, the first student from each team rushes to the board and writes *G* or *I* after one of the expressions on his list, then quickly passes his/her chalk or marker to the next team member. Succeeding players can either identify another word or can choose to correct an incorrect answer left by one of his/her teammates. The first team to finish the list with all answers correct is the winner.

3. BOARD GAME

Materials: Worksheet 79
Markers for each student, a die for each group

Dynamic: Groups

Time: 20 minutes

BLUE

Procedure:

1. Arrange the students in groups of four. Give each group a die and a copy of the worksheet, and give a marker to each student.

2. When a student lands on a space with a sentence, he/she must provide the correct form (gerund, infinitive, or base form) of the underlined verb. The other players are judges. If the space is blank, the student stops and waits for his/her next turn.

3. The first player to reach the end wins.

4. STORYTIME

BLUE

Materials:	Worksheet 80
Dynamic:	Small groups
Time:	15 minutes
Procedure:	

1. Arrange students in groups of three or four and give each student a worksheet.

2. Have the students read the summaries and discuss the questions, then write answers, using either a gerund, an infinitive, or a simple form. Make sure students write answers on only one worksheet, working together.

3. Go around the groups and share some of the answers. You may want to have the groups write some of their answers on the board for critiquing.

   NOTE: *You may want to use summaries of soap operas (as in the worksheet), TV shows, movies, fairy tales, fables, or a personal story.*

be interested	accuse	be capable
be dedicated	forgive	be known
approve	be worried	be innocent

insist	be fond	object
forget	prevent	be prepared
be tired	complain	be concerned

count	be addicted	be excited
feel	dream	excuse
be proud	prohibit	be done

What is _____ strong enough to carry?

What is _____ old enough to do?

What is _____ young enough to do?

What is _____ too young to do?

What is _____ too old to do?

What is _____ tall enough to do?

What is _____ too short to do?

What is _____ crazy enough to do?

What is _____ too shy to do?

What is _____ too smart to do?

What is _____ too tired to do?

What is _____ too nervous to do?

What is _____ hungry enough to eat?

What does _____ have enough money to buy?

it's disappointing	not to receive any mail
not receiving any mail	is disappointing
it's crazy	to wear a heavy coat in August
wearing a heavy coat in August	is crazy
it is polite	to listen to your teacher
listening to your teacher	is polite
it is frightening	to walk in downtown Los Angeles at night
walking in downtown Los Angeles at night	is frightening

it's unusual	to wear pink shoes
wearing pink shoes	is unusual
it is dangerous	to drink and drive
drinking and driving	is dangerous
it is impolite	to speak your native language in English class
speaking your native language in English class	is impolite
it is easy	to ride a bicycle
riding a bicycle	is easy

With your partner, decide which of the meanings at the bottom of the page best matches the meaning in each sentence.

1. I <u>remembered to pay</u> my bills this past weekend. _____

2. I often <u>forget to put</u> money in the parking meter. _____

3. I <u>remember watering</u> my garden when I lived in England. It took three hours because the garden was so big. _____

4. How can you <u>forget visiting</u> Thailand? _____

5. I'll never <u>forget buying</u> my first car. _____

6. <u>I regret to tell you</u> that Arthur Ashe has died. I know how much you admired him. _____

7. She <u>regrets to tell</u> us that she can't come to our party. _____

8. I <u>regret starting</u> to smoke when I was 13 years old. _____

9. We <u>regret moving</u> to New York City. _____

10. I <u>have tried to learn</u> Spanish, but I'm not a good student. _____

11. He <u>tries to exercise</u> every day. _____

12. Andrea <u>tried sleeping</u> on the floor, but her backache continued. _____

13. If you burn yourself, <u>try putting</u> ice on the burn immediately. _____

---

a. duty or responsibility

b. to recall or not recall the past

c. wishing you had not done something in the past

d. telling bad news

e. experiment with new approaches or solutions

f. make an effort

1. What must you remember to do before you leave home?

2. What have you forgotten to bring to class?

3. What do you remember doing on your last vacation?

4. What can you never forget eating?

5. What do you regret not doing in the past?

6. What news would you have for your parents that might start out "I regret to tell . . ."?

7. If you have a sunburn, what could you try doing?

8. What have you tried to do but were not successful at?

Choose the best answer to each of your teacher's five questions. Then discuss your choices with your group. Your teacher will repeat a question if there is disagreement within your group.

1. a. John stopped to buy premium gas last week.
   b. John stopped buying premium gas last week.

2. a. Mary remembered to lock the door before she left.
   b. Mary remembered putting the cat out before she left.

3. a. I regret telling you the secret about Jennifer.
   b. I regret to tell you that I wrecked your car.

4. a. Thu was very hot, so she tried to turn on the air conditioner.
   b. Thu was very hot, so she tried turning on the air conditioner.

5. a. Kim did not forget to tell you about the test.
   b. Kim did not forget receiving your letter.

Situation #1

Plan a birthday party, complete with entertainment and food, for a classmate.

Verb suggestions: advise, stop, consider, recommend, enjoy, ask, plan, prepare, remember, want, (don't) forget, promise

Situation #2

A classmate wants to be accepted at a prestigious university, but he/she is nervous about the oral interview. Give advice.

Verb suggestions: advise, avoid, finish, (don't) delay, mention, practice, remember, dislike, (don't) quit, decide, need, want, wait

Situation #3

Complain about the rising cost of living such as health care, car insurance, etc. Try to end the conversation on a positive note.

Verb suggestions: admit, deny, anticipate, dislike, can't help, regret, tolerate, claim, afford, hesitate, pretend, understand, learn, want, appreciate, wish

Situation #4

Give advice on (a) losing weight and (b) gaining confidence to make a good impression on people (boss, spouse, girlfriend/boyfriend, etc.).

Verb suggestions: advise, avoid, keep, (don't) miss, postpone, suggest, expect, hope, seem, need, struggle, learn, offer, want, plan

Go boating	Go bowling	Go camping
Go dancing	Go fishing	Go hiking
Go jogging	Go running	Go sailing
Go window shopping	Go shopping	Go sightseeing
Go skating	Go water-skiing	Go skiing
Go skydiving	Go swimming	Go birdwatching
Go canoeing	Go hunting	Go mountain climbing

What is something you can't stand _____ ?

What have you asked a friend _____ ?

What would you be happy _____ for me?

What did you promise your parents not _____ when you left home?

What are you afraid of my _____ ?

A person can lose weight by _____ what?

What are you interested in _____ while you're in the U.S.?

What is something your parents told you not _____ ?

What are you too embarrassed _____ ?

What are you thinking about _____ this weekend?

What are you worried about your family's _____ ?

What have you seen children _____ ?

What did you hear a family member/roommate _____ last night?

What do you prefer _____ in the evenings?

What have you noticed me _____?

What do you think I should begin _____?

What would you keep _____ even if your parents asked you to stop?

What do you often postpone _____?

What do you recommend _____ tonight?

What have you agreed _____ for a friend?

What would you like to quit _____?

What do you enjoy _____ on vacations?

What do you suggest _____ after class?

What are you considering _____ when you return home?

What have you been angry enough _____?

What are you too young _____?

START ➡	I'm used <u>study</u> English.	**ROLL AGAIN**	I quit <u>smoke</u> a year ago.	**LOSE A TURN**	She avoids <u>do</u> laundry. ⬇
Are you going <u>shop</u> today? ⬇		I resent your <u>answer</u> for me.		She pretends <u>listen</u> to you.	⬅
➡	Have you decided <u>buy</u> a new car?	She opened the jar by <u>twist</u> the lid.		**GO BACK 3 SPACES**	I was sorry <u>hear</u> the news. ⬇
I forgot <u>tell</u> you about the test. ⬇	I was sad <u>see</u> you leave.		She came here <u>get</u> a good education.	This box is too heavy for me <u>lift</u>.	**GO AHEAD 3 SPACES** ⬅
➡	It is easy <u>fool</u> by his lies.			She encouraged us <u>get</u> married.	His not <u>know</u> the answer was unusual. ⬇
ROLL AGAIN ⬇		I let her <u>ride</u> my bike.	He got me <u>go</u> with him.	I am lucky <u>have</u> you as a friend.	⬅
➡ She made me <u>feel</u> sorry for her.	**GO BACK 2 SPACES**	I warned you <u>study</u> harder.	We look forward <u>see</u> you next quarter.	She helped me <u>choose</u> a new school.	**LOSE A TURN** ⬇
⬇	I heard it <u>rain</u> last night.		He got an A by <u>work</u> hard.		Do you mind not <u>smoke</u> in here? ⬅
➡ She is still young enough <u>spank</u>.	**ROLL AGAIN**	We're thinking about <u>go swim</u> next week.		He refused <u>help</u> us with our problem.	**GO BACK 2 SPACES** ⬇
FINISH!!!	What do you know about <u>ski</u>?		**GO AHEAD 2 SPACES**	I'm trying <u>learn</u> Chinese.	I dared him <u>jump</u>. ⬅

Answer the questions based on the summaries below. Use either a gerund, an infinitive, or a simple form in your answer.

1. *One Life to Live*

   Maggie, who teaches children at a school for the deaf, meets Max when she comes to Llanview to visit her cousin, Andrew. Max, a friend of Andrew's, is a widower with one-year-old twins. After Maggie spends some time with the twins, she suspects that one of them, Frankie, is partially deaf. She tells Max that he must take Frankie for testing. Max refuses to believe that his son is deaf and tells Maggie to stay out of his family's business. Maggie, who grew up with a deaf brother, pursues the matter, even setting up an appointment for Frankie without Max's knowledge. When Max finds out about the appointment, he is furious at Maggie.

   a. Why did Maggie come to Llanview?

   b. Why is Max angry at Maggie?

   c. What is Maggie determined to do?

2. *General Hospital*

   Jason is in a car accident when the car he is riding in (his brother, A.J., is driving) hits a tree. Jason was not wearing a seat belt and was thrown from the car. He experiences memory loss as a result of the accident. He can't remember anyone and gets particularly angry at his family and his girlfriend when they tell him what he was like and how he used to act before the accident. Jason is from a wealthy family and had been a premed student. Because he knows he can't match his family's expectations, he leaves home, rents a room, and takes a blue-collar job.

   a. What is Jason angry about?

   b. What did Jason decide to do?

   c. What can't Jason remember?

   d. What did Jason stop doing?

Fun with Grammar   **249**

CHAPTER

13

Comparatives and Superlatives

13.1 COMPARATIVES

1. COMPARISON CARDS 1

Materials:	Worksheet 81 or 3″ x 5″ cards
Dynamic:	Groups
Time:	10 minutes

RED BLACK

Procedure:

1. Make as many copies of the worksheet as you have groups. Cut the worksheets up into cards to make sets for each group. Arrange the class into groups of three or four and give each group a set of cards.

2. One student in each group draws a card and makes a comparative sentence using the two nouns and adjective on the card.

   Example:　　My legs　　　　　(short)
   　　　　　　　　Your legs

   Student sentence:　My legs are shorter than your legs.

   The other students in the group judge whether the sentence used the correct comparative form and decides if it is logical/correct.

3. The students take turns in the group choosing cards and making sentences until they finish all the cards or time is up. The students can keep score in their groups to see who makes the most correct sentences.

   SUGGESTION: *Make some of your own cards, using names of students in the class.*

2. COMPARISON CARDS 2

Materials:	Small pictures
Dynamic:	Pairs
Time:	15 minutes

RED BLACK

Procedure:

1. Arrange students in pairs, and give each pair two or more pictures to compare. (You may want to stick to one topic, such as famous people, or have several types of pictures.)

2. Each pair writes comparisons of the two pictures.

   Example:　A bear is shorter than a giraffe.

3. When everyone has finished, have the pairs show their pictures and read their sentences. You might ask the other students whether they agree or disagree. This is interesting when students use a subjective adjective (such as *beautiful*) as their point of comparison.

NOTE: *If you use famous people, you can write the names of the people under the picture for the students, or have them say simply "the man in picture A," etc.*

3. MATCH

RED   BLACK

Materials: Worksheet 82

Dynamic: Pairs

Time: 15 minutes

Procedure:

1. Put students into pairs, and give each pair a copy of the worksheet. Go over the words on the list and explain any with which the students are unfamiliar.

2. Call out an adjective or phrase from the list below. The students choose two of the words or expressions on the worksheet and write a comparison sentence. Continue until all the words on the paper have been matched.

   Adjectives to use with the worksheet:

clean	expensive	noisy	slow
cold	good pet	quick	spicy
dangerous	hard	short	tall
easy to use	large		

   Example: Instructor says: "spicy"
   Students write:
   "Mexican food is spicier than Italian food."

3. Go over the sentences by having the pairs write them on the board or read them aloud. The other students decide if the sentences are logical and grammatical.

252

4. MAGAZINE SEARCH

RED   BLACK

Materials: Magazines or catalogs

Dynamic: Small groups

Time: 15 minutes

Procedure:

1. Put students into groups of three. Give each group several magazines or catalogs that can be cut up. (Or, for a previous homework assignment, ask the students to bring in magazines or catalogs.)

2. In their magazines, the groups look for pictures to compare, then write comparison sentences. The number of sentences you assign will depend on how long you want to devote to this activity.

3. The groups take turns showing their pictures and reading their sentences aloud.

5. IT'S BIGGER THAN A BASEBALL

BLACK   BLUE

Materials: None

Dynamic: Pairs

Time: 25 minutes

Procedure:

1. Use the following riddle as a model, or make up one of your own, using comparisons.

   > It is bigger than a baseball.
   > It is as round as the moon.
   > It is as orange as a carrot.
   > It is as hard as a melon.
   > It is not as sweet as fruit.
   > Answer: *A pumpkin.*

2. The students work in pairs and use the structure above to make their own riddles. Circulate and answer questions. Make sure the students' riddles are not too ambiguous; that is, the answer should be clear by the time students get to the end of the riddle.

3. When they finish, do one of the following:

   a. Tape the riddles to the wall. The students circulate and write answers before discussing them as a class.

   b. The students exchange papers and discuss the answers with their partners.

   c. The students read their riddles aloud for the rest of the class to guess.

SUPERLATIVES

1. THE SUPERLATIVE TASTE TEST

RED   BLACK

Materials: Worksheet 83, three kinds of mints

Dynamic: Pairs/Small groups

Time: 20 minutes

Procedure:

1. Place three dishes of mints on a table, enough for each student to have one of each flavor. Put students in groups of two or three. Give each group a copy of the worksheet. One student from each group will be the recorder. You may need to go over the worksheet vocabulary words before the students begin the taste test.

2. Each student eats one mint from each dish, noting qualities such as color, taste, and texture. Group members discuss these qualities with each other and decide which mint ranks best in each area. Then the group writes two sentences about each mint, using the superlative.

   Examples: Mint #1 is the smoothest tasting.
   Mint #2 has the blandest taste.

   Then the group decides which mint they liked the best overall.

3. Circulate to make sure that everyone is on task and is using the correct forms of the superlatives.

4. Call on each group to share results with the class.

   NOTE: *Other types of food can be used. You can use three of the same kind of food (such as three different brands of potato chips) or have three very different food items, such as pickles, pretzels, and hard candy.*

2. SURVEY

BLACK

Materials: Worksheet 84 (two pages)

Dynamic: Pairs/Small groups

Time: 30 minutes

Procedure:

1. Divide the class into pairs or groups of three or four. Give each group 11 copies of a different section of the worksheet.

2. Have the students go over the words on their list and decide if they would use *most* or *-est* to form the superlative. Do NOT allow

them to use dictionaries. Even if they are unfamiliar with some of the words, they should be able to apply rules they know for forming the superlative.

3. Send them out to ask 10 native speakers about which form they think is correct, either in class time or as a homework activity. If it is done during class hours, set a time limit. If it is not possible to interview native speakers, the students should interview people who are fluent or use English in their jobs.

4. The students tabulate their results and compare them to their group's answers. Each group then makes a short presentation to the class and says what they think the best choice is and why. An effective way to do this is to put the worksheet with the words for each group on an overhead projector. The class will be able to follow the oral reports more easily.

3. CLASSMATE QUESTIONNAIRE

RED BLACK

Materials: Worksheet 85

Dynamic: Pairs

Time: 25 minutes

Procedure:

1. Put students into pairs. Give each pair a copy of the handout.

2. Have students answer the questions in complete sentences. Some students will be able to answer without talking to their classmates, but others will require asking their classmates questions.

Variation: To take less time, have students answer the questions in pairs without talking to their classmates. They can begin the sentences with "We think . . ." or "We guess . . ." Then have the pairs read their answers. (Have all pairs give their answers for question 1 before going on to the next question.) Determine who has written the correct answer. You may want to do this as a competition and assign points for every correct answer.

4. THE COMPLIMENT GAME

Materials: 3″ x 5″ cards with an adjective written on one side, paper

Dynamic: Whole class

Time: 20 minutes

RED BLACK

Procedure:

1. Review the rules for superlatives, if necessary. Give each student a card and a piece of paper. Tell the students to write, on the reverse of their cards, the superlative form of the adjective on the front.

Suggested adjectives (for a lower-level class, you will of course choose easier adjectives):

attractive	delightful	modern	terrific
beautiful	funny	nice	unique
bright	happy	pleasant	wonderful
comfortable	interesting	pretty	
cute	large	small	

2. The students are to imagine that they are rich aristocrats at a party. They are to act very formally and give compliments to everyone they meet. They are to go up to other "guests" and show them the word on their card. Each "guest" approached (Student B) then compliments the "guest" who approached him or her (Student A), using the correct superlative form of the word he or she is shown.

Example:

> **Student A**'s card: beautiful
> **Student B**'s compliment: You are wearing the most beautiful dress in the room.

If Student B's compliment uses the correct form of the superlative, Student A signs Student B's paper. If Student B's compliment does not use the superlative correctly, Student A does not sign Student B's paper. At the end of the alloted time, the student with the most signatures (that is, the student who used the superlative correctly the most) wins.

13.3 REVIEW

1. READING QUESTIONS

BLACK

Materials: Reading handout or book used in reading class

Dynamic: Pairs/Small groups

Time: 30 minutes

Procedure:

1. Arrange students in pairs or groups of three.

2. Have each group make up 10 questions based on a short story or novel they are using in their reading class. The questions can elicit either the comparative or superlative form. If the students are in different reading classes or if you do not have access to their reading material, give them something short to read for homework. Keep it short and relatively simple, as the focus of this activity is to use the comparative and superlative, not to concentrate on reading comprehension. Then discuss the reading before the students make up their questions.

3. Have the groups exchange question papers with each other and answer the questions they receive.

4. The groups then return the questions papers (now with answers) to the groups who made them up to be checked.

   SUGGESTION: *You may want to set a time limit for making the questions.*

2. WORD SEARCH

RED   BLACK

Materials: Worksheet 86A or 86B

Dynamic: Pairs/Small groups

Time: 10 minutes

Procedure:
1. Put students into pairs or groups of three. Give each group one copy of the worksheet.

2. Students work together to find all the comparative and superlative forms. The forms may be up, down, forward, backward, or diagonal. You may prefer not to include the word list on the worksheet.

3. You may set a time limit, or tell the students that the first group to find all the forms wins.

   SUGGESTION: *A good way to go over where the hidden forms are is to use an overhead after the game.*

3. COMPARE THEM

RED   BLACK

Materials: None

Dynamic: Pairs

Time: 15 minutes

Procedure:
1. Put students into pairs. Assign each pair a different topic of comparison.

   Examples: Two fast-food restaurants
   Two famous people
   Two cars
   Two animals
   Two grocery stores
   Two brands of soda

2. On the board, make a list of adjectives. Students choose from the list to write 10 comparisons of their two items, using either comparative or superlative forms.

You may want to choose from the following list of adjectives:

bad	funny	new	quiet	tasty
beautiful	good	nice	rich	ugly
bright	handsome	noisy	serious	wise
busy	messy	old	short	wonderful
empty	neat	pretty	tall	young

SUGGESTION: *In a higher-level class, the pairs can write a paragraph instead of individual sentences.*

4. WHO'S THE WORST (BEST)?

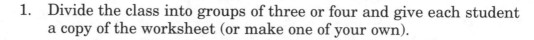

Materials:	Worksheet 87
Dynamic:	Small groups
Time:	30 minutes

BLACK

Procedure:

1. Divide the class into groups of three or four and give each student a copy of the worksheet (or make one of your own).

2. After they read the story, the students in each group rate the characters in the story from 1 to 4 as to who has the worst character (#4 is the worst). There may be disagreement in the group, so the students should express their reasons for their choices ("Maria is the worst because . . .").

3. After the group reaches an agreement, a member of each group comes to the board and list the four characters in descending order, #4—worst to #1—best.

4. Have the class compare the answers and discuss the differences. Each group should be prepared to state why they listed the characters in the order in which they did.

Worksheet 81: COMPARISON CARDS

✂

my legs (short) your legs	biology (interesting) history
the weather here (bad) the weather in my hometown	comics (funny) novels
grammar (difficult) spelling	a skyscraper (tall) a gas station
a giraffe's neck (fat) an elephant's neck	my old shoes (comfortable) my new shoes
a tree (thin) a stick	our grammar book (easy) our writing book
a mouse (small) an elephant	your hair (long) my hair
winter (good) summer	my eyes (dark) my teacher's eyes
a motorcycle (expensive) a bicycle	a chocolate bar (fattening) an apple

Your teacher will give you an adjective. Choose two words in this list and write a sentence using the two words and the adjective.

airplane	cat	dog	ladder	rock
ant	chalk	fog	lake	snow
bee	charge cards	giraffe	Mexican food	stilts
bus	checks	Italian food	mud puddle	wolf

1. _____

2. _____

3. _____

4. _____

5. _____

6. _____

7. _____

8. _____

9. _____

10. _____

You have been selected by the Magnificent Marketing Company to taste-test three new mints before they go on the market. The company wants to know which mint the public prefers, and why.

Taste each mint. Describe its qualities, such as color, taste, and texture. Write at least two sentences about each mint in the space provided, using superlatives. Decide with your group which mint is best.

You may want to use some of these words in your sentences. You may use a dictionary to find their meaning and/or a thesaurus to find other words to use.

delicious   tasty   smooth   creamy   sweet   rich   flat   bland

MINT #1

1.

2.

MINT #2

1.

2.

MINT #3

1.

2.

We think the best mint is # _____ .

Using the list your teacher assigns your group, decide together if you would use most or -est to form the superlatives of the words. Then use the other 10 copies to survey native speakers about which form they think is correct.

GROUP 1:

	most	-est
1. old	_____	_____
2. famous	_____	_____
3. busy	_____	_____
4. important	_____	_____
5. sweet	_____	_____
6. gross	_____	_____
7. handsome	_____	_____
8. rough	_____	_____
9. listless	_____	_____
10. young	_____	_____

GROUP 2:

	most	-est
1. wise	_____	_____
2. clever	_____	_____
3. pretty	_____	_____
4. beautiful	_____	_____
5. wet	_____	_____
6. keen	_____	_____
7. difficult	_____	_____
8. queasy	_____	_____
9. tired	_____	_____
10. tough	_____	_____

GROUP 3:

	most	-est
1. slow	_____	_____
2. gentle	_____	_____
3. friendly	_____	_____
4. serious	_____	_____
5. late	_____	_____
6. windy	_____	_____
7. confusing	_____	_____
8. funky	_____	_____
9. helpful	_____	_____
10. plain	_____	_____

GROUP 4:

	most	-est
1. thin	_____	_____
2. active	_____	_____
3. happy	_____	_____
4. courageous	_____	_____
5. wild	_____	_____
6. yummy	_____	_____
7. orderly	_____	_____
8. fast	_____	_____
9. comfortable	_____	_____
10. narrow	_____	_____

Using the list your teacher assigns your group, decide together if you would use most *or* -est *to form the superlatives of the words. Then use the other 10 copies to survey native speakers about which form they think is correct.*

GROUP 5:

	most	-est
1. red	_____	_____
2. common	_____	_____
3. heavy	_____	_____
4. expensive	_____	_____
5. weak	_____	_____
6. shy	_____	_____
7. humid	_____	_____
8. safe	_____	_____
9. delicious	_____	_____
10. shallow	_____	_____

GROUP 6:

	most	-est
1. new	_____	_____
2. pleasant	_____	_____
3. dry	_____	_____
4. dangerous	_____	_____
5. soft	_____	_____
6. uncanny	_____	_____
7. unpopulated	_____	_____
8. fat	_____	_____
9. boring	_____	_____
10. appetizing	_____	_____

GROUP 7:

	most	-est
1. small	_____	_____
2. silly	_____	_____
3. valuable	_____	_____
4. nervous	_____	_____
5. loud	_____	_____
6. merry	_____	_____
7. polluted	_____	_____
8. dark	_____	_____
9. relaxed	_____	_____
10. joyous	_____	_____

GROUP 8:

	most	-est
1. sour	_____	_____
2. noisy	_____	_____
3. embarrassing	_____	_____
4. homesick	_____	_____
5. sad	_____	_____
6. hungry	_____	_____
7. discouraged	_____	_____
8. quiet	_____	_____
9. popular	_____	_____
10. ghoulish	_____	_____

Answer the questions about your classmates in complete sentences.

1. Who is wearing the most jewelry today? _____

   _____

2. Who has the curliest hair? _____

   _____

3. Who has the longest name? _____

   _____

4. Who has the largest shoe? _____

   _____

5. Who has the nicest car? _____

   _____

6. Who has the most brothers and sisters? _____

   _____

7. Who brings the most books to class? _____

   _____

8. Who is the best singer in the class? _____

   _____

9. Who has studied English the longest? _____

   _____

10. Who traveled the farthest to come to this country? _____

   _____

Find the comparative and superlative forms of the words on the list. The forms may be listed up, down, forward, backward, or diagonally.

```
F  E  E  M  W  B  F  R  F  R
A  S  S  R  O  T  U  E  E  L
R  R  L  B  R  S  R  H  W  M
T  O  E  E  R  E  T  T  E  B
H  W  A  S  S  R  H  R  R  E
E  A  S  T  A  S  E  U  O  S
S  S  T  F  B  E  S  F  M  T
T  E  W  O  R  S  T  R  A  F
```

Word list:

AS
BEST
BETTER
FARTHER
FARTHEST
FURTHER
FURTHEST
LEAST
LESS
MORE
MOST
WORSE
WORST

Fun with Grammar **265**

Find the comparative and superlative forms of the words on the list. The forms may be listed up, down, forward, backward, or diagonally.

```
W   D   A   L   I   M   I   S   E   L
O   I   E   L   O   O   F   A   L   L
F   F   B   R   A   L   I   M   I   S
U   F   E   W   O   R   S   E   O   R
R   E   T   T   A   R   K   W   R   E
T   R   T   F   H   I   O   E   W   H
H   E   K   I   L   A   T   M   O   T
E   N   R   E   S   T   N   O   R   R
S   T   S   A   E   L   E   S   S   A
T   S   E   B   R   E   S   T   T   F
```

Word list:

ALIKE	LESS	WORSE
AS	LIKE	WORST
BEST	MORE	
BETTER	MOST	
DIFFERENT	OF ALL	
FARTHER	SAME	
FURTHEST	SIMILAR	
LEAST	THAN	

Rate the characters from 1 to 4, with 4 being the worst person in the story.

Maria, Sachie, Toshie, and Ana shared an apartment near the college that they attended. Maria needed to buy a book for her history class, but she didn't have enough money. She had a test in three days, and she needed the book to study. Maria knew that Sachie always kept quite a bit of money in an envelope in her desk drawer. Maria decided to take enough money from Sachie's desk to buy the book. Maria told herself that she would return the money before Sachie noticed it was missing.

The next day, Sachie discovered that some money was missing from her desk. None of her roommates was home, so she looked around the apartment. On Toshie's bed, she found a bag from a clothing store. Inside the bag was a new blouse with a sales receipt. The price of the blouse was only slightly less than the amount of the missing money. Sachie assumed that Toshie had taken her money to buy the new blouse. Sachie decided to teach Toshie a lesson, and she poured catsup all over Toshie's new blouse.

When Toshie returned home, she found her ruined blouse. When she asked Sachie what had happened, Sachie asked her about the missing money. Toshie told Sachie that she had not taken her money, but Sachie didn't believe her.

Ana returned home, and Toshie told her that Sachie had ruined all her clothes by putting catsup on them. Ana decided that Sachie was a troublemaker and that she didn't want her living in the apartment anymore. Ana decided to call the apartment manager and tell him Sachie was keeping stolen goods at the apartment for her boyfriend so that she would have to move out.

CHAPTER

14

Relationships Between Ideas

14.1 PARALLELISM

1. MEMORIZE IT

BLACK   BLUE

Materials: Worksheet 88

Dynamic: Whole class

Time: 10 minutes

Procedure:

1. Make copies of the handout. Give half of your class Part A and the other half, Part B. Do not tell the students that there is a difference between the sentences in the two parts.

2. Tell the students to memorize the sentences for about 30 seconds and then turn over their papers. On the backs of their papers, or on another piece of paper, have them write the sentences exactly as they remember them.

3. Students now turn their papers back to the front and check their answers with the sentences. Did anyone get all the sentences correct?

4. Reveal that there is a difference between the sentences in the two parts and have a student with Part A compare papers with a student who has part B. Ask them which one was easier to remember and why. Talk about where the parallel structure is in each sentence in Part A.

NOTE: *Those students with Part A usually have an easier time memorizing the sentences because of the parallel structure. Occasionally, however, you may have a student who can memorize Part B completely. In that case, talk about how some people have a good ability to memorize, but that it is easier for most of us if there is some kind of structure.*

JOINING IDEAS

1. *EITHER/NEITHER/TOO*

BLACK

Materials: 3″ x 5″ index cards

Dynamic: Whole class

Time: 15 minutes

Procedure:
1. Write out two kinds of cards: one set has sentences; the other set has short answers that agree or disagree. Each sentence in Set One has only one matching answer in Set Two.

Example:	**Set One**	**Set Two**
	I'm having a good time	I am, too.
	I'm not having fun.	I'm not either.
	The U.S. president lives in Washington, D.C.	His wife does, too.
	I don't have a headache.	Neither do I.
	I didn't do the homework.	Neither did I.
	You're a good student.	You are, too.

2. Divide the students into two groups. Each student receives one card. The students circulate and look for their match. They can say their sentences to each opposite group member until they find the appropriate matching answer.

3. Students can then invent their own sentences and see if their classmates can give an appropriate answer.

2. USING CORRELATIVE CONJUNCTIONS

BLACK   BLUE

Materials: Worksheet 89

Dynamic: Pairs

Time: 15 minutes

Procedure:
1. Put students into pairs. Fill the blanks in the worksheet with your students' names. Give one copy of the worksheet to each pair of students.

2. Have the pairs work together to write one sentence, joining the pairs of sentences on the paper with an appropriate correlative conjunction (*both . . . and*, *not only . . . but also*, *either . . . or*, and *neither . . . nor*).

Example:

> Guillermo has black hair. Jorge has black hair.

Possible combinations:

> Both Guillermo and Jorge have black hair.
> Not only Guillermo but also Jorge has black hair.

Variation: Use the worksheet as a model only. Write your own sentences containing information about students in your class. This will make it seem less like an exercise and more fun for your students.

3. SAME / DIFFERENT

BLACK   BLUE

Materials: Worksheet 90

Dynamic: Pairs

Time: 20 minutes

Procedure:

1. Put students into pairs and give each student a copy of the worksheet. The students ask each other the questions on the worksheet. Then they write a sentence, using an appropriate correlative conjunction to compare themselves with each student who answered each question.

    Example:

Question:	What month were you born in?
Student A's answer:	June
Student B writes:	<u>Both</u> Student A <u>and</u> I were born in June.
or	<u>Neither</u> Student A <u>nor</u> I was born in September.

2. Circulate to check on student progress. When all pairs have finished, you may want to have volunteers give a few example sentences.

4. CONNECTING IDEAS

BLACK   BLUE

Materials: Board, paper

Dynamic: Small groups

Time: 10 minutes

Procedure:

1. Write a list of connecting words on the board (for example, *because*, *although*, *for*, *before*, *so*). You may want to concentrate on just one type (conjunctions, adverbial subordinators, or transitions) or mix them.

2. Divide the class into groups of approximately three or four. Set a time limit (perhaps 5 minutes), and have the groups write a logical and grammatical sentence for each word on the board. Each sentence must have a different meaning. (This avoids such sentences as *I went to bed after I finished my homework, I went to bed before I finished my homework, I went to bed because I finished my homework*.)

3. For each word on the board, have the groups read their sentences. Give the groups a point if a sentence is both grammatical and logical. (If it is not correct, have other students correct it.) If you are also looking for correct punctuation, have a student from each group write some of the group's answers on the board.

NOTE: *The time limit will vary depending on the level of the class and the number of words you list on the board. If you want, you can give the class a topic to base their sentences on, although this can lead to similar sentences, as noted in step 2 above.*

5. PANTOMIME

Materials: 3″ x 5″ cards with instructions on them

Dynamic: Whole class

Time: 15 minutes

BLACK   BLUE

Procedure:
1. Write one situation on each card.

   Suggestions: starting a car on a cold morning
   receiving a letter from a good friend
   eating something you don't like
   making scrambled eggs
   trying to study next to a noisy person

   Hand out cards, face down, to the most outgoing students, who will be your "actors." They should not show their cards to anyone.

2. Be sure the class understands the meaning of "pantomime." Then call the first student to the front of the class to act out his/her card.

3. Ask the class to explain what the "actor" did by using adverbials of time and sequence and adverbial clauses of time.

   Example: "First, she sat down at the table. Then she took her books out of her bag. As soon as she began to study, another student sat down next to her."

4. Encourage students to shout out possibilities for each action. Do not focus on guessing what the "actor" was doing, but rather on describing how he/she did it.

272

6. COMBINATIONS

Materials:	Worksheet 91
Dynamic:	Small groups
Time:	15 minutes

BLUE

Procedure:
1. Put students into groups of three or four. Give each group one copy of the worksheet.

2. Have students work together to choose the best answer for each sentence. (Remember, the directions state to find the expressions that can <u>not</u> be used in the sentences.) In each case, two answers are correct and one is not. The students are looking for the expression/word that is <u>not</u> possible in the sentence, considering both appropriate meaning and appropriate punctuation.

7. COMPLETE THE SENTENCE

Materials:	Worksheet 92
Dynamic:	Teams
Time:	15 minutes

BLUE

Procedure:
1. Cut up the worksheet and divide the class into two teams.

2. The students on each team take turns drawing slips of paper that contain a clause beginning or ending with a coordinator or subordinator.

   Examples: He went to class although . . .
   Because he was all wet . . .

3. If the student completes the sentence correctly, he/she scores a point for his/her team.

   NOTE: *You may want only the student who draws the slip to respond, or you may allow the teammates to help. Either way, accept the answer only from the student who drew the slip.*

   This activity can also be used with intermediate students if you limit the coordinators and subordinators to those used in their text.

8. JUST BECAUSE

Materials:	Worksheet 93
Dynamic:	Pairs
Time:	15 minutes

BLACK   BLUE

Procedure:
1. Arrange students in pairs and give each pair a copy of the worksheet.

2. Using the randomly listed independent clauses, the students work together to write logical and grammatical sentences by combining two of the clauses with *because*. Punctuation also counts!

3. You can award one point for each correct sentence, or one point for a logical combination of clauses and one point for correct punctuation. Collect the written sentences and grade them immediately, if possible. The pair with the most points wins. If you do not want to do this activity as a competition, go around the room and have the pairs share some of their sentences as a closure.

4. As a follow-up activity, use the students' combination and punctuation errors for an error analysis worksheet.

Variation: Read an independent clause from one of the lists on the worksheet. The students, working in small groups, supply a logical completion to your sentence, using *because*. The first group to produce a good completion scores a point. Alternatively, ask all groups for a completion and give points for all correct answers.

9. *OTHERWISE . . . OR ELSE*

Materials: None

Dynamic: Whole class

Time: 15 minutes

BLUE

Procedure:

1. Explain that you will write a sentence such as *I have a headache* or *I have to work* on the board after a student volunteer leaves the room.

2. Send a volunteer out of the room. With the rest of the class, brainstorm several possible logical clauses to complete the sentence, beginning with *otherwise* or *or else*.

3. Erase the sentence on the board and have the volunteer return. The other students offer their responses. The student volunteer tries to construct the sentence that had been written on the board.

   Example:

   Possible responses: Otherwise, I would be scared.
   Otherwise, I would worry about my valuables.
   Otherwise, someone could break in.

   Sentence on the board (which
   the volunteer must guess): I always lock my doors.

PART A

1. Mary liked to dance, bowl, and swim.

2. I admire Bob for his intelligence, honesty, and cheerfulness.

3. By getting a job and saving money, Marcia paid for her dance lessons.

PART B

1. Mary liked to dance and bowl, and she is a good swimmer.

2. I admire Bob for his intelligence and honesty, and he has a cheerful disposition.

3. By getting a job and she was able to save her money, Marcia paid for her dance lessons.

Fun with Grammar

Write one sentence joining the two ideas with a correlative conjunction (both . . . and, not only . . . but also, either . . . or, and neither . . . nor).

1. _____ isn't from Hong Kong. She isn't from Mexico.

2. Someone just bought a new car, but I can't remember who. Maybe it was _____. Maybe it was _____.

3. _____ lost her passport. She lost her driver's license too.

4. We have an essay due next Tuesday. We have a grammar test next Tuesday.

5. I enjoy this class. I am learning lots of new things. I am meeting new people.

6. _____ doesn't like to cook. He doesn't like to eat out in restaurants.

7. _____ likes cats. She likes cocker spaniels.

8. Chocolate can make some people hyperactive. It can keep people awake at night.

© 1997 Prentice Hall Regents. Duplication for classroom use is permitted.

Ask your partner these questions. Then use correlative conjunctions (both . . . and, not only . . . but also, either . . . or, neither . . . nor) to write sentences about the two of you.

1. What month were you born in?

   _____

2. Do you have a boyfriend/girlfriend?

   _____

3. Are you married?

   _____

4. Do you drive?

   _____

5. Are you the youngest in your family?

   _____

6. Can you play the piano?

   _____

7. Do you have American friends?

   _____

8. Do you like cats?

   _____

9. Have you ever studied in another foreign country?

   _____

10. Can you speak more than four languages?

    _____

Cross out the words or expressions that can <u>not</u> be used in the sentences without a change in meaning or punctuation.

1. (Although / Because / Even though) Sue is a good student, she did not receive a good grade.

2. It was hot today. (Although / However / Nevertheless), I still ran for five miles.

3. I went swimming (despite / even though / in spite of) the cold weather.

4. Mary is rich, (but / however / whereas) John is poor.

5. (However / Whereas / While) John is poor, Mary is rich.

6. I always eat breakfast. (Nevertheless / However / Therefore), I still get hungry.

7. It was raining today. (But / Consequently / Therefore), we stayed home.

8. This university, (for example / for instance / such as), has an excellent ESL program.

9. (Besides / Furthermore / In addition to) working at the restaurant, Kim works on campus.

10. I had a terrible headache today. (Furthermore / As well as / In addition), I was very tired.

My friend went to class although

Since the dog was all wet,

I got a raise at work; consequently,

Not only does the president like to go running, but

Because my boyfriend thinks he is God's gift to women,

My friend found a new job last week, so

I had fun at the beach this weekend; nevertheless,

Neither my sister nor her children

Both Indonesia and Thailand

Even though my brother has five children,

The population of the United States is increasing, for

Despite the fact that I didn't go to my friend's party last Saturday,

Because Kim lost her car keys,

I went to class even though

Before I called my mother,

Since I had lived there for five years,

I was born in Mexico, yet

Every day there is more information about the dangers of smoking; therefore,

My brother got involved with bad people; as a result,

I don't like the taste of carrots, nor

While my mother likes to stay home and watch movies on TV,

While I was walking down the street,

As long as you are happy,

He seemed happy; however,

With your partner, select two sentences from the list and combine them using because. *Be sure your sentences are logical and grammatical. Remember to punctuate correctly.*

I'm not going to go camping.

She has six children.

I had to go to work.

Don't eat too much for lunch.

My in-laws are coming for a visit.

It's impossible to see out the front window.

More and more people are driving alone.

We are going to a great restaurant for dinner.

You should wash your car.

It's been raining all day.

I spent the day cleaning the house.

She studied hard for her final exams.

She took aspirin.

Air pollution in California is increasing.

The bus was late.

My sister doesn't work outside the house.

I was late for work.

She has a migraine headache.

She wants to get into a good university.

I ate breakfast at 7:00 A.M.

CHAPTER

15

Clauses

15.1 ADVERB

1. GUESS WHO?

BLACK BLUE

Materials:	None
Dynamic:	Whole class/Groups
Time:	20 minutes
Procedure:	1. Write 10 phrases on the board.

* **Examples:**

borrow money	eat pizza
have my first kiss	eat too much
go to a movie	go to bed
go out to eat	go dancing
go to the mall	stay up late

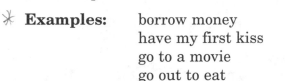

    2. Instruct the students to write a sentence using each of the phrases and an adverbial subordinator. The sentences may use any logical tense/time. You may want to list adverbial subordinators on the board.

    Examples: I borrowed money after I lost my wallet.
                       I had my first kiss when I was 14 years old.

    3. Collect individual papers as they are completed. You can be noting unusual sentences to read aloud and have the class guess who wrote them.

Variation 1: As a follow-up activity, you can use the students' sentences to create a game to review adverbial subordinators at the end of the unit. Divide the sentences into two columns with the main clause on the left and the dependent clause (with the adverbial subordinator) on the right. Cut them apart and mix them up. Divide the class into teams and hand out the strips containing clauses to the teams. Have the students make as many logical sentences as possible. (It is not necessary to duplicate the original sentences as long as the ones they create as a team are logical.) The team with the most logical sentences wins.

Variation 2: Give 20 cards or slips of paper to each group. Have them write 10 sentences, with the adverb clause on one paper and the independent clause on another. Collect the 20 papers from each group and give them to a different group. Tell the groups to match the independent and dependent clauses written by the other group. The first group who matches all the clauses to form logical sentences wins. (It is not absolutely necessary to match every sentence as it was written, but it may not be possible to come up with 10 logical sentences otherwise.)

2. FINISH THIS

Materials: None

Dynamic: Small groups

Time: 15 minutes

RED   BLACK   BLUE

Procedure:

1. Divide the class into groups of three or four. Each group makes a list of clauses containing an adverbial subordinator. (The number of clauses you want your students to list will depend on how much time you have for this activity.)

   Examples: I get scared when
   Before I got to class,
   I always eat pizza after

2. To play a round, Group 1 reads one of its clauses for Group 2. Group 2 must complete the sentence. If they do so correctly, they get a point.

3. Group 2 then reads a sentence for Group 3 to complete. Continue until all clauses have been completed.

15.2   ADJECTIVE

1. DEFINITION COMPETITION

Materials: Slips of paper, a noun written on each
A paper bag

Dynamic: Teams

Time: 15 minutes

BLACK   BLUE

Procedure:

1. Use a variety of nouns that denote things, people, places, time periods (months or holidays), and so on. Put the slips of paper into the bag and divide the class into two teams.

2. A student from the first team comes to the front and picks a paper from the bag. The student then gives his/her teammates one clue about the noun, using the phrase "I'm thinking of a thing (person/place/animal/etc.) . . ." and an adjective clause to complete the clue. It is helpful if you write this starting phrase on the board.

   Sample clue: I am thinking of an animal that is orange with black stripes.

3. After the first clue has been given, the first person on the clue-giver's team to raise his/her hand can guess the noun. If the answer is correct, his/her team gets a point. If the answer is incorrect, the clue-giver gives another clue, again using an adjective clause. This time, anyone on either team may guess, and the team of the person who answers correctly gets the point.

4. Repeat steps 2 and 3 with a student from the other team. Continue alternating between teams. The team with the most points at the end wins.

2. PICTURE SENTENCES

Materials: Large pictures

Dynamic: Pairs

Time: 10 minutes

BLUE

Procedure:

1. Try to find full-page ads that can be seen when held up. Put students into pairs, and give each pair a picture.

2. Have the pairs write a sentence containing an adjective clause about their picture.

    Example: The man who is next to the president is holding a book.

3. The pairs hold up their pictures and read their sentences to the class.

4. Last, the pairs write a reduction of their sentence, if possible.

    Example: The man next to the president is holding a book.

3. WHO AM I?

Materials: Slips of paper, each containing the name of a different student in the class

Dynamic: Whole class

Time: 25 minutes

BLACK   BLUE

Procedure:

1. Tell the students that you are going to take on the identity of one of them. Choose a student and then describe yourself as if you were that student. Use physical and personality details and the structure "I am someone who . . ." or "I am the kind of person who . . ."

2. Distribute the slips of paper. Each student is to take on the identity of the name on his/her paper and write five sentences to describe himself/herself, using the structure indicated above.

3. Have the class get up and circulate. They must try to find themselves in the crowd by listening to other students describe themselves in the new identity. (You can circulate and listen for examples and errors.)

4. The first person to find himself/herself is the winner, but have everyone find himself/herself before you stop play if time permits.

NOTE: *This activity works best with a class that has worked together for awhile and who are familiar with one another.*

NOUN

1. SONG

BLACK BLUE

Materials: Worksheet 94
Tape player and music

Dynamic: Pairs

Time: 10 minutes

Procedure:

1. Tell students that you are going to play a song. They are to listen for noun clauses and count them. Remind the students that there can be clauses where "that" has been eliminated. Play the song once.

2. Ask how many noun clauses were heard. Get several answers. Play the song again, if desired, and recount.

3. Put students in pairs and give each pair a copy of the worksheet.

4. Have the pairs go through the song lyrics and underline all the noun clauses.

5. Go through the words together and have the students identify each noun clause as you come to it.

NOTE: *The lyrics to "Amie" (Craig Fuller, sung by Pure Prairie League) are provided in the worksheet as an example. If you do not have the music, you could read it to your students, but it is best to find a song with noun clauses for which you have the music. Another good song to use is "Don't Pass Me By" (Richard Starkey, sung by the Beatles).*

2. COMPLETIONS

BLACK   BLUE

Materials: Worksheet 95

Dynamic: Pairs

Time: 10 minutes

Procedure:

1. Put the students in pairs. Give each pair a copy of the worksheet containing the six sentence fragments that they should complete with a noun clause. Encourage them to use the names of students from the class in their completions and to be silly if they want. You may also suggest a topic for the sentences.

    SUGGESTIONS: your classmates
    elephants
    outer space
    another country
    the opposite sex
    unusual animals

2. Go around the class and have the pairs read their sentence completions. You may also want to see if any of the students can respond to a completed sentence. For example, if one pair writes "I wonder why Marissa was absent today," you may ask if anyone knows why.

3. RESPOND TO THE QUESTION

BLACK   BLUE

Materials: Worksheets 96, cut into strips

Dynamic: Whole class/Teams

Time: 10 minutes

Procedure:

1. Give each student a strip with a question on it. If you use the worksheet, fill in the blanks with the names of students from your class. The students are to respond to the question, using a noun clause.

    Example:

    On the strip: How many people live in Miami?

    Possible responses:

    I don't know how many people live in Miami.
    I don't care how many people live in Miami.
    Who knows how many people live in Miami? etc.

2. Have students take turns reading their question and their answer.

Variation: Divide the class into teams and have the students draw strips alternately. If a student answers the question correctly (correct noun clause form), the team gets a point. If you allow the team to work together on the answer, accept the answer only from the student who drew the strip.

4. THE FACT THAT

Materials: Worksheet 97

Dynamic: Pairs

Time: 15 minutes

BLUE

Procedure:

1. To review noun clauses using *the fact that*, divide the class into pairs. Give each pair a copy of the worksheet and have them work together to combine the two sentences using "the fact that."

2. Have each pair write one answer on the board. The other students will critique the answers (Do the sentences combine the two sentences grammatically? logically?).

5. MATCH GAME

Materials: Worksheet 98

Dynamic: Small groups

Time: 20 minutes

BLACK   BLUE

Procedure:

1. To review noun clauses, put students into groups of three to five. Cut up the worksheet and randomly distribute cards to the groups. Because the groups need to make matches, give an even number of cards to each group even if one or two groups receive two more cards than another group.

2. Each group tries to match its cards to make sentences that are both grammatical and logical, observing the capitalization on the cards (that is, they cannot change the capitalization).

3. Because cards were given out randomly, some of the cards will not form matches. After making all the matches they can within their groups, the students try to trade with other groups. They <u>cannot</u> just take a card from another group, but must trade them. If one group is unwilling to trade a certain card, the other group cannot force them.

4. When one group has made all its matches and feels they are correct, the game stops. One member of the group reads out the matches to see if the class accepts the match. (You may need to referee if the class rejects a logical, grammatical answer. Sometimes this happens if the class does not want the group to win [and thus the game to end].)

5. If all matches are accepted, the group wins. If any of the matches is rejected, the game continues until another (or the same) group feels it has matched all cards. There can be no unmatched cards.

6. SOLVE THE MYSTERY

Materials: Worksheets 99A and 99B or a 3″ x 5″ card for each student and a list of information the students must obtain
A piece of paper for each student

Dynamic: Whole class

Time: 30 minutes

BLACK   BLUE

Procedure:
1. Copy and cut Worksheet 99A, making sure there will be one card for each of your students. The first seven cards must be used. Use as many of the others as you have students in the class. (You may have to duplicate the worksheet or make others yourself if you have a large class.) If you choose not to use the worksheet, make cards with similar information on them.

2. Have the students number their papers 1–7, and ask them to write the following information:
   1. the name of a student in the class
   2. the name of a thing that can be carried
   3. the name of another student in the class
   4. a money amount
   5. complete the sentence: *He/She did it because* . . .
   6. the name of another student in the class
   7. a location in your house

3. Collect the papers and draw seven at random. Use a different student paper to fill in the information on the first seven cards on the worksheet. (Take the name of a student in the class from the first paper, the name of a thing that can be carried from the second paper, the name of another student in the class from the third paper, and so on.)

4. Distribute the cards randomly so that seven students have a clue card (with the blank now filled in) and the rest of the students have the other cards from the worksheet. Tell the students that a crime has been committed and they must solve the crime by finding the answer to the questions on Worksheet 99B. Either give each student a copy of the questions, or write the questions on the board or on an overhead transparency.

5. The students circulate and ask each other the questions, making sure to preface each question with an expression such as "Can you please tell me . . .?" or "Do you know . . .?" with the rest of the question converted into a noun clause.

Example: "Whose was it?" becomes "Do you know whose it was?"

If the question is not phrased properly, the student being asked may refuse to answer the question. Students who have the requested information must respond to a correctly worded question truthfully. Students who do not have the answer must use the phrase on their cards, followed by a noun clause.

Example: I don't know how much it costs.
I don't have the foggiest idea who stole it.

6. The first student to acquire all of the requested information wins.

7. ORDERS → SUBJUNCTIVE

BLUE

Materials:	Worksheet 100
Dynamic:	Teams
Time:	10 minutes

Procedure:

1. Cut up the worksheet. Divide the class into two teams and have them line up on either side of the room.

2. The first student from Team 1 comes to the front desk and draws a slip of paper with an order on it. The student then puts that order into a subjunctive sentence. Tell students not to repeat the same verb used by their classmates, but to use a variety: *demand, tell, order, ask*, etc.

   Example:

   Paper: Teacher to student: "Shut the door."
   Student response: She demanded that the student shut the door.

3. If the student answers correctly, he/she scores a point for his/her team. Then the other team takes a turn.

4. Repeat until all orders have been put into the subjunctive. The team with the most points wins.

8. QUESTION DRAW (Subjunctive form)

BLUE

Materials:	Worksheet 101
Dynamic:	Teams
Time:	10 minutes
Procedure:	

1. Cut up the worksheet. Divide the class into two teams and have them line up on either side of the room.

2. The first student from Team 1 comes to the front desk, draws a slip of paper with a question on it, and reads it to the first student on Team 2. That student answers the question, using the subjunctive in a noun clause.

   Example:
   Question: What is it necessary that a person wear to class?
   Answer: It is necessary that a person wear shoes to class.

3. If the student answers correctly, he/she scores a point for his/her team. Then a student from the other team takes a turn.

4. Repeat until all questions have been chosen. The team with the most points wins.

   NOTE: *Having one team read the question to the other team ensures that everyone can hear the question.*

9. CHANGE IT (Quoted/Reported speech)

BLACK BLUE

Materials:	Worksheet 102
Dynamic:	Teams
Time:	10 minutes
Procedure:	

1. Cut up the worksheet. Divide the class into two teams and have them linc up on opposite sides of the room.

2. A student from Team 1 comes to the front of the class and draws a slip of paper with a sentence or question in quoted speech. The student reads it to the first student in Team 2, who puts the statement into reported speech.

   Example: **Student A:** "Where can I meet you?"
   Student B: She asked where she could meet me.
   Student A: "Come here!"
   Student B: He ordered me to go there.

3. After all members of Team 2 have responded, reverse roles so that the students in Team 2 ask the questions.

10. INTERVIEW (Quoted/Reported speech)

Materials:	Worksheet 103
Dynamic:	Pairs
Time:	30 minutes
Procedure:	

BLACK   **BLUE**

1. Review quoted speech, making sure students understand how quoted speech is represented in English for statements, questions, and commands. Divide the students into pairs.

2. The partners use the worksheet to collect samples of quoted speech from each other. Then they rewrite their partner's quoted speech as reported speech.

   NOTE: *You can wait until you have covered all the relevant reported speech structures in the book before you assign this task, or you can have the students do each section as they learn it.*

REVIEW

1. COMBINATIONS

Materials:	Worksheet 104
Dynamic:	Pairs
Time:	15 minutes
Procedure:	

BLUE

1. Have students work in pairs. Give each pair one copy of the worksheet.

2. The students are to combine the sentences as directed on the worksheet.

3. When all pairs have finished, go over the worksheet together by asking for volunteers to read or write their sentences on the board.

   NOTE: *For a high-level class, eliminate the instructions regarding what type of clause to use.*

Worksheet 94: SONG

"Amie"

I can see why you think you belong to me;
I never tried to make you think or let you see
One thing for yourself.
But now you're off with someone else and I'm alone.
You see, I thought that I might keep you for my own.

REPEAT

Amie, what 'choo wanna do?
I think I could stay with you
For awhile, maybe longer, if I do.

Don't you think the time was right for us to find
All them things we thought weren't proper
Could be right in time.
And, can you see
Which way we should turn together or alone.
I can't never tell what's right or what is wrong.
(It'd take too long to see)

REPEAT

Well, now it's come to what you want; you've had your way.
And all the things you thought before just faded into gray.
And can you see
A-That I don't know if it's you or if it's me.
If it's one of us, I'm sure we both will see
(Oh, won't you look at me and tell me)

REPEAT

I just keep falling in and out of love with you,
Falling in and out of love with you,
Don't know what I'm gonna do,
I keep falling in and out of love with you.

"Amie," words and music by Craig Lee Fuller
©1971, 1975 McKenzie Music & Unichappell Music, Inc. (BMI)
All Rights Administered by Unichappell Music, Inc. (BMI)
All Rights Reserved   Used by Permission
WARNER BROS. PUBLICATIONS U.S., INC., Miami, FL 33014

Fun with Grammar   **293**

I'd like to know . . .

I wonder . . .

Can you tell me . . .

Please tell me . . .

Do you know . . .

I don't know . . .

I'd like to know . . .

I wonder . . .

Can you tell me . . .

Please tell me . . .

Do you know . . .

I don't know . . .

I'd like to know . . .

I wonder . . .

Can you tell me . . .

Please tell me . . .

Do you know . . .

I don't know . . .

How many people live in Miami?

How old is your grandmother?

How often does _____ study?

What is _____'s telephone number?

Why was _____ absent yesterday?

What did _____ eat for dinner yesterday?

Where is the head of our program today?

Why is _____ always smiling?

Where is Omaha?

What is _____'s middle name?

What is the capital of Japan?

How many brothers and sisters does _____ have?

What is _____'s favorite color?

How did _____ meet her husband?

What is _____'s favorite animal?

When is the next test?

Why do classes start at 8:00?

How many girlfriends does _____ have?

How tall is the Empire State Building?

How many hours does it take to drive from San Diego to San Francisco?

Who was that guy with _____ last night?

How many legs does a centipede have?

Who is the best cook in the class?

What is the average rainfall in Panama?

Who was the oldest U.S. president?

How old is the teacher?

What is the best place to go on vacation?

How much does _____ weigh?

Combine the two sentences in each set, using the fact that. *Be sure your resulting sentence is grammatical and logical.*

1. A big dog lives on my street.

   That scares me.

2. The bus didn't come.

   Because of that, I was late.

3. Yoichi didn't study but got 100 percent.

   I wonder about that.

4. My mother forgot my birthday.

   That made me sad.

5. It's cold today.

   In spite of that, I'm going to the beach.

6. Ahmed was wearing a tie today.

   I was stunned by that.

7. Hitoshi seemed sincere.

   I wasn't convinced by that.

8. The pyramids were built without the aid of machines.

   That really amazes me.

9. My daughter graduated at the head of her class at Harvard.

   That takes my breath away.

10. My dog chewed up my new book.

    In spite of that, I still love her.

Where Bob eats lunch	I don't know	I wonder
It's a miracle	We don't care	We need to find out
How many husbands she had	How much money I earn	The fact that no one has seen Brian
Everyone wants to know	It bothers me	What he has on
It's a fact	No one knows	Let's ask him
That she was in an accident	I can't imagine	Could you tell me
is too bad	was a secret	is strange

what he is really like	is a mystery	where he lives
how old she is	that you forgot my birthday	if she has a sister
is scary	if he knows how to get to the ocean	that she agreed to go on a date with you
whether or not she's busy tonight	where the party will be	is none of your business
what you were like as a child	that he stole the money	how often he goes jogging

_____ stole it.	He/She stole a _____ .	It was _____ .
It cost _____ .	He/She stole it because _____ .	He/She stole it from _____ .
Now it's _____ .	I don't have any idea . . .	I don't know . . .
I haven't the foggiest idea . . .	No one told me . . .	I can't imagine . . .
I'd like to know . . . too.	I wish I knew . . .	It's none of my business . . .
No one knows . . .	I can't remember . . .	It's a mystery to me . . .

© 1997 Prentice Hall Regents. Duplication for classroom use is permitted.

Worksheet 99B: SOLVE THE MYSTERY

Who stole something?	Who stole something?
What did he/she steal?	What did he/she steal?
Whose was it?	Whose was it?
How much did it cost?	How much did it cost?
Why did he/she steal it?	Why did he/she steal it?
Who did he/she steal it from?	Who did he/she steal it from?
Where is it now?	Where is it now?

Who stole something?	Who stole something?
What did he/she steal?	What did he/she steal?
Whose was it?	Whose was it?
How much did it cost?	How much did it cost?
Why did he/she steal it?	Why did he/she steal it?
Who did he/she steal it from?	Who did he/she steal it from?
Where is it now?	Where is it now?

Who stole something?	Who stole something?
What did he/she steal?	What did he/she steal?
Whose was it?	Whose was it?
How much did it cost?	How much did it cost?
Why did he/she steal it?	Why did he/she steal it?
Who did he/she steal it from?	Who did he/she steal it from?
Where is it now?	Where is it now?

Fun with Grammar **301**

Mother to child: "Be careful!"	Teacher to student: "Stay after class."	Teacher to student: "Study for the test."
Mother to son: "Be home by 5:00."	Friend to friend: "Drive more carefully."	Father to child: "Eat your vegetables."
Mother to daughter: "Get your hair cut."	Friend to friend: "Be here in an hour."	Father to son: "Don't spend all your money."
Museum official to visitor: "Don't touch that!"	Sister to sister: "Don't tell anyone my secret."	Test official to worker: "Don't admit anyone after 1 P.M."
Teacher to student: "Take the Institutional TOEFL."	Mother to child: "Clean up your mess."	Friend to friend: "Buy a new car."
Friend to friend: "Tell me the truth."	Father to child: "Don't lie to me!"	Advisor to student: "Apply to colleges early."

What have your parents insisted that you do?	What do you suggest your brother do?	What is it important that students do?
What is it vital that a doctor do?	What do you propose that we do after class?	What does the teacher recommend that you do?
What have you asked that your parents do?	What is it necessary that a pilot have?	What do you advise that your friend do?
What has a doctor suggested that you take?	What has someone requested that you do?	What is it necessary that a teacher do?
What is it vital that the government do to decrease crime?	What do you request that your friends call you?	What is it essential that a person do before going to a foreign country?
What is it imperative that a driver do when he/she hears a fire engine coming?	What have you asked that your boyfriend/ girlfriend/spouse do?	What meal is it most important that a person eat?

✂ -

"Read chapter 6 for homework."	"Pick up your clothes!"	"You should drive more carefully."
"It will rain tomorrow."	"I'm watching the news."	"I was angry yesterday."
"I've already read this book."	"Do you have an extra pencil?"	"I have already seen that movie."
"I have a headache."	"Put that back!"	"I have to work tonight."
"Are you still studying?"	"I am going to take a bath now."	"Can I have those French fries?"
"Is that your sister?"	"I ate dinner at 10:00."	"I must go now."
"Do you have any money?"	"I might go out tonight."	"I may be late."

A. Statements: *Ask your partner these questions and write his/her answers in the space provided. Make sure you use the correct punctuation for quotes.*

1. What is one thing you did this weekend?

2. What do you think about _____? (*fill in with placename*)

3. What will you do after you finish this program?

4. What is one thing you would like to change about this program?

5. Do you think money is the most important thing in life?

6. Have you been to _____ yet? (*fill in with placename*)

B. Questions: *Ask your partner three* yes/no *questions (ex: Are you going to eat lunch today?) and three* wh-*questions (ex: Where is my book?). In the space below, write the questions that your partner asks you, making sure to use the correct punctuation for quotes.*

1.

2.

3.

4.

5.

6.

C. **Commands:** *Imagine that you are a teacher or a parent. Tell your partner three commands that you would give to your students or children. (ex: Write your name on your test. Get off the table!). Write your partner's commands below, using the correct punctuation for quotes.*

1.

2.

3.

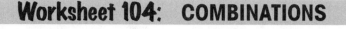

Combine the information by changing one of the sentences into an adjective, adverb, or noun clause as directed. Use any additional words necessary to form your sentence.

1. He teaches a class for students. Their native language is not English. (*adjective clause*)

   _____

   _____

2. She gave several reasons. Only a few of them were valid. (*adjective clause*)

   _____

   _____

3. I don't know. What should I do? (*noun clause*)

   _____

   _____

4. She doesn't understand spoken English. That is obvious. (*noun clause*)

   _____

   _____

5. John's glasses broke yesterday. He was playing basketball during that time. (*adverb clause*)

   _____

   _____

6. The Civil War has ended. A new government is being formed. (*adverb clause*)

   _____

   _____

CHAPTER
16

Conditionals and Wishes

16.1 TRUE IN THE PRESENT/FUTURE

1. SUPERSTITIONS

Materials: None

Dynamic: Small groups

Time: 15 minutes

BLACK BLUE

Procedure:

1. Write a few superstitions on the board. Here are some examples.

   If a black cat crosses your path, you'll have bad luck.
   If your palm itches, you're going to receive money.
   If you break a mirror, you'll have seven years bad luck.
   If you step on a crack, you'll break your mother's back.

   Look at the verb forms in the *if*-clause and result clause together. Ask students to generate a rule (if this is an introduction) or review the rule (if you have already introduced this form).

2. Break students into small groups and have them discuss superstitions from their countries. They should list three or four to share with the rest of the class.

3. As a whole group, share the superstitions and discuss which are universal and which seem to exist only in one or two cultures. Students often have similar superstitions in their countries and like to share them, and it is interesting to compare slight variations.

4. For further review of forms, you may want to write several of the students' superstitions on the board and analyze them (Were they written correctly?).

2. SUPERSTITIONS MATCH A

Materials: Worksheet 105

Dynamic: Whole class

Time: 15 minutes

BLACK BLUE

Procedure:

1. Cut up the worksheet or make your own. Give each student half of a superstition, that is, one card.

2. The students circulate and try to find the missing half of their superstition. When students feel they have a match, they sit down. You will probably have to check student matches and advise them

to sit down or find a different match. (In case you are unfamiliar with some of the superstitions in the worksheet, the *if*-clause on the left matches the result clause directly across from it.)

3. Go over the superstitions together, talking about meaning and form.

3. SUPERSTITIONS MATCH B

BLACK   BLUE

Materials: 3" x 5" cards, or paper cut into strips at least 2" x 4"

Dynamic: Groups

Time: 15 minutes

Procedure:

1. Follow steps 1 and 2 for **Superstitions**, page 309.

2. Have the students write their superstitions on the cards or paper strips so that one half of the superstition is on one card and the other half is on a different card. (Each group should produce only half as many superstitions as there are members in their group, so that a group of four students will write two superstitions, a total of four cards. In step 2 of Activity 1, students may have generated many superstitions, so instruct them to choose the ones they like best.)

3. Collect and shuffle the cards. Hand one card to each student. Students circulate and try to find their match. (The student who wrote the superstition will have to be the judge of whether or not the match is good because you will probably be unfamiliar with several of the superstitions.)

4. As a class, go over the superstitions and check (as a group) to see if the correct grammar forms were used.

4. JUST THE FACTS

BLACK   BLUE

Materials: Worksheet 106

Dynamic: Whole class

Time: 10 minutes

Procedure:

1. Cut up the cards in the worksheet or prepare your own. Distribute one to each student, who must construct a sentence that uses the true conditional form.

Example: Add lemon to milk

Example fact (by student):   If you add lemon to milk, it curdles.

2. Arrange students in a circle, and have each say his/her sentence.

Variation: To avoid students' losing interest, do step 2 as a memory round. Each student says his/her sentence and repeats all those that came before his/hers.

5. EXPERIMENT REPORT

Materials: None

Dynamic: Small groups

Time: 10 minutes

BLACK   BLUE

Procedure:
1. Divide the class into groups of three or four. Assign each group an experiment.

   Suggested experiments: putting a spoon in the microwave
   mixing blue and yellow paint
   boiling eggs in water with onion skins
   touching your tongue to a frozen
       surface
   shaving your eyebrows
   frowning all the time

2. The students discuss what they think the result will be. Then each group reports to the class, using some conditional sentences.

   (If you intend to have the students act out the experiments in class or for homework, obviously there are some in the list above you would not want to assign.)

   NOTE: *Because the results of these experiments can be perceived as a habitual result or as a predictable fact, either the present or the future can be used in the result clause.*

6. DIRECTIONS

Materials: A map (Worksheet 107) and a handout (either A or B) per student

Dynamic: Pairs

Time: 15 minutes

BLACK   BLUE

Procedure:
1. Break the class into pairs and give a map and two worksheets to each pair. Each student handout contains both locations and routes as indicated in Worksheet 107.

2. Student A begins and asks Student B for directions to the first location. Student B looks at the map and the list of routes on his/her handout and gives advice in a conditional sentence.

Example:

> **Student A:**   How can I get to Bethesda?
> **Student B:**   If you take Route 190, you will get to Bethesda.

3. After Student A has asked for directions to all the locations on 107 Part A, Student B asks for directions to the location on his/her handout (107 Part B). Student A now gives the advice.

NOTES: *Locations and the ways to get there are not in order. Students must match them. A local map also works well because the students are familiar with places and highways. Pattern the handouts after Worksheet 107, in that case.*

Variation: For a higher-level class, provide locations only and have the partner search the map for a route that goes to the requested location.

UNTRUE IN THE PRESENT

1. MEMORY GAME

BLACK   BLUE

Materials: 3″ x 5″ cards

Dynamic: Whole class

Time: 25 minutes

Procedure:
1. On each card write an adjective in large letters so that it can be seen around the room.

   SUGGESTIONS: *sad, drunk, lonely, stranded, nauseous, hungry, thirsty, nervous, angry, rich, sick, sleepy, famous, tired, poor, lost, married, single, scared*

   (Include a few new words that will be challenging even for higher-level students, such as *jilted* or *stranded*.) Have students sit or stand in a circle while you distribute the cards. (If you use adjectives like *married* or *single*, be sure to give them to students who are not!)

2. Ask who has the best memory and then start with the person next to him/her. If you know you have a weak student, you may want to start with that person. The first student holds up his/her card and composes a sentence, using the untrue present conditional.

   Example card: lonely

   Example sentence: If I were lonely, I would call my family.

3. The second student says his/her sentence and repeats student one's sentence. Continue around the circle, with each new student

adding a sentence and repeating all the previous sentences. The last student will have to remember the sentences from all the other students. It is important that students hold their cards toward the circle at all times because they serve as clues. Also, don't let any of the students write. Students may cue their classmates through gestures. The only correction allowed is to emphasize *were* rather than *was*.

NOTE: *If your class is large, divide it into two groups and play two rounds. The same cards can be used, but different sentences must be created. The game has been played with up to 14 in a low-level class and up to 22 in a high-level class.*

2. CLUE

BLACK   BLUE

Materials: None

Dynamic: Whole class

Time: 10 minutes

Procedure:
1. One student volunteers to leave the room and, when he/she returns, will guess the word chosen by the class from clues given by the rest of the class. The volunteer can ask questions if they are in the form of the untrue present.

2. While the volunteer is out of the room, decide on a category (suggestions: occupations, food, school material). Have the class choose a word in that category. Brainstorm together the kinds of clues that can be given. They must be in the form of the untrue present conditional.

Example 1:	Food server
Clues:	If I were you, I would wear a uniform.
	If I were you, I'd never have dirty hands.
	If I were you, I would talk to many people.

Also, decide which clues should be saved for last. (For example: "If I were you, I would serve customers quickly in order to get a good tip.")

Example 2:	mustard
Clues:	If I were you, I'd be careful not to get this on my clothes.
	If I were you, I'd never eat this by itself.
	If you were a waitress, you would put this on the table next to the ketchup.
Last clue:	If I were you, I would always put it on hot dogs.

3. When the volunteer returns, students take turns offering clues, but they must be in the form of the untrue present conditional.

313

3. BUILDING AROUND

BLACK BLUE

Materials: None

Dynamic: Large groups

Time: 15 minutes

Procedure:
1. Put students into groups of five to seven.

2. One student begins with a sentence in the untrue present conditional.

    Example: If I lived in France, I would speak French.

3. Each student builds on the story by taking the result of the previous sentence and turning it into an *if*-clause.

    Example:

Student 1:	If I lived in France, I would speak French.
Student 2:	And if I spoke French, I would speak the same native language as Florence.
Student 3:	And if I spoke the same native language as Florence, we would be good friends.
Student 4:	And if we were good friends, we would go to parties together.

4. Encourage the students to correct/help each other within the groups.

4. SONG

BLACK BLUE

Materials: Lyrics to a song, handout with questions (optional)
Tape player (optional)

Dynamic: Pairs/Small groups

Time: 30 minutes

Procedure:
1. Choose a song that has several examples of the untrue present conditional.

    SUGGESTIONS: "If I Were a Carpenter"
    "If I Had a Hammer"
    "If I Could Save Time in a Bottle"

    Type up the lyrics, but leave blanks for the conditional forms—just provide the verb.

2. The students, working in pairs, fill in the missing verbs.

3. Listen to the song to check answers.

Variation: Add some questions that make use of the conditional or allow students to think about why the conditional was used. For the song "If I Were a Carpenter," questions can include:

a. What kinds of jobs are mentioned?

b. Does the man hold any of these jobs? How do you know?

c. The man asks a lot of questions about occupations, but what does he really want to know from his girlfriend? Write a conditional sentence to express what he wants.

5. LINE-UPS

Materials: Worksheet 108 or 3″ x 5″ cards

Dynamic: Whole class

Time: 20 minutes

BLACK BLUE

Procedure:

1. Use the cards in the worksheet or prepare your own cards with similar questions. If you make your own cards, it is advisable to make each set a different color so you can assemble students in lines more easily. ("Everyone with a pink card, stand against the board. If you have a yellow card, stand in front of someone with a pink card.") Have all the students holding one of the colors come to the front of the room and stand against the board (or wall). Have the other students stand in front of one of these students.

2. The students in the line against the board ask their questions of the student standing in front of them. When the students in the "answer line" have answered the question, they move on to the next "questioner." The students in the "question line" do not move.

3. When the students in the "answer line" have talked to every student in the "question line," it is time to change positions. Continue as specified in step 2.

4. To wrap up this activity, ask each student to share some of the responses he/she received.

   NOTE: *If you have an uneven number of students, have one student wait at the end of the line until the students move. One student will always be without a partner, but because the students will answer the questions at different rates, it will always appear as if several students are waiting. If you have a very large class, divide the class in two and do the line-ups both in front and in back of the class.*

6. VALUES

Materials: Worksheet 109

Dynamic: Groups

Time: 20 minutes

BLACK BLUE

Procedure:

1. Prepare two sets of cards from Worksheets 109A and 109B. Break the class into small groups. Give each group a values card and a YES or NO card. Stress that they cannot let any of the other groups know if their card says YES or NO.

2. Each group is presented with a situation. They must change the wording on the card into a conditional sentence. They then choose one classmate in another group who they feel will give them the answer on their YES/NO card.

   Example:

   The card says: You find a wallet with $50 and an ID inside. Do you keep it?

   Sentence made by the group: If you found a wallet with $50 and an ID inside, would you keep it?

   YES/NO card: YES

   Task: Decide which of their classmates not in their group will answer YES to the question they generated. They must make an educated guess based on what they know of their classmates.

3. Check with each group to make sure they have chosen a classmate. When all groups have done so, play a round: the first group picks a student and asks its question. If the student's answer matches the group's card, the group receives a point. Go on to the next group.

4. Play another round.

7. IMAGINE THAT! (*Might* and *Would*)

Materials: None

Dynamics: Groups

Time: 15 minutes

BLUE

Procedure:

1. Write a result on the board that is either unusual or funny. Ask students when or why they <u>might</u> do that action. Generate as many *if*-clauses as possible.

Suggested results (can be used for teacher example and for groups):

> go skinny dipping
> call 911
> paint my body
> hop on one foot
> climb on the roof
> attract a lot of attention
> climb a tree

2. Divide the students into groups. Give each group a different result and have them brainstorm *if*-clauses using *might*.

3. After each group writes as many *if*-clauses as possible, have the students in each group decide which one of the *if*-clauses <u>would</u> produce the result they have been working with. The groups should try to reach a consensus, but that may not be possible.

4. Share sentences (or *if*-clauses) with the class.

   Example: attract a lot of attention

   Student sentences:

   > I might attract a lot of attention if I screamed in class.
   > I might attract a lot of attention if I dyed my hair green.
   > I might attract a lot of attention if I sang a song on the street corner.

5. As a whole class, look at the sentences each group has chosen to share with the class. Decide as a whole class which sentence would most likely produce the result.

   SUGGESTION: *If you do this game as a competition, have the class vote on the best sentence. The group that receives the most votes gets a point for that round. Then go on to another round of sentences. The only danger here is that students may vote for their own sentence and then no one group would ever win. This could be avoided by telling students that they cannot vote for their own sentence.*

8. *AS IF/AS THOUGH* PICTURES

Materials: Magazines

Dynamic: Small groups

Time: 10 minutes

BLUE

Procedure:

1. Arrange students in groups of three or four. Find, copy, and distribute magazine pictures that have people with unusual expressions.

2. Have students discuss several pictures, making sentences using *as if* or *as though*. ("He looks as if he ate a lemon." "He looks as if he were sick.")

3. Each group takes turns holding up a picture and describing it by using their sentences.

Variations: Have students find their own pictures, perhaps as homework. Or have them each bring a magazine to class and look through them in their groups for a good picture. (In this case, you may want to have some back-up pictures just in case.)

16.3 UNTRUE IN THE PAST

1. BUILDING AROUND

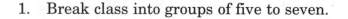

Materials:	None
Dynamic:	Large groups
Time:	15 minutes

BLACK   BLUE

Procedure:
1. Break class into groups of five to seven.

2. Have one student begin with a sentence in the untrue past conditional. Follow the steps in **Building Around**, 16.2.3.

   Example:

   Student 1: If I had gotten married after high school, I would not have come to the United States.
   Student 2: If I had not come to the United States, I would not have visited the Grand Canyon.
   Student 3: If I had not visited the Grand Canyon, I would not have taken so many pictures. (etc.)

2. STORY SAGAS

Materials:	Worksheet 110
Dynamic:	Small groups
Time:	20 minutes

BLACK   BLUE

Procedure:
1. Have students work in groups of three or four. Give each group a story summary. If you plan to give each group a different summary, give each group a handout with all the summaries and then assign one per group. (There is a handout of sample summaries in Worksheet 110.)

2. The students read the summary and then write five conditional sentences based on the information in the summary.

Example:

> Blair lied and told Todd she was pregnant with his child so that he would marry her. She knew what he didn't: that he was about to inherit $28 million. As a result of her deception, Cord, the man she really loved, was disgusted with her. Since the marriage, Blair has discovered that she is now, in fact, pregnant, and Todd has discovered that he is a millionaire. Blair's mother, who is in a psychiatric center, knows the truth about the marriage and has a habit of saying whatever comes to mind.

Sample Sentences:

> If Blair had not lied to Todd, he wouldn't have married her.
> If Blair had not married Todd, she could have married Cord.
> If Todd had known about the $28 million before his marriage, he might have suspected Blair.

Variation: Instead of using soap opera summaries, use a story the class has read. If this is a multiskills class, you know what material the class has read. If the reading class is separate, you can check with the reading instructor. Follow the same procedure, but write conditional sentences based on the story. You can also use fairy tales or fables.

16.4 MIXED CONDITIONALS

1. WHAT IF

Materials: None

Dynamic: Pairs/Small groups

Time: 15 minutes

BLUE

Procedure:

1. Break the class into pairs or groups of three or four.
   Explain (or review) that some actions have results not only in the time they happened, but can also carry over into the present or future.

   Example: If I had eaten more *last night* . . . I wouldn't be hungry *now*.

2. Give each group or pair several *if*-clauses—things that happened in the past. Tell them this activity has results in the present and that they should make sentences with a past condition and a present result.

   SUGGESTIONS: If I had written my essay last weekend
   If I had gone to bed earlier last night
   If I had washed my hair yesterday
   If I had gone to the movies with my friends last night
   If I had studied more English in my own country

If I hadn't gone to Morocco ...

If I hadn't drunk so much Tequila last night ...

(I'm the youngest of 6) *If my parents hadn't had 5 children ...*

result → in present

2. COMIC STRIP ADVICE

Materials: Worksheet 111

Dynamic: Small groups

Time: 15 minutes

BLUE

Procedure:

1. Distribute copies of the comic strip *Cathy* (Worksheet 111) to each group.

2. After they read the comic strip, have the groups work together to complete the *if*-clauses. They can use the information provided by the mother in the strip or just make a logical ending.

   Example: **Cathy says:**   If only I weren't so fat.

   Student results: I could wear my new dress.
   I would have had more boyfriends.
   I would feel better.

REVIEWING THE CONDITIONAL FORMS

1. REVIEW MATCH

Materials: Worksheet 112

Dynamic: Small groups

Time: 20 minutes

BLACK   BLUE

Procedure:

1. Divide the class into small groups. Give each group the same number of cards. Be sure to give an <u>even</u> number to each group. If this is not possible, give one group one pair more than the others. Use the cards in Worksheet 112 or make your own.

2. Each group should make as many matches as possible. Group members should take the remaining unmatched cards to other groups and try to make a trade. (Important: They cannot give away a card without receiving one in exchange, and they cannot take a card unless the other group agrees to the trade.)

3. When one group has matched all its cards, the game stops. A group member reads the matches, and the rest of the class must agree that they are logical. If all matches are accepted, that group is the winner. If one or more matches is rejected, the game proceeds until the next group feels it is finished.

   NOTE: *Because of mixed conditionals, there will not necessarily be matches for all cards.*

2. DEAR ANNIE

BLUE

Materials: Worksheet 113

Dynamic: Whole class

Time: 30 minutes

Procedure:
1. Have students pick one of the seven situations on the worksheet and write a letter to "Dear Annie" in which they explain their situation and ask how it can be avoided in the future or how it could have been avoided.

2. Collect the students' "Dear Annie" letters. Randomly redistribute them to the class, making sure that no one receives his/her own letter.

3. Have students pretend they are Annie and respond in writing to the letter they received. They must use whichever conditional structures are appropriate to the situation described in the letter.

4. Have several students read to the class the original letter they wrote along with their (Annie's) response. Return the letters and the responses to the authors of the original letters.

 16.6 WISHES

1. ALADDIN'S LAMP

BLACK   BLUE

Materials: Worksheet 114

Dynamic: Groups

Time: 20 minutes

Procedure:
1. Discuss the meaning of Aladdin's lamp if necessary. (A poor boy named Aladdin found an old lamp. When he rubbed it, a genie appeared and granted him three wishes.)

2. Tell students they have each found Aladdin's lamp and been granted three wishes. Have them write their wishes down.

3. Break students into groups of about five. Pass out one worksheet per group and have the students compare their wishes and answer the survey questions.

4. Each group can report its findings to the class.

if you sleep with a mirror under your pillow	you will dream of what your future husband looks like
if you trip on a flight of stairs	you will have triplets
if your cat washes its face	company is coming
if your eyebrows grow together or your arms are hairy	you will be very rich
if the bottom of one of your feet itches	you are going to take a trip
if your nose itches	you'll kiss a fool

if a cat licks its tail	it will rain
if your ears burn	someone is talking about you
if you find a four-leaf clover	you will have good luck
if you walk under a ladder	you will have bad luck
if you use the same pillow your dog uses	you will dream what he dreams
if you step on your shadow	you will have bad luck
if you want to do well on a test	use the same pencil you used for studying because it will remember the answers

✂ -

drive with your eyes closed	eat five pizzas at once
use sunscreen	heat water to 100°C
fly east from here	put ice cubes in the sun
have a baby	never study
read a lot	do not eat
overwater plants	pour oil on water
pass this class	take scuba diving lessons

© 1997 Prentice Hall Regents. Duplication for classroom use is permitted.

A

I. Can you tell me how to get to . . . ?
   The Goddard Space Flight Center
   The White House
   Georgetown University

II. If you take . . . you will get to . . .
   395
   495
   16th Avenue

B

I. If you take . . . you will get to . . .
   MacArthur Boulevard
   Route 214
   The Baltimore–Washington Parkway

II. Can you tell me how to get to . . . ?
   The University of Maryland
   The National Zoo
   The Pentagon

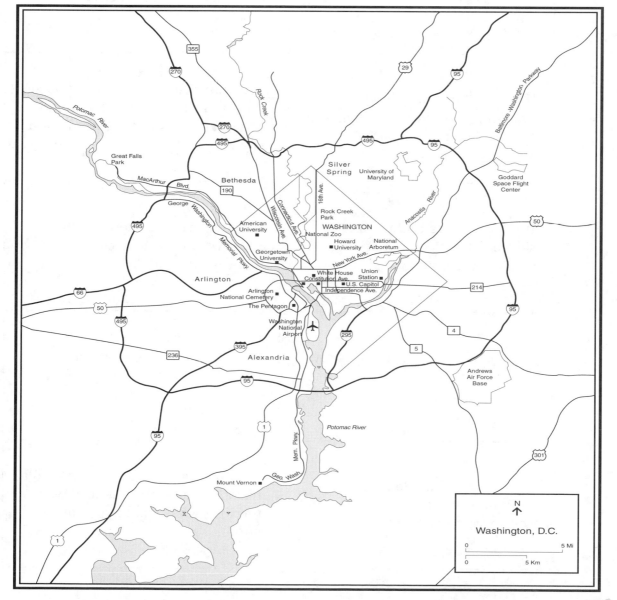

If you lost your homework and your teacher did not believe that you had done the work, what would you do?	If you discovered, after eating dinner at a restaurant, that you had no money or credit cards with you, what would you do?
If you disliked your sister's new boyfriend, what would you say to her?	If you saw your friend cheating on a test, what would you do?
If you had a choice between finishing your essay and going to a party, what would you do?	If you arrived at a friend's house for dinner and realized you had the wrong night, what would you say?
If your parents told you not to see your boyfriend/girlfriend, what would you do?	If your parents asked you to return to your home country, what would you do?
If your friend gave you a puppy for your birthday, what would you do?	If a classmate asked you a personal question, what would you say?
If your friend made mistakes in grammar while speaking, would you correct him/her?	If you were invited for dinner to a friend's house and the food was terrible, what would you say or do?

You accidently break your host family's remote control. Do you confess?

Your best friend's boyfriend/ girlfriend asks you out. Do you accept?

You see your teacher's car hit a parked car and leave. You know the owner of the damaged car. Do you tell him/her?

A new acquaintance invites you to a party, and everyone there goes skinny-dipping. Do you join them?

You know that a friend's boyfriend is involved with another man. Do you tell her?

You see a friend shoplift something inexpensive. Do you talk to him/her about it?

Your friend is copying someone else's homework instead of doing it himself/herself. Do you talk to him/her?

The cashier overcharges you by 15 cents. Do you complain?

You see your sister's husband kissing another woman. Do you tell her?

You run over your neighbor's dog. Do you confess?

The waiter forgets to charge you for your dessert. Do you tell him?

Your parents tell you to stop seeing your boyfriend/girlfriend. Do you see him/her in secret?

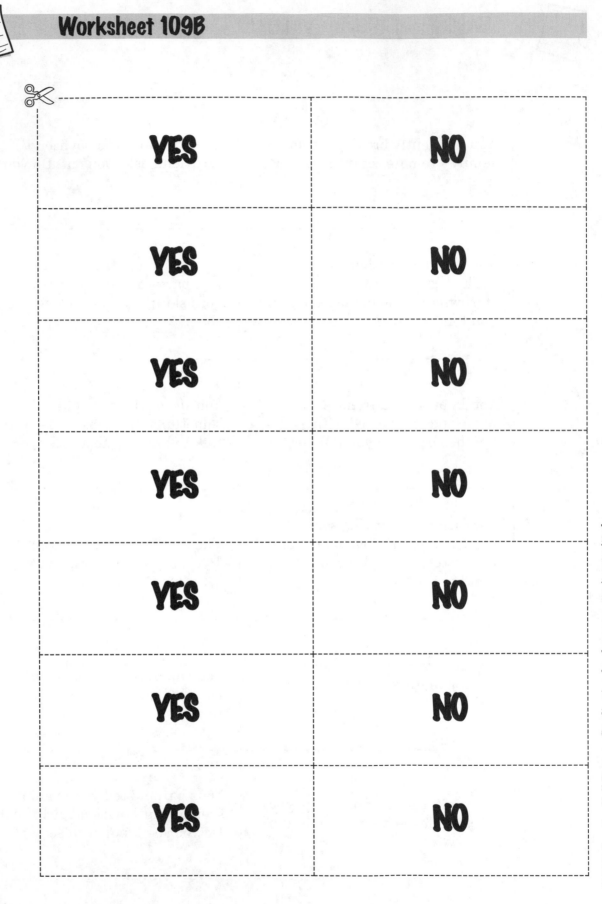

YES	NO
YES	NO
YES	NO
YES	NO
YES	NO
YES	NO
YES	NO

Sample Summaries:

From *General Hospital:*

Catherine is accused of murdering Damian even though no body has been found. (Damian has disappeared under mysterious circumstances.) Lucy remembers seeing Catherine parked outside her building at 11 P.M., which does not match the prosecution's case. Lucy agrees to testify for Catherine. When asked how she happened to look outside at 11 P.M, Lucy says that her pet duck was quacking. This amuses the jury and the lawyers, who laugh at Lucy. Embarrassed, Lucy tries to defend her duck, which only makes matters worse. After her testimony, Catherine is angry at Lucy for mentioning the duck because it made Lucy look foolish and caused the jury to disregard her testimony.

From *All My Children:*

Charlie and Hailey were dating, but break up over a difference of opinion regarding her domineering father. Meanwhile, Cecily's newly famous movie star husband divorces her. She returns to Pine Valley and begins to work for Charlie. An attraction begins to develop between them, which they both deny. Charlie is surprised when Hailey announces only weeks after their break up that she is engaged to Alex.

From *One Life to Live:*

Eighteen-year-old Joe falls in love with a much older woman, Dorian. Although she swears that she really loves Joe, everyone warns him that Dorian is just using him and that he will be hurt. Joe's mother makes a deal with Dorian. Dorian's part of the deal is to drop Joe and marry David, who agrees to marry Dorian for money.

David impersonates Vicki and Tina's brother to inherit a fortune. When he falls in love with Tina, he is forced to reveal the truth to her. She agrees to conceal the truth to help David inherit. David and Tina marry in secret. When Tina's ex-husband, Cord, learns about the marriage, David must confess he is not the true heir. To save Tina from possible conspiracy charges and to help her retain custody of her children, David tells Tina he never loved her, and he divorces her. Having had to give up Tina, whom he really did love, he agrees to Dorian's plan to marry Dorian.

if you catch a cold	you need to take some medicine and keep warm
if I had been tired	I would have taken a nap
if I had a dog	I would take him for a walk
if you eat a lot of ice cream	you will gain weight
if I had been as sick as you	I wouldn't have gone to school
if you study hard	you get good grades
if I had had a dog	I wouldn't have been afraid to be alone

✂

if I found a wallet	I would return it
If I find your wallet	I will return it to you
If I had found your wallet	I would have returned it to you
if I had eaten the whole box of chocolates	I would have had an upset stomach
if you had asked me	I would have helped you
If I had had enough money	I would have lent you some
if I am sick tomorrow	I will stay home

if I had eaten a lot of ice cream	I would have felt sick
if I am angry	my face turns red
if your skin turns green	you have a serious problem
if you ask me	I will tell you the truth
if you need me	I will be there
if I were bitten by a dog	I would go to the hospital
If my feet hurt	I would rub them

Part A

Choose one of the situations. For the situation you choose, write a letter to "Dear Annie" explaining your situation. Ask her for advice about how your situation could have been prevented or how it can be prevented in the future.

1. You forgot to lock your car and as a result, your books were stolen from the back seat. How could you have avoided having your books stolen?

2. You were absent from class on Monday when the teacher told the class there would be a test on Tuesday. How could you have avoided failing the test?

3. Your dog always barks late at night. As a result, your neighbor has threatened to kill the dog. What will save your dog's life?

4. You were out having a good time. On your way home, a policeman gave you a ticket for speeding. How could you have avoided getting a speeding ticket?

5. Although you know that you are not a very good cook, you prepared dinner for all of your friends. As a result, all of your friends got sick and had to be taken to the hospital. How could this situation have been avoided?

6. While you were playing, you left a little ball on the stairway. When your mother came down the stairs, she fell and broke her leg. How could this have been avoided?

7. Every time you go shopping, you go at 5:00 when the store is busiest. As a result, you always have to stand in a long check-out line. How can you avoid standing in a long line the next time you go to the store?

Example:

Dear Annie,

Help! A terrible thing has just happened to me! Yesterday after my classes, I went to the mall to go shopping. I forgot to lock my car, and as a result, my books were stolen from the back seat. I have a test this Friday, but now I can't study because I don't have my book. I am very upset. Could you tell me how I could have prevented this terrible situation?

Sincerely yours,

Going to Fail in Buffalo

© 1997 Prentice Hall Regents. Duplication for classroom use is permitted.

Part B

You write an advice column in the paper and sign yourself "Dear Annie." You have received a letter that describes a situation and asks your advice on how the situation could have been prevented/avoided or how it can be prevented/avoided in the future. Write a response, using the appropriate conditional constructions. If you are asked about how a situation could have been avoided, use the untrue in the past conditional. If you are asked about how a situation can be avoided, use the present/future conditional. You may also use other conditional constructions in your response.

Example:

Dear "Going to Fail,"

If you <u>had remembered</u> to lock your car in the first place, your books <u>wouldn't have been stolen</u> and you <u>wouldn't be</u> in this terrible situation! Perhaps in the future you should keep your books in the trunk of your car. That way, if you <u>forget</u> to lock your car again, your books <u>won't be stolen</u> and you <u>won't fail</u> any more tests.

Yours truly,

Annie

P.S. If you <u>tell</u> your teacher about your situation, I'm sure he/she'll <u>help</u> you find a book to study with.

Answer the questions based on the wishes in your group.

1. How many were past wishes?

2. How many were wishes for the present?

3. How many were wishes for the future?

4. How many wishes were about family members?

5. How many wishes were about money?

6. How many wishes were about the environment?

7. How many wishes were about stopping some habit?

8. Did any group members have the same wish?

9. What was the most popular topic of the wishes?

10. What was the most popular time for the wish (past, present, future)?

# Answer Key

Note: The answers to cloze exercises using songs can be found in the section **Lyrics** on page 349.

Worksheet 6   HOW OFTEN?
Part 2:

1.	John seldom works.	True	**False**
2.	John usually plays with his sons.	**True**	False
3.	John's wife never works.	True	**False**
4.	She rarely studies.	True	**False**
5.	She almost never works late.	True	**False**

Worksheet 10   DETECTIVE 1

A thief stole a computer and printer from an office on campus Saturday at 10:00. Sandy __was__ in the parking lot across from the office, standing next to her car. She only saw him for a few minutes, but she __was__ sure she could identify him. The police officers __were__ happy to have a witness, but they __weren't__ sure how much she saw from the parking lot. Sandy __was__ positive she could answer the detective's questions.

Questions:

1.	Were	7.	was
2.	were	8.	Were
3.	Was	9.	Were
4.	Were	10.	was
5.	was	11.	Was
6.	was		

Worksheet 18   LINE-UPS (Present perfect)

1. What have you __eaten__ this morning?
2. What have you __forgotten__ to do?
3. Where have you __gone__ shopping?
4. How much money have you __lent__ a friend?
5. What habit have you __quit__?
6. What have you __told__ a family member more than once?
7. Who have you __spoken__ to before class today?
8. What have you __thought__ about doing after class?
9. What have you __given__ a friend?
10. What have you __sent__ to your family recently?
11. How often have you __been__ to the movies this month?
12. What have you __lost__ recently?

Worksheet 18   (continued)

How often have you __seen__ your family since you came to this school?

What have you __drunk__ more than once today?

How many essays have you __written__ in writing class?

How often have you __bought__ a soft drink in the last week?

What is the longest you have __slept__ since coming to this school?

What have you __broken__ more than once?

Who have you __known__ since you were a child?

Who have you __told__ a secret to more than once?

What have you __done__ more than once today?

How many people from your country have you __met__ in this class?

What have you __begun__ to do since coming to the U.S.?

How much money have you __spent__ on lunch this past month?

How have you __felt__ this week?

Who have you __sat__ next to in class more than once this week?

338   Answer Key

Worksheet 19   LINE-UPS (Past perfect)

Where _had you studied_ English before you _came_ to this school?

What _had you heard_ about this school before you _came_ here?

What _had you already done_ before you _left_ home this morning?

When you _left_ for class this morning, _had the sun come up_ ?

What _had you never seen_ before you _went_ to a museum?

Where _had you been_ before you _got_ home yesterday?

Who (if anyone) _had you known_ in this class when you _started_ to study here?

How many times _had you seen_ a movie in English before you _came_ to this city?

What _had you already eaten_ before you _came_ to class?

Who _had already gotten up_ when you _left_ home this morning?

What _had you never eaten_ before you _went_ to a Mexican restaurant?

Before you _went_ to bed last night, what _had you already done_ ?

Worksheet 25C   FAIRY TALES

1. Both.
2. "The Three Little Pigs." (I'll blow your house down.)
3. "The Little Red Hen." (Who will help me plant the wheat?)
4. No.
5. Yes. "The Little Red Hen." (Who will help me plant the wheat? I won't.)
6. In "The Little Red Hen," the hen is asking if any of the other animals would be willing to help her. They are not willing until she has made the bread. Then they are willing to eat it. In "The Three Little Pigs," the wolf states what he is going to do and what the result of that action will be (he predicts that the pigs' houses will fall down).

Worksheet 27B   (Part II)

1. Future progressive.
2. It describes an action that is in progress for some time. It takes a long time to come around a mountain.
3a. Yes.
3b. "Going out to meet" someone is a short, completed action like starting or stopping. It does not continue for some time.
4a. Simple present.
4b. Whenever a sentence expresses a future time, the verb in the dependent (time) clause must be in the simple present form.

Worksheet 28A   ERROR ANALYSIS DRAW (Low level)

He **doesn't** eat lunch with us.
My cousin **lives** very far away.
CORRECT for adding emphasis. Or eliminate *do*.
What time **do you go** to class every day?
How many dogs **do** you have?
Is **your sister pretty**?
Sam and his father **were** happy to see us.
Was/Is your aunt a teacher?
I **am** going to the grocery store after class today.
My brother **is singing** right now.
My brother is home because he usually **does** his homework in the afternoon.

Worksheet 28B   ERROR ANALYSIS DRAW (Higher level)

We **haven't** been very lucky recently.
She will have gotten married before she **moves** to New York.

A pencil **is** made of lead and wood.

My husband and I **have been** married since 1985.

The news **is** exciting these days.

He hadn't met many famous people in Los Angeles before he **left.**

Chris **is** from Switzerland.

She is the laziest person I have **ever** met.

Worksheet 32A ERROR ANALYSIS (Lower level)

1. My brother **doesn't** like coconut. Can you believe it? I never met anyone else in my life who felt this way. It **seems** very strange to me. What **is** there about coconut that he **doesn't** like? It **seems** very inoffensive to me. Perhaps he says he **doesn't** like it in order to get attention. When he **refuses** to eat a coconut cookie or cake with coconut frosting, he gets a lot of attention and people try to figure out why he **dislikes** it so much. Of course, my brother always **denies** this, but I think that is the real reason.

2. When I first **moved** here 10 years ago, it **got** cold in December and January. In fact, the first two years, we **had** a freeze which killed all of my outdoor plants. As a result, I **decided** not to try to grow anything else. Now, however, it **stays** pretty warm all winter. In fact, just the other day I **wore/was wearing** shorts and a T-shirt. The sun **was shining,** and I felt as if it were summer! I couldn't resist calling my family and friends back home to brag about the good weather here.

3. Last week my brother-in-law **took** me to the desert about 45 minutes away, and we **stayed** there a couple of days. One of the reasons why we went there **was** to shoot rifles just for fun. He **set** up some cans and bottles for targets and shot at them. He also **let** me shoot his rifle. It **was** the first time I **shot** a gun, and I **felt** very scared. Even though I can see how much he **enjoys** target practice, I **think** gun ownership should be limited.

Worksheet 32B ERROR ANALYSIS (Higher level)

1. I first **learned** about this English program from a teacher at my school back home. I was surprised that it **wasn't** my English teacher, but rather my history teacher. He **had attended** this program when he was a university student. He told me how good this school **was** and what an interesting city this **was.** However, he **warned** me that he **had** been a student here many years ago and that sometimes things **change.** I have noticed some changes, but basically, I **have** found this to be a good program with friendly teachers. I also **enjoy** living in this city.

2. One of the most important decisions in life is deciding on a job. I first **came** to this country without knowing any English. Therefore, I **had** a hard time finding a job. I applied everywhere, but no one **called** me for a job. For that reason, I **attended** college and **took** some classes that **helped** me to have a good career. Now I have almost gotten my AA degree. After I **had attended** college for one year, I applied at a shoe store, and they **hired** me right away. My plan is to transfer to the university; after that, I can easily **find** a better job.

3. My son **has become** a "snackaholic." There was a time when he ate three big meals a day. Now, he only **wants** to snack. Popcorn, cookies, candy, soft drinks: these are his favorite foods. He **seems** to want to eat constantly, but only sweets or chips. What has happened to my good little eater? Could it be that he **is following** the example of his parents? I **guess** we better look at our own eating habits!

Worksheet 37A WHAT'S THE QUESTION 2?

1. What did John watch?
2. Where did Mary study?
3. Whom was she talking to?
4. When did the movie begin?
5. Why did Ali go to the dentist?
6. How much did your watch cost?
7. What did you buy?
8. Why did they miss the party?
9. When are you going to the zoo?
10. What did Akiko see last night?

Worksheet 37B   WHAT'S THE QUESTION 2?

1. What did Jeremy play?
2. Where did Jose ride his bike?
3. Who were you writing a letter to?
4. When does class begin?
5. Why did Ken stay home last night?
6. How many sisters does Kenji have?
7. How much did you spend on gifts for your family?
8. Why were your parents angry?
9. When is Mohammed going to visit you?
10. What did Yuko buy at the mall?

Worksheet 38   TAG QUESTIONS

1. weren't you
2. don't you
3. won't you
4. didn't you
5. aren't you
6. shouldn't they
7. don't you
8. can't you
9. haven't you
10. won't you

Worksheet 39A   FILL-IN CHART (Lower level)

cities	men	mothers	lives
keys	pans	brothers	lines
tomatoes	fish	these	foxes
radios	wishes	kisses	locks
mice	feet	those	
houses	boots	hats	

Worksheet 39B   FILL-IN CHART (Intermediate level)

kisses	men	zoos	shells
these	pans	potatoes	shelves
those	boots	geese	boxes
hats	feet	sheep	
mice	teeth	cacti	
houses	booths	classes	

Worksheet 39C   FILL-IN CHART (Higher level)

boxes	thieves	kisses	bans
oxen	lice	bats	blouses
heroes	houses	those	geese
pianos	teeth	roots	
autos	booths	boots	
chiefs	these	men	

Worksheet 40   MOUSE STORY

1. friends
2. NO CHANGE
3. roots
4. vegetables
5. NO CHANGE
6. ants

7. insects
8. things
9. NO CHANGE
10. cookies
11. pastries
12. apples

13. rolls
14. children
15. mice
16. kids
17. NO CHANGE
18. luxuries

Worksheet 42A   ERROR ANALYSIS (Lower level)

A. Clothes can tell a lot about a person, but we can't judge a person by the clothes **he/she wears.** In my country, a lot of **people judge** a person by what name brand of clothes **he/she wears.** A lot of times, **people talk** about what clothes their friends **wear** or **say** some **people wear** inappropriate clothes to high school.

B. Now I'm in California where it is warm all through the year and where there **are** many beautiful **beaches.** When you take a walk on the beach, you see people wearing baggy clothes–at least two **sizes** larger than what they should be wearing. **These** people are surfers. Personally, I believe that the reason surfers **wear** baggy clothes **is** they always **have** wetsuits in order to be ready for waves.

C. We have some important **decisions** to make in our lives. We can't run away from them and we **need** to choose what is best for us. The three most important decisions for me are where to study, choice of **job,** and who to marry. All of them **are** important, but perhaps marriage is the most important **one.** We **have** to choose whether we will marry or not. If we **don't** marry, it **means** that we will not have a family–including our own children. The decision about who we'll marry **is** difficult to make also. In **conclusion,** we can't predict what will happen and how our lives will be influenced by those **decisions,** but we **have** to decide even if it **turns** out bad.

D. There **are** a lot of important **things** in a lifetime. The most important thing for a young **person** is to get a good **education.** A good education **helps** you to get a good job later on. You **need** a good job to earn enough money to live comfortably. It is not as important to have a really high-paying job as it is to be happy in your **choice** of occupation. Also, everyone **needs** to settle down by having a **family** because it is important in order for civilization to continue. However, being happy with oneself is truly the most important thing in life.

Worksheet 42B   ERROR ANALYSIS (Higher level)

A. I **have** lived in Poland most of my life, and there is a **place** that I **remember** very well. It is a short, dark **street** with **buildings** on both **sides.** The buildings are very tall–at least four **floors.** There **is** an entrance but no exit from these **streets.** The windows **look** dirty, but shadow and window coverings **make** them look dark. Most people keep them clean and nice. I **think** about these **places** often because I spent most of my **life** there with many good **friends.**

B. Explorers **have** lived in almost all times and in almost every **country.** There **are** many interesting books written and lots of adventure **movies** made about them. We can see that an explorer's life is not just interesting, but it is also dangerous. In my opinion, explorers should be strong and brave, smart and experienced, and also **have** a sense of adventure.

C. All the **governments** of democratic nations **make** laws according to the necessity of the social life of the country at the **moment** the law is enacted. After many **years,** some of **those** laws **become** inadequate, and there **is** an attempt by **citizens** to change them. This is what is happening in the United States now regarding gun control. In my opinion, a law that **controls** guns is necessary because it **reduces** slaughters, gun accidents, and violence in general.

D. Dreams–**this** interesting topic **has** been on people's minds for a long time. Everybody **has** the ability to dream in one way or another. Some **people** even **say** that dreaming is a sign that we are sleeping the perfect sleep. Throughout time, it **has** always been a top **priority** to figure out the nature of dreams. Although our knowledge of dreams **is** still in a primitive stage, we **have** already managed to divide them into **categories.** The majority of people will agree that nightmares, daydreams, and visions are the most common types of **dreams.**

Worksheet 43   ARTICLE PASS-ALONG

1. **The** yellow dog that belongs to my brother is **an** old dog.
2. Does Yasuyuki drive **a** truck or **a** car?
3. My sister's boyfriend works at **a** restaurant across from **the** school he attends.
4. My new watch is made of ø gold.
5. When Martha heard **the** terrible news, she was filled with ø sadness.
6. ø Women generally live longer than ø men.
7. Many people return to ø college after working for several years.
8. **The** teacher said, "You may take **a** break if you have finished **the** rest of **the** test."
9. I'm going to **the** market on Hill Street. Can I get you anything?
10. After Thanksgiving weekend, you would probably agree that ø football is **the** most popular sport in North America.
11. I hope to get **a** degree in ø computer science by **the** end of this year.
12. What is more important to you—ø good health or ø money?
13. If **the** telephone in **the** kitchen rings, will you pick it up?
14. ø Radio had **the** biggest influence on ø people until **the** invention of television.
15. One reason Rafael bought his house is that **the** backyard is **a** good place for his kids to play.
16. What is **the** quickest way to get to **the** mall?

Worksheet 44   ERROR ANALYSIS DRAW

Japanese eye contact between women and ø men is impolite. or **a woman and a man**

Eyes, hands, and **the** entire body help express what we want to say.

When people meet for the first time, they shake hands. **CORRECT.**

Gestures are used by many people, such as ø teachers and policemen.

If a guy and a girl are sitting together on a sofa and talking about something, and suddenly the girl is moving and tossing her hair, this signals her interest in the guy. **CORRECT.**

When we are talking, we like to see ø people's eyes.

Body language is part of our system of communication. **CORRECT.**

The gestures mentioned earlier are also important to interpret nonverbal communication. **CORRECT.**

The misinterpretation of nonverbal signals can cause serious ø problems between cultures.

The way a person stands or sits can reflect his self image. **CORRECT.**

This example reminds me of the memories of the past 24 years. **CORRECT.**

People can tell by the wrinkes on others' faces what they have done in the past. **CORRECT.**

Worksheet 45   POSSESSIVES

1. I have **yours**.
2. Is she **yours**?
3. Do you have **mine**?
4. That new car is **theirs**.
5. This is **yours**; it isn't **mine**.
6. This is **mine**.
7. Did you bring **his**?
8. Those aren't **ours**. We have **ours**.
9. Did you see **hers**?
10. **Mine** is leather; **hers** is straw.
11. **Yours** is nice, but **ours** is nicer.
12. The winning science project is **mine**.
13. I like **yours** better than **mine**.
14. **His** experience was worse than **hers**.
15. May I borrow **yours**? I broke **mine**.
16. Those brownies are **theirs**.
17. The books on the table are **theirs**.
18. I sold **mine**.
19. That cocker spaniel is **ours**.
20. **Theirs** are outside.

A GROUP OF FRIENDS

I have a friend named John who is a student. John has two brothers. **His** older brother, Tad, now lives in San Francisco. **It** is a beautiful city, as you know. I met **them** (the two brothers) when **we** were all working at the mall after school. John and Tad's younger brother, Paul, lives in Austin, Texas. **He** is a swinging, single guy with two girlfriends. One girlfriend is a singer, and **she** sings every night with **her** twin sister. The other girlfriend lives in an apartment with **her** pet dog. **It** is a huge German shepherd. This dog likes to go camping with **them**, so **they** take **it** with them every chance **they** get. **It** is pretty much a "people" dog. By that, I mean **it** doesn't like to be left alone. Now that **you** know a little bit about John, **his** two brothers, and **me**, read on to find out more about **us**.

NUISANCE

Once upon a time, there was a tomcat named Nuisance. **He/It** lived with a wonderful woman named Lisa, but for some reason, **he/it** seemed to like everyone but **her**. The harder Lisa tried to please **him/it**, the more Nuisance thought of things **he/it** could do to annoy **her**. One day Lisa's friend brought over a beautiful hanging plant. **She/they** hung it in **her** bedroom window. Then the two friends went out to dinner. When **they** returned, **they** found the plant on the floor. "What happened to **it**?" asked **her** friend, but Lisa knew and **you** do too, don't **you**? That Nuisance! Another time, **he/it** ran away and was gone for three months. Lisa asked the people in the apartment building to help search for **him/it**. **They** all agreed to help, but no one found Nuisance. Just when **she/they** had given up hope, **he/it** turned up. Nuisance spent **his/its** whole life doing things like this to Lisa, but she always forgave **him/it**.

across	down
3. them	1. you
6. ours	2. he
8. I	4. hers
9. theirs	5. mine
11. me	7. she
12. yours	9. they
	10. it
	13. us

1. Correct
2. Incorrect (*next to*)
3. Incorrect (*in*)
4. Correct
5. Incorrect (*next to*)
6. Correct
7. Correct
8. Incorrect (*hamburgers*)
9. Correct
10. Correct

Worksheet 52A PREPOSITION BEE (Lower level)

1. in
2. next to/behind/in front of/near/close to/in back of
3. over/on top of
4. at
5. in
6. in
7. next to/between/in back of/in front of/near/close to
8. at/in
9. near/next to/close to/behind/in back of/in front of
10. under/on

11. from . . . to
12. at
13. in
14. in
15. above/over
16. over
17. on
18. around
19. behind/in back of
20. out/outside
21. to

Worksheet 52B PREPOSITION BEE (Higher level)

1. at
2. away
3. over
4. near/next to/beside
5. on/under/near/next to
6. into
7. on
8. during
9. off/down
10. from
11. with/among/around
12. after/during
13. from . . . to
14. without
15. within/in/outside
16. on
17. on
18. between/next to/beside
19. beyond
20. in/inside
21. around/over

Worksheet 54 PREPOSITION BEE (Phrasal verbs)

1. out
2. up
3. up . . . out
4. over
5. along with
6. off
7. out
8. out of
9. up
10. down

11. back
12. out . . . away
13. around
14. over/through
15. up
16. up
17. on
18. up
19. over
20. into

Worksheet 66   MOVIES

1. Sand was placed in the bag.
2. He was frightened by spiders.
3. He had already been killed.
4. It was replaced with the bag of sand.
5. He was almost flattened/squashed.
6. He had already been shot with an arrow/dart.
7. He was chased by a boulder.
8. He was surrounded by Indians.
9. It was taken away from Indiana.
10. He was chased and shot at by the Indians.
11. He was scared by a snake.
12. He will be flown back to his country. (Various answers possible.)

Worksheet 67B   BUSY PICTURES

1. A menu was being read by the old man.
2. The drink was poured by the man.
3. A tray is being carried by the waitress
4. The table is set by the waiter.
5. The silverware has been placed on a table by a waiter.
6. The menus are being read by two women.
7. The order was written by the waiter.
8. The rolls have already been set on the table.
9. A drink is being drunk by a man.
10. An order is being listened to (or is being taken) by the waiter.

Worksheet 69   STORYTIME

1. General Hospital
   a. Kevin is worried about Lucy.
   b. Lucy is attracted to Norma.
   c. Kevin and Mac are taken out by Lucy.
   d. Kevin and Mac are taught a lesson by Lucy.

2. General Hospital
   a. Sonny's share of the company is sold to Edward.
   b. The control of the company is taken away from Lois and Brenda.
   c. Brenda is lied to about some legal papers.
   d. Brenda is pressured to sign some papers.

Worksheet 70   REVIEWS

A Walk in the Clouds is an **interesting/exciting** movie starring Keanu Reeves. The movie takes place after World War II in the wine country of California. The characters are **surrounded** by the beautiful scenery. Keanu's character is married to a woman he met right before going overseas. They don't really know each other, nor are they **interested** in the same things. He is a traveling salesman, and on his first trip after returning home he meets a **confusing/fascinating** woman on the train. Every time he runs into her, he gets into trouble. She is **embarrassed** to have caused him so many problems, but he notices that she is very **frightened/depressed**, and finally she tells him that she is pregnant and unmarried. This is an especially **humiliating** position to be in at this time because her parents are very strict and will be **shocked** by this news. She is very **depressed** and doesn't know what to do. Keanu's character offers to pose as her husband who will then have a fight with her and leave the **confused/humiliated** woman. Her family, however, will believe she is married and that the husband is a **disgusting** person. They will feel sorry for her. Before the two can carry out this somewhat **confusing** plan, they start to really fall in love. Watch the movie to find out the **exciting** ending!

Worksheet 74A   EXAMPLES

1.	a	6.	d	11.	f
2.	a	7.	d	12.	e
3.	b	8.	c	13.	e
4.	b	9.	c		
5.	b	10.	f		

Worksheet 75   WHICH IS IT?

1. a
2. b
3. a
4. b
5. a

Worksheet 80   STORYTIME

1. *One Life to Live*
   a. Maggie came to Llanview to visit/see her cousin.
   b. Max is angry at Maggie for making an appointment for his son.
   c. Maggie is determined to help Frankie.

2. *General Hospital*
   a. Jason is angry about people telling him what he was like.
   b. Jason decided to leave home.
   c. Jason can't remember being in an accident.
   d. Jason stopped living at home.

Worksheet 86A   WORD SEARCH (Lower level)

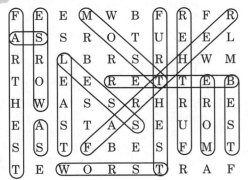

Worksheet 86B   WORD SEARCH (Higher level)

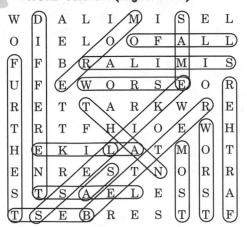

Worksheet 91 COMBINATIONS

These words cannot be used in the sentences:

1. Because
2. Although
3. even though
4. however
5. However
6. Therefore
7. But
8. such as
9. Furthermore
10. As well as

Worksheet 97 THE FACT THAT

1. The fact that a big dog lives on my street scares me.
2. Because of the fact that the bus didn't come, I was late.
3. I wonder about the fact that Yoichi didn't study but scored 100 percent.
4. The fact that my mother forgot my birthday made me sad.
5. In spite of the fact that it's cold today, I'm going to the beach.
6. I was stunned by the fact that Ahmed was wearing a tie today.
7. I wasn't convinced by the fact that Hitoshi seemed sincere.
8. The fact that the pyramids were built without the aid of machines really amazes me.
9. The fact that my daughter graduated at the head of her class at Harvard takes my breath away.
10. In spite of the fact that my dog chewed up my new book, I still love her.

Worksheet 104 COMBINATIONS

1. He teaches a class for students whose native language is not English.
2. She gave several reasons, only a few of which were valid.
3. I don't know what I should do. / I don't know what to do.
4. That she doesn't understand spoken English is obvious.
5. John's glasses broke yesterday while he was playing basketball.
6. Because the Civil War has ended, a new government is being formed.

Worksheet 110 STORY SAGAS

Suggested answers:

General Hospital:

1. If Lucy had not seen Catherine outside her building, she wouldn't have had to testify.
2. If Lucy had not mentioned her duck, the jury would not have made fun of her.
3. If Catherine had not been accused of Damian's murder, Lucy would not have talked about her duck.
4. If Lucy had not told Catherine about her testimony, Catherine would not have gotten angry.

All My Children:

1. If Hailey's father had not interfered, Charlie and Hailey would still be together.
2. If Cecily had not gotten divorced, she might not have returned to Pine Valley.
3. If Charlie and Hailey had not broken up, Charlie would not have become involved with Cecily.
4. If Charlie and Hailey had not broken up, she would not have become engaged to Alex.

One Life to Live:

1. Joe might not have gotten involved with Dorian if everyone had left him alone.
2. If Dorian had really loved Joe, she would not have dropped him.
3. Dorian would not have married David if Joe's mother had not forced her to.
4. David would not have married Dorian if she were poor.

1. David would not have admitted his impersonation if he had not fallen in love with Tina.
2. David and Tina would not have married in secret if David were not impersonating her brother.
3. David would not have agreed to marry Dorian if he had not given up Tina.
4. If Tina had not had children, David would not have given her up.

 348 Answer Key

Lyrics

Worksheet 22 SONG

"Some of These Days"

Some of these days

You *'ll miss* me baby

Some of these days

You *be* so lonely

You *'ll miss* my kissing

You *'ll miss* my hugging

You *'ll miss* me baby

When I'm far away

Well, I feel so lonely

For you only

Ah, but honey,

You had your way.

When you leave,

I know it *'s gonna grieve* me

You *'re gonna miss* me baby

When I'm gone.

Worksheet 26 SONG (Time Clauses)

"When Johnney *Comes* Marching Home"

When Johnny *comes* marching home again, Hurrah! Hurrah!

We*'ll give* him a hearty welcome then, Hurrah! Hurrah!

The men *will cheer*, the boys *will shout*, the ladies

    they*'ll all turn out*

And we*'ll all feel* gay when Johnny *comes* marching home.

Worksheet 27A   SONG (Future Progressive &Time Clauses)

"She'll Be Comin' Round the Mountain"

She*'ll be coming* round the mountain when she __*comes*__
She*'ll be coming* round the mountain when she __*comes*__
She*'ll be coming* round the mountain,
She*'ll be coming* round the mountain,
She*'ll be coming* round the mountain when she __*comes*__ .

She*'ll be driving* six white horses when she __*comes*__ .
She*'ll be driving* six white horses when she __*comes*__ .
She*'ll be driving* six white horses,
She*'ll be driving* six white horses,
She*'ll be driving* six white horses when she __*comes*__ .

Oh, we*'ll all go* out to meet her when she __*comes*__ .
Oh, we*'ll all go* out to meet her when she __*comes*__ .
Oh, we*'ll all go* out to meet her,
Oh, we*'ll all go* out to meet her,
Oh, we*'ll all go* out to meet her when she __*comes*__ .

Worksheet 47A   Songs

"He Stopped Loving Her Today"

He said, "**I**'ll love **you** 'till **I** die."
She told **him**, " **You**'ll forget in time."
As the years went slowly by,
She still preyed upon **his** mind.

He kept **her** picture on **his** wall
And went half crazy now and then;
But **he** still loved **her** through it all,
Hoping **she**'d come back again.

Kept some letters by **his** bed,
Dated nineteen-sixty-two;
He had underlined in red
Every single "**I** love **you**."

I went to see **him** just today.
Oh but **I** didn't see no tears.
All dressed up to go 'way.
First time **I**'d seen **him** smile in years.

REFRAIN

He stopped loving **her** today.
They placed a wreath upon **his** door.
And soon **they**'ll carry **him** away,
He stopped loving **her** today.

You know, **she** came to see **him** one last time,
Oh, and **we** all wondered if **she** would.
And **it** kept running through **my** mind
This time, **he**'s over **her** for good.

REFRAIN

"The Erie Canal"

I've got a mule, **her** name is Sal,
Fifteen miles on the Erie Canal.
She's a good ol' worker and a good ol' pal,
Fifteen miles on the Erie Canal.

We've hauled some barges in our day,
Filled with lumber, coal and hay.
And **we** know every inch of the way
From Albany to Buffalo.

REFRAIN

Low bridge, everybody down!
Low bridge, for **we**'re coming to a town!
And **you**'ll always know **your** neighbor,
You'll always know **your** pal,
If **you**'ve ever navigated on the Erie Canal.

We better get along on our way, ol' gal,
Fifteen miles on the Erie Canal.
'Cause **you** bet **your** life
I'd never part with Sal,
Fifteen miles on the Erie Canal.

Get up there, mule, here comes a lock
We'll make Rome about six o'clock,
One more trip and back **we**'ll go,
Right back home to Buffalo.

REFRAIN

"Red River Valley"

From this valley they say you are going,
We will miss **your** bright eyes and sweet smile,
For **they** say **you** are taking the sunshine,
That brightens **our** pathway awhile.

REFRAIN

Come and sit by **my** side if **you** love me,
Do not hasten to bid me adieu,
But remember the Red River Valley
And the girl that has loved **you** so true.

Won't **you** think of the valley **you**'re leaving?
Oh, how lonely, how sad **it** will be,
Oh think of the fond heart **you**'re breaking,
And the grief **you** are causing **me**.

REFRAIN

From this valley **they** say **you** are going,
When **you** go, may **your** darling go, too?
Would **you** leave **her** behind unprotected?
When **she** loves no other but **you**?

REFRAIN

I have promised **you**, darling, that never
Will a word from **my** lips cause **you** pain;
And **my** life, **it** will be **yours** forever
If **you** only will love **me** again.

Worksheet 94 SONG

"Amie"

I can see <u>why you think you belong to me;</u>
I never tried to make you think or let you see
One thing for yourself.
But now you're off with someone else and I'm alone.
You see, I thought <u>that I might keep you for my own</u>.

REPEAT

Amie, what 'choo wanna do?
I think <u>I could stay with you</u>
For awhile, maybe longer, if I do.

Don't you think <u>the time was right for us to find</u>
All them things <u>we thought weren't proper</u>
Could be right in time.
And, can you see
<u>Which way we should turn together or alone.</u>
I can't never tell <u>what's right or what is wrong</u>.
(It'd take too long to see)

REPEAT

Well, now it's come to <u>what you want</u>; you've had your way.
And all the things <u>you thought before</u> just faded into gray.
And can you see
<u>A-That I don't know if it's you or if it's me.</u>
If it's one of us, I'm sure <u>we both will see</u>
(Oh, won't you look at me and tell me)

REPEAT

I just keep falling in and out of love with you,
Falling in and out of love with you,
Don't know <u>what I'm gonna do,</u>
I keep falling in and out of love with you.

Index 1: Grammar

Index 2: Games